Electronic and Digital Media

Electronic and Digital Media

Reuben Chapman

Willford Press
www.willfordpress.com

Published by Willford Press,
118-35 Queens Blvd., Suite 400,
Forest Hills, NY 11375, USA

ISBN: 978-1-64728-352-0

Cataloging-in-Publication Data

Electronic and digital media / Reuben Chapman.
p. cm.
Includes bibliographical references and index.
ISBN 978-1-64728-352-0
1. Digital media. 2. Digital communications. 3. Online journalism. I. Chapman, Reuben.
HM851 .E44 2021
302.231--dc23

For information on all Willford Press publications
visit our website at www.willfordpress.com

Willford Press

Contents

Preface

The media which uses electronics or electromechanical audience to access the content is known as electronic media. The devices, which are used in electronic communication process are also regarded as electronic media. It can be either in digital electronic data format or analogue electronic data format. The media which are encoded in digital electronic format are known as digital media. It can be designed, shared, viewed, modified and saved on digital electronic devices. There are several examples of digital media such as digital videos, software, databases and video games. This book is compiled in such a manner, that it will provide in-depth knowledge about the theory and practice of electronic and digital media. The topics included in this book on electronic and digital media are of utmost significance and bound to provide incredible insights to readers. Those in search of information to further their knowledge will be greatly assisted by this book.

Given below is the chapter wise description of the book:

Chapter 1- A type of media which can be used to propagate and spread information to the people with the help of electronic devices is called electronic media. Any media which can be encoded in computer readable format is termed as digital media. This is an introductory chapter which will briefly introduce management of electronic and digital media.

Chapter 2- Audience can be defined as masses of people with whom communication is performed through every medium. Clients in business, customers in market, members of an organization, etc. can be referred to as audience. The topics elaborated in this chapter will help in gaining a better perspective about audience research.

Chapter 3- Information stored in digital format is defined as digital content. This chapter delves into different ways in which digital content can be distributed such as, radio broadcasting, radio programming, television programming, broadcast syndication, paid promotion, etc., to provide an extensive understanding of the subject.

Chapter 4- Advertising and marketing are of the publicity strategies used by firms and organizations to reach their target audience. The diverse applications of advertising and marketing such as digital advertising and marketing; video, email and radio marketing, cinema and television advertising, digital billboards, paid media, etc. have been thoroughly discussed in this chapter.

Chapter 5- Media that can be created and shared by people in a social network is termed as social media. This chapter deals with various aspects of social media management such as business models in social media, social media marketing, social media advertising, paid social media advertising, social competitive analysis, social media sentiment analysis, etc.

Chapter 6- Freshly received notable information, related to important events, is called news. News broadcasting, online newsroom, news media, video news release, electronic news-gathering, news management, electronic newspaper, etc. are some of its components. This chapter closely examines these components of news and news management to provide an in-depth understanding of the subject.

At the end, I would like to thank all those who dedicated their time and efforts for the successful completion of this book. I also wish to convey my gratitude towards my friends and family who supported me at every step.

Reuben Chapman

1

Electronic and Digital Media: An Introduction

A type of media which can be used to propagate and spread information to the people with the help of electronic devices is called electronic media. Any media which can be encoded in computer readable format is termed as digital media. This is an introductory chapter which will briefly introduce management of electronic and digital media.

Electronic Media

Electronic media is the media that one can share on any electronic device for the audiences viewing, unlike static media (Printing) electronic media is broadcasted to the wider community. Examples of Electronic media are things such as the television the radio, or the wide internet.

- Broadcasting: To transmit or sent information through the use of various Electronic media devices.
- Media: The wide world of mass communication through Electronic media.

Electronic media or not, most or almost all business use electronic media in some way to attract new or more customers, just say one choose to advertise using Facebook which is a basic electronic media module which one can use to owner advantage, businesses usually use the "check-in" method where if one check into their store they will give one something in return, either a discount or some points on a membership card, this generates more customer flow to the store and in turn allows more profit to be made.

Electronic media is the basis of e-commerce marketing, firstly one will need a method of approach whether one would like to use online marketplaces or social/mail like places to promote owner business, then soon after obtaining online contacts one will be seeing customers showing up to owner business or buying from owner online market.

Electronic media is a way for owner business to be heard but not only heard, seen too. As owner Business becomes its own entity online, one have a brand and owner brand has a face, if managed well it is sure to increase revenue. If not then owner business may struggle to get back up from the floor with many other competitors.

What is the purpose of using electronic media?

The purpose of using electronic media can be for many reasons, one of the reasons is that one can use it to market owner self and anything else from businesses to products and so on. Electronic media is an efficient way to communicate to one another, either by the use of media devices and networks or social media sources such as Television or the Internet these are a few of the many ways one can use Electronic media to owner advantage.

What are the different types of Electronic media?

There is a wide range of Electronic media that broadcast a variety of different things like advertisements and promotions. Different Electronic media types are below:

- Television,
- Radio,
- Internet,
- Shops.

Television is one of the most used Electronic media devices because franchises can pay for advertisements to show millions of people, thus bringing in more business for the franchise owner.

The Radio is similar but does not give the audience visuals, just sound. This method of Electronic media can be effective and much more affordable than Television but does not engage the listeners as much as visual ads.

The Internet is one of the most profitable Electronic media devices, with a single click of a button ads will fill the webpage and is definite to catch a few glimpses for fellow web surfers. This not only spreads through Electronic media but can profit the creator of the web page throughout time.

Shops have Electronic media in most places, whether it is on an electric billboard or ATM screen Electronic media is sure to be in almost everywhere one go.

Electronic media or for that matter media, in general, continue to play an influential role in our society today-careers are made and destroyed, depending on what gets published in the media. Take Kevin Spacey for example, at one point he was the leading Hollywood icon but when stories of him trying to take advantage of underage actors made the rounds, well, that's the last nail on his career, so as to speak. This only goes on to show one that electronic media can indeed play a pivotal role as it had in the past but it is time that we took a closer look at the same and reviewed the positive and negative impact of electronic media.

The Positive Impact of Electronic Media

- Information: Electronic media is one of the effective methods by which one can disseminate information within seconds. So if one wanted certain information including information about an impending tsunami, then electronic media is owner best bet to get that information out there, within a short space of time. That's why most politicians utilize all forms of electronic media to publicize themselves and to enable them to reach out to brand new voters.

- Educational: Electronic media provides one with a host of information and certain agencies have started using the same to educate their oneng students. With the help of electronic media oneng students can learn more about the news, about the process and how reporters often have to report on it while facing a lot of stress and pressure. Some institutions also feature educational modules based on electronic media which can prove to be invaluable for those seeking to establish a career in the same.

- Behavioral: various studies have already established that television and other forms of electronic media do continue to influence behavioral patterns in oneng children. And this can be a positive thing as it helps them to relate to the context and as a result, modify their behavior, As a –parent, one would be required to monitor all their electronic media interaction to ensure that they are not led astray.

The Negative Impact of Electronic Media

- Psychological: Again various studies have established the fact that the more oneng children are exposed to scenes of gratuitous violence in television programs, the more likely they are, to act it out. And moreover, television, as well as social media, can have a psychological effect on oneng viewers and cause them to become more reclusive, and to become addicted to select programs. As a result, this can impact their health in the long run.

- Behavioral: Oneng children often tend to imagine that television programs are for real and naturally when they see explicit scenes and even violent ones, this can have a direct impact on their behavior. This is why it is important for parents to regulate all forms of electronic media; after all, it is for their own benefit. And remember, all it takes is for one show to alter owner little one forever.

- Health: Being exposed to electronic media 24/7 is not good, not in any sense of the word. For one, binge-watching television programs can impair owner vision and even affect owner hearing. If that wasn't enough, one would most likely put on more weight as a result of all that inactivity and this can even play a causative role in one developing diabetes.

- Social interaction: As a result of being obsessed with electronic media and communication devices, one are more likely to lead a life of a recluse with little or no interaction with others. Soon, one would feel comfortable only when one is sitting in front of owner laptop or television which is indicative that one have a major problem.

These are some of the positive and negative impacts of television and other forms of electronic media in our society. This is why we must be on our guard and ensure that our children do not get addicted to the various forms of electronic media from newspapers to androids. One need to carefully monitor owner children so that one can be sure that they are watching the right programs, the sort that is educational and nothing gruesome.

Radio

Radio is the sound communication by radio waves usually through the transmission of music, news, and other types of programs from single broadcast stations to multitudes of individual listeners equipped with radio receivers. From its birth early in the 20th century, broadcast radio astonished and delighted the public by providing news and entertainment with an immediacy never before thought possible. From about 1920 to 1945, radio developed into the first electronic mass medium, monopolizing "the airwaves" and defining, along with newspapers, magazines, and motion pictures, an entire generation of mass culture. About 1945 the appearance of television began to transform radio's content and role. Broadcast radio remained the most widely available electronic mass medium in the world, though its importance in modern life did not match that of television, and in the early 21st century it faced yet more competitive pressure from digital satellite- and Internet-based audio services.

Based on the human voice, radio is a uniquely personal medium, invoking a listener's imagination to fill in mental images around the broadcast sounds. More readily and in a more widespread fashion than any other medium, radio can soothe listeners with comforting dialogue or background music, or it can jar them back into reality with polemics and breaking news. Radio also can employ a boundless plethora of sound and music effects to entertain and enthral listeners. Since the birth of this medium, commercial broadcast companies as well as government organs have made conscious use of its unique attributes to create programs that attract and hold listeners' attention.

Radio's Digital Future

At the turn of the 21st century, the most important on-going change was the inception of digital radio. In the 1990s countries in Europe had inaugurated digital audio broadcasting (DAB), which was distributed both by ground transmitters and by means of orbiting communication satellites.

Late in 2002 the FCC authorized an American terrestrial digital radio service. But digital radio grew very slowly, because receivers were expensive and there was little original programming to attract listeners. Moreover, the U.S. government did not set a deadline (as it had for television) for stations to convert to digital transmission; all stations would retain their existing AM or FM channels even after going digital. The slow changeover led some critics to argue that radio broadcasters were missing an important chance to play a part in an increasingly digital media landscape.

In late 2001 and early 2002 two American digital satellite services, XM and Sirius, began operating from satellite systems, each providing 100 channels of specialized music and talk programming, some with no advertising. Would-be listeners had to pay a monthly subscription fee (paying for audio content that most had long considered to be "free"), and they also had to purchase special receivers and antennas for listening in cars (the primary market) or at home or the office. In 2009 U.S. government officials allowed the two services to merge, eliminating their overlapping channels. The satellite radio audience (chiefly in automobiles) continued to grow slowly, and it seemed likely that satellite radio would remain a niche service.

Both terrestrial and satellite radio faced competition from new ways to transmit audio programming—the Internet and mobile services. Most radio broadcasters had a presence online by the start of the 21st century, nearly all of them simply streaming their over-the-air signal. Streaming made it possible to reach new listeners, enabling stations to extend their appeal beyond local markets and into other countries. Indeed, stations that were once "local" could now be heard anywhere. Internet distribution also promoted further splintering of radio formats—and their audiences—into even more specialized minicategories. Some "broadcasters" appeared only on the Internet and thus avoided much of the trouble and expense of station operation, including the need to get a license.

Generally free for users, and sometimes lacking commercial interruptions, countless Web audio services began to tempt many onetime broadcast listeners to "tune in" with their computers. Moreover, Web-only services such as Pandora, which had its debut in 2000, allowed users to "program their own station" by selecting only the music they wanted to hear—and without a word of talk to interrupt. In addition, portable media players such as Apple Inc.'s iPod, introduced in 2001, created a growing market for carrying recorded music, and perhaps radio-type services, wherever the consumer went. Many people simply downloaded music (legally or otherwise) for use on their mobile devices, further threatening broadcasters. The many Internet music (and other) services thus constituted the most serious competitive threat facing radio broadcasting since the advent of television.

AM Radio and FM Radio

AM is mostly talk radio and FM is mostly music." While this is somewhat true (there are exceptions with both), it's certainly not the main characteristic that sets them apart from one another. While AM and FM radio function and operate in the same ways and by the same principles, the biggest difference between the two is the way in which the carrier waves are modulated.

AM Radio

AM stands for "Amplitude Modulation", as AM radio signals vary their amplitude to adapt to the sound information that is being broadcasted through the wavelengths. While changes in amplitude occur on FM radio as well, they are more noticeable in AM radio because they result in audible static. So, essentially, when you're switching the channels on an AM radio, you're hearing changes in amplitude, which is why distant broadcasts with weak signals will come across as very faint with the sound largely dominated by static.

FM Radio

FM stands for "Frequency Modulation," and, unlike AM radio, sound is transmitted through changes in frequency. While both FM and AM radio signals experience frequent changes in amplitude, they are far less noticeable on FM. During an FM broadcast, slight changes in amplitude go unnoticed because the audio signal is presented to the listener through changes in frequency, not amplitude. So, when you're switching between stations, your FM antenna is alternating between different frequencies, and not amplitudes, which produces a much cleaner sound and allows for smoother transitions with little to no audible static.

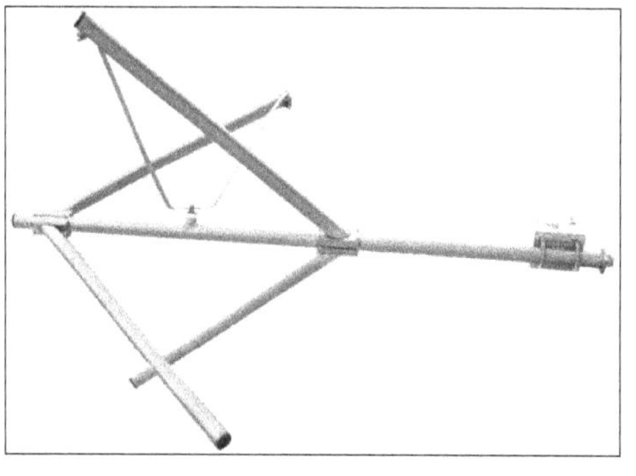

There are pros and cons of both AM and FM radio, but the better sound quality of FM radio makes it more desirable for those who want to transmit clear and clean sounding audio. And while AM radio has a lower bandwidth and can accommodate more stations, FM radio is generally preferred by those who want to start their own low power broadcast.

If you're interested in broadcasting on your own low power FM radio station, Progressive Concepts has everything you need to produce a professional sounding show, whether you plan on transmitting mostly spoken word, or recorded or live music.

Differences in Sound Quality

The difference in the way AM and FM radio signals are encoded means differences in sound quality, performance, and broadcast range between the two types of station. This explains why FM stations sound better than AM stations, but AM stations can be heard from further away.

AM radio varies the amplitude of the broadcast signal so the power at which that signal is broadcast is also changed, since amplitude represents the strength of the signal. Some receivers can't pick up low amplitude signals at all. FM radio, always remains at constant amplitude, so signal strength does not change.

FM uses a higher frequency range and a bigger bandwidth than AM. AM radio operates from 535 kHz (kiloHertz) to 1605 kHz. When you tune the dial on your radio, the number changes by 10 kHz each time. This means that each station has 10 kHz of bandwidth on which to broadcast. FM radio on the other hand operates between 88 MHz (MegaHz) and 108 MHz, and your radio increments every 200 kHz.

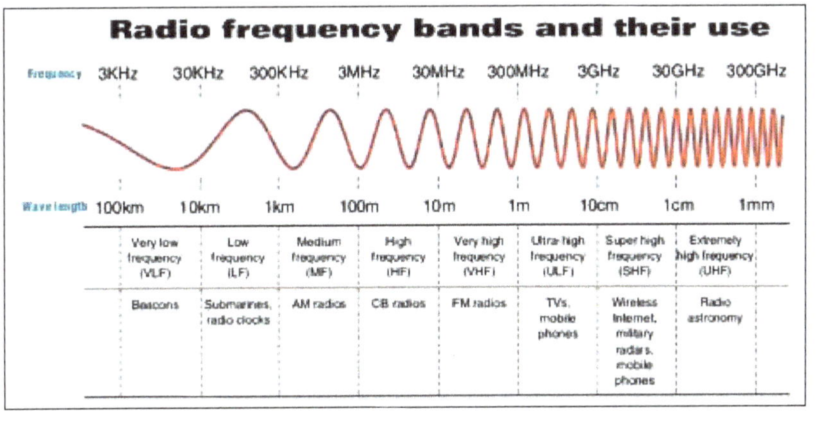

Each FM station is allocated 150 kHz of bandwidth, which is 15 times that of an AM station. This means that an FM station can transmit 15 times as much information as an AM station and explains why music sounds so much better on FM. Since music has more electrical information contained within it than a monophonic voice audio signal, FM typically broadcasts music and AM generally sticks to talking programs.

Satellite Radio

Satellite radio is a type of digital broadcast which transmits audio signals over large areas with greater clarity and consistency than conventional radio.

A satellite radio service works by transmitting its signal from a ground-based station to one or more satellites orbiting the Earth. The satellite bounces the signal back to specialized receivers on the ground, commonly located in automobiles and home stereo systems. Because the signal is broadcast from outer space, it can reach across an entire continent. Ground-based repeaters augment the signal in urban areas where tall buildings might cause interference. In the United States, satellite radio operates on the 2.3 gigahertz (GHz) S band of the electromagnetic spectrum; elsewhere, it often uses the 1.4 GHz L band.

Most satellite radio services operate on a subscription model. A consumer buys a proprietary receiver, which is activated with the purchase of a subscription. Once activated, a receiver can decode the satellite's encrypted digital signals. Satellite radio typically offers a much clearer signal and greater dynamic range than conventional radio, often approaching the sound quality of compact discs (CDs). Services typically offer a hundred or more channels, including music, news, talk, and sports. Many channels are free of advertising.

In the United States, rivals XM Satellite Radio and Sirius Satellite Radio, launched in 2001 and 2002, respectively, competed to attract exclusive talent, such as television host Oprah Winfrey and radio star Howard Stern. However, the splitting of marquee stars between the two services, along with a similar split in sports programming, hampered both companies. Laden by debt, the two companies merged in 2008, and the newly formed company, named Sirius XM Radio, became the sole American satellite radio provider (they remained separate entities in Canada). Another major broadcaster, 1worldspace, serves Asia and Africa, with plans to expand to South America and Mexico.

Internet Radio

Internet radio has been around since the late 1990s. Traditional radio broadcasters have used the Internet to simulcast their programming. But, Internet radio is undergoing a revolution that will expand its reach from your desktop computer to access broadcasts anywhere, anytime, and expand its programming from traditional broadcasters to individuals, organizations and government.

How Internet Radio Works

Freedom of the Airwaves

Radio broadcasting began in the early '20s, but it wasn't until the introduction of the transistor radio in 1954 that radio became available in mobile situations. Internet radio is in much the same place. Until the 21st century, the only way to obtain radio broadcasts over the Internet was through your PC. That will soon change, as wireless connectivity will feed Internet broadcasts to car radios, PDAs and cell phones. The next generation of wireless devices will greatly expand the reach and convenience of Internet radio.

Uses and Advantages

Traditional radio station broadcasts are limited by two factors:

- The power of the station's transmitter (typically 100 miles).
- The available broadcast spectrum (you might get a couple of dozen radio stations locally).

Internet radio has no geographic limitations, so a broadcaster in Kuala Lumpur can be heard in Kansas on the Internet. The potential for Internet radio is as vast as cyberspace itself (for example, Live365 offers more than 30,000 Internet radio broadcasts).

In comparison to traditional radio, Internet radio is not limited to audio. An Internet radio broadcast can be accompanied by photos or graphics, text and links, as well as interactivity, such as message boards and chat rooms. This advancement allows a listener to do more than listen, a listener who hears an ad for a computer printer ordered that printer through a link on the Internet radio broadcast Web site. The relationship between advertisers and consumers becomes more interactive and intimate on Internet radio broadcasts. This expanded media capability could also be used in other ways. For example, with Internet radio, you could conduct training or education and provide links to documents and payment options. You could also have interactivity with the trainer or educator and other information on the Internet radio broadcast site.

Internet radio programming offers a wide spectrum of broadcast genres, particularly in music. Broadcast radio is increasingly controlled by smaller numbers of media conglomerates (such as Cox, Jefferson-Pilot and Bonneville). In some ways, this has led to more mainstreaming of the programming on broadcast radio, as stations often try to reach the largest possible audience in order to charge the highest possible rates to advertisers. Internet radio, on the other hand, offers the opportunity to expand the types of available programming. The cost of getting "on the air" is less for an Internet broadcaster, and Internet radio can appeal to "micro-communities" of listeners focused on special music or interests.

Creating an Internet Radio Station

What do you need to set up an Internet radio station?

- CD player,
- Ripper software (copies audio tracks from a CD onto a computer's hard drive),
- Assorted recording and editing software,
- Microphones,
- Audio mixer,
- Outboard audio gear (equalizer, compressor, etc.),
- Digital audio card,
- Dedicated computer with encoder software,
- Streaming media server.

Getting audio over the Internet is pretty simple:

- The audio enters the Internet broadcaster's encoding computer through a sound card.
- The encoder system translates the audio from the sound card into streaming format. The encoder samples the incoming audio and compresses the information so it can be sent over the Internet.
- The compressed audio is sent to the server, which has a high bandwidth connection to the Internet.
- The server sends the audio data stream over the Internet to the player software or plug-in on the listener's computer. The plug-in translates the audio data stream from the server and translates it into the sound heard by the listener.

There are two ways to deliver audio over the Internet: Downloads or Streaming Media. In downloads, an audio file is stored on the user's computer. Compressed formats like MP3 are the most popular form of audio downloads, but any type of audio file can be delivered through a Web or FTP site. Streaming audio is not stored, but only played. It is a continuous broadcast that works through three software packages: The encoder, the server and the player. The encoder converts audio content into a streaming format, the server makes it available over the Internet and the player retrieves the content. For a live broadcast, the encoder and streamer work together in real-time. An audio feed runs to the sound card of a computer running the encoder software at the broadcast location and the stream is uploaded to the streaming server. Since that requires a large amount of computing resources, the streaming server must be a dedicated server.

Organizational Structure of a Radio Station

The First Radio Companies

The first true commercial radio broadcasts were still dependent on the government for authorization to use the air waves, which had taken control of all two-way transmitting to prevent wartime enemies from spying. The Westinghouse Company, General Electric and Western Electric received licensing from the government to build transmitters and receivers, and AT&T received permission to broadcast signals over the air waves. This paved the way for more commercial-based programming by newcomers such as the National Broadcasting Company (NBC) and the Columbia Broadcasting System (CBS) in the 1920s. The concept of organizing of a radio station began at this point.

Organization Template of a Radio Station

The basic structure of a radio station is much like any business model. Ownership is at the top, whether it is a sole proprietor or a board of directors. The responsibility of delegating labor and financial operations falls to upper management, who are supported by administrative staff. This would be the station manager or the program director of a radio station. Employees charged with the daily operation of the business itself are the on-air talent, the sales staff and receptionists or other front office staff. Additional staff in a radio station consists of special programming and production staff, if any, and engineers who look after the technical operation of the station.

For-profit vs. Nonprofit Organization

The goal of any radio station, regardless of its profit structure, is to gain and maintain listeners. The station must provide what its audience wants, whether it is news, talk, classical music, or Top 40 programming. For-profit stations depend on advertising revenue to finance their operation, other than in-house promotions such as sponsored concerts or special live remote broadcasts. This requires a larger and more intensive sales effort and the staff to handle it. Nonprofit stations rely on listener contributions, corporate sponsorship and funding from government agencies or private institutions. This type of station will have a staff specifically focused on fundraising, grant writing and community-based communication in order to maintain financial support to stay on the air.

Legal Issues for a Radio Station

Licensing aspects require all radio stations to direct elements of staff to maintain the legal status of the station. This applies to both operating licensing, overseen by the Federal Communications Commission (FCC), and content licensing. Content refers to music that a station includes on its playlists or other programming that is owned under copyright, such as syndicated sports programs and special music broadcasts. The staff that handles this aspect can be a legal team, as in the case of large corporate stations, or management staff, such as the station manager.

The Broadcast Clock

Most radio stations today operate on a 24-hour basis. The actual daytime operation starts at around 6 a.m. with the "morning drive" program, followed by the mid-morning show that often runs through the noon hour. The afternoon programs generally run from 2 to 6 p.m. (known as the "afternoon drive"), when programming is broken up either into a 6 to 10 format or a 6 to midnight format. After-hours are not regulated by the FCC, and this is generally when a station offers programs that are unique and specific to their target audience.

Television

Television is a widely used telecommunication system for broadcasting Television (often abbreviated to TV or idiot box in British English is a widely used telecommunication system for broadcasting and receiving moving pictures and sound over a distance. The term may also be used to refer specifically to a television set, programming or television transmission.

Since it first became commercially available from the late 1930s, the television set has become a common household communications device in homes and institutions, particularly in the first world, as a source of entertainment and news.Since the 1970s, video recordings on VCR tapes and later, digital playback systems such as DVDs, have enabled the television to be used to view recorded movies and other programs.

A television system may be made up of multiple components, so a screen which lacks an internal tuner to receive the broadcast signals is called a monitor rather than a television. A television may be built to receive different broadcast or video formats, such as high-definition television (HDTV). The elements of a simple broadcast television system are:

An image source. This is an electrical signal representing the visual image, and may be from a camera in the case of live images, a video tape recorder for playback of recorded images, or a film chain-telecine-flying spot scanner for transmission of motion pictures (films).

A sound source. This is an electrical signal from a microphone or from the audio output of a video tape recorder or motion picture film scanner.

A transmitter, which generates radio signals (radio waves) and encodes them with picture and sound information.

An antenna coupled to the output of the transmitter for broadcasting the encoded signals. An antenna to receive the broadcast signals. A receiver (also called a tuner), which decodes the picture and sound information from the broadcast signals, and whose input is coupled to the antenna.

A display device, which turns the electrical signals into visual images. An audio amplifier and loudspeaker, which turns electrical signals into sound waves (speech, music, and other sounds) to accompany the images. Practical television systems include equipment for selecting different image sources, mixing images from several sources at once, insertion of pre-recorded video signals, synchronizing signals from many sources, and direct image generation by computer for such purposes as station identification. The facility for housing such equipment, as well as providing space for stages, sets, offices, etc., is called a television studio, and may be located many miles from the transmitter. Communication from the studio to the transmitter is accomplished via a dedicated cable or radio system.

Television signals were originally transmitted exclusively via land-based transmitters. The quality of reception varied greatly, dependent in large part on the location and type of receiving antenna. This led to the proliferation of large rooftop antennas to improve reception in the 1960s, replacing set-top dipole or “rabbit ears” antennas, which however remained popular. Antenna rotors, set-top controlled servo motors to which the mast of the antenna is mounted, to enable rotating the antenna such that it points to the desired transmitter, would also become popular.

In most cities today, cable television providers deliver signals over coaxial or fiber-optic cables for a fee. Signals can also be delivered by radio from satellites in geosynchronous orbit and received by parabolic dish antennas, which are comparatively large for analog signals, but much smaller for digital. Like cable providers, satellite television providers also require a fee, often less than cable systems. The affordability and convenience of digital satellite reception has led to the proliferation of small dish antennas outside many houses and apartments.

Digital systems may be inserted anywhere in the chain to provide better image transmission quality, reduction in transmission bandwidth, special effects, or security of transmission from reception by non-subscribers. A home today might have the choice of receiving analog or HDTV over the air, analog or digital cable with HDTV from a cable television company over coaxial cable, or even from the phone company over fiber optic lines. On the road, television can be received by pocket sized televisions, recorded on tape or digital media players, or played back on wireless phones (cell or “mobile” phones) over a high-speed or “broadband” internet connection.

Cable TV

Cable television is generally, any system that addition to an initial installation fee.

Since the mid-1970s there has been a proliferation of cable-television systems offering special services. Besides bringing high-quality signals to subscribers, the systems provide additional television channels. Some of these systems can deliver 50 or more channels because they distribute signals occurring within the normal television broadcast band as well as nonbroadcast frequencies. A frequency-conversion device is connected to the television set of the subscriber to accommodate these signals of nonbroadcast frequencies. The increased number of channels allows expanded programming, including broadcasts from distant cities, continuous weather and stock-market reports, programs produced by community groups and educational institutions, and access to pay-TV program materials such as recent motion pictures and sports events not telecast by other broadcasters.

Another feature offered by more and more cable operators is two-way channel capability, which enables subscribers to communicate with programming facilities or information centres within the system. Using the cable connection, home viewers can, for example, participate in public-opinion polls or call up various kinds of written and graphic materials (e.g., citations from reference books, concert schedules, and recipes). The latter feature is offered by systems called videotex, which were first introduced in Great Britain and West Germany. Two-way cable-television systems increasingly allow subscribers with home computers to link up with computer networks, giving the subscribers access to data banks and permitting them to interact with other online users. Cable operators have also experimented with video compression, digital transmission, and high-definition television (HDTV).

In the United States, government deregulation of the cable-television industry in the 1990s allowed cable companies to experiment with telephony and allowed telephone companies to distribute cable-television programming.

Satellite TV

Satellite TV is a type of television programming that is wirelessly delivered to TV sets across the world via a network of radio signals, communications satellites, broadcast centers and outdoor antennas. Broadcast signals are transmitted from satellites orbiting the Earth and received by local and regional satellite TV systems.

Working of a Satellite TV

Satellite TV technology makes use of specialized antennas known as satellite dishes. These satellite dishes transmit signals to a satellite receiver such as a set-top box or satellite tuner module within a TV set. The programming source transmits signals to a satellite provider broadcast center and these waves are then picked up by a compact satellite dish and broadcast onto television sets.

Satellite TV service can also be referred to as direct-broadcast satellite (DBS or DBSTV) service. A DBS provider will select programming—often a wide range of channels and services—and will then broadcast this content to satellite TV subscribers as part of a larger TV package. DBS programming can either be sent to a digital satellite receiver or an analog satellite receiver. Analog satellite television is slowly being replaced by digital satellite programming. Digital satellite television has become increasingly available in better quality known as HD TV (high-definition television). Digitally-broadcast content is characterized by greater picture and sound quality.

Satellite stations and broadcast television stations both transmit TV programming through radio signals. Years ago, the first satellite television TV technologies were broadcast in the C-band radio frequency range. Today, digital satellite TV content is transmitted in the Ku frequency range.

To further understand the technology behind direct-broadcast satellite systems, it is important to review the top features and elements involved in direct-broadcast satellite TV video content delivery: programming sources, satellite provider broadcast centers, satellites, satellite dishes and the satellite receivers. Programming sources refer to networks or channels that offer TV shows and movies for the enjoyment of subscribers. A broadcast center plays an integral role in video content delivery. At broadcast centers, TV providers receive and send broadcast signals to satellites orbiting the Earth. Before sending out a signal, a broadcast center will convert programming into a digital stream of content. Once satellites have received and processed all of these uncompressed signals, they ultimately rebroadcast them to satellite dishes on Earth. Next, a subscriber's outdoor satellite dish will pick up the broadcast signal and transmit it to the satellite receiver located inside of a home. A satellite receiver then completes the information transmission by processing the signal and passing it on to a viewer's television set.

Cable vs. Satellite: TV Service Comparison

When it comes to TV service and programming, does cable or satellite come out on top? Years ago, it was much harder to get satellite TV service in homes across the country. Now, satellite TV technology is recognized as an available option for television viewers throughout the United States. Satellite providers offer quality programming, but are subject to weather-related disruptions.

Cable TV vs. Satellite TV

Availability

Satellite TV providers primarily service subscriber homes that have an unobstructed view of the sky, which allows for continual network coverage and uninterrupted connection via an antenna and satellite dish. Cable TV programming is available in neighborhoods where a provider can run a cable into homes. You can contact your satellite provider or satellite company directly with questions about service availability in your region.

Permission

The installation of a satellite dish and antenna on one's property may not be approved by a landlord, homeowners association or building owner. Throughout the years, restrictions have been imposed by the Federal Communications Commission (FCC) on the exact placement of direct-broadcast satellite antennas. Tenants living in multi-dwelling units, condominiums, apartment buildings, townhouse communities or cooperatives should review the latest FCC guidelines and regulations before installing antennas and satellite dishes.

Reliability and Reception

If a satellite dish or antenna is knocked out of place by inclement weather, homeowners may need to climb a roof to adjust these settings

Equipment

Satellite dishes are required for satellite TV service and these large dishes are affixed prominently to one's roof. If you reside in a rental property location and your landlord approves a satellite dish installation on your property, this dish may then become customer-owned equipment for you to take with you should you move. You may have to assume responsibility for any of the damage the satellite dish may have left on the property's roof, shingles or building frame. Furthermore, you may need to purchase additional satellite equipment in order to receive HD signals. Cable TV requires a cable box or DVR box with your subscription, and some cable companies will allow you to rent these items. It is recommended that you closely compare equipment costs before confirming your subscription or service order.

Bundle Services

Bundling services like television, Internet, phone and home security is often a very convenient option for customers. One advantage of bundled service is a single bill. While cable TV providers frequently offer bundles, satellite TV companies may need to partner up with other carriers in order to provide Internet, phone and other services to their customers.

Online Streaming Service

If you are interested in streaming live TV and watching video content online, you may want to carefully review package details to ensure you sign on with a provider—whether Internet, cable or satellite—that offers a wide array of live TV streaming content, both in-home and on-the-go. Do you want to stream your favorite TV shows and movies online or would you prefer to watch live TV on your mobile devices?

Organizational Structure of a TV Station

Despite the rise of online media, traditional broadcast television stations still deliver news and entertainment via cable and satellite. It takes a veritable army of managers and employees to keep these stations humming. Television stations are organized into five basic departments under the guidance of a company president and a general manager. These departments are news, programming, engineering, sales and advertising, and business administration.

News

The news department is the local face of any television station. News anchors, reporters, meteorologists and sports anchors usually become recognizable personalities in their communities. But behind the scenes are several people that facilitate news coverage, including the news director, makeup artists and a variety of producers, editors and content writers. Entry-level staffers at the news assignment desk, for instance, are on the front lines of the news-gathering operation. They man news-tip phone lines, listen to police scanners, wade through emails and press releases and assist editors and producers in assigning stories and scheduling interviews.

Programming

Programming departments have a manager and assistant staff. The manager coordinates with other departments, especially the production or engineering department, to ensure scheduling and local television listings are accurate and up to date. This person also negotiates with parent companies to secure airing rights for new shows. However, the National Broadcasters Association reports that many large stations have reduced programming departments due to content being pre-determined at higher corporate levels. Another department with a similar function is the traffic department, which sets the advertising schedule and helps develop and edit a station's master list of programming.

Engineering

This department handles the technical aspects of broadcasting and on-air time. Under a chief engineer, otherwise known as director of broadcasting operations, there are a host of managers, engineers and studio crew members, including show directors, cameramen, audio board operators, teleprompter operators, photographers, videographers, tape room editors and engineering technicians. Master control supervisors oversee the master control room and all switchboard operators. They monitor transmitter readings, align satellite receiver equipment and make sure video airs in proper sequence.

Sales and Advertising

This is the department of the television station that generates revenue. The director of sales oversees sales managers, including the national sales manager and local sales manager. The former handles sales representatives from national advertising firms, working on tight deadline to book air time for high-profile clients. The latter supervises a sales staff comprised of account executives. Often working on commission, account executives focus on the local market, making contacts with businesses and other organizations in the community to sell advertising. Advertising departments might also have production staffs that include art directors, electronic graphic artists and voice talent, as well as market researchers who review and interpret ratings.

Business Administration

The business administration department handles the day-to-day business of a TV station. Office managers or station managers work under the general manager and oversee clerks, receptionists and other help staff. Controllers, usually certified public accountants, are responsible overseeing the station's financial transactions, reports and budgets. They consult with other department heads regarding cash flow and expenditures. The human resources or personnel manager hires employees and ensures a safe workplace in all departments. Business administration might also house building maintenance workers who take care of the facility, from the studio to the restrooms.

Digital Media

Digital media is digitized content that can be transmitted over the internet or computer networks. This can include text, audio, video, and graphics. This means that news from a TV network, newspaper, magazine, etc. that is presented on a Web site or blog can fall into this category. Most digital media are based on translating analog data into digital data. The Internet began to grow when text was put onto the Internet instead of stored on papers as it was previously. Soon after text was put onto computers images followed, then came audio and video onto the Internet. Digital media has come a long way in the few short years to become as we know it today and it continues to grow.

In earlier times, messages were once distributed by one particular source to their audience. The audience gathered their sources through a certain form of distribution, whether it was newspapers, magazines, radio, or television. Publishers had a great source of power over the information distributed and how it was perceived by the public. However, all that began drastically change with the rise of computers and more importantly the Internet.

Internet and Computers in Digital Media

Calculation and programming served as the main purposes for earlier computers. However, over time computers began to play a more personal role in humans' lives. No longer were computers being associated with governments or large corporations. As technology grew, people found out that storing information on a computer was convenient and provided good structure. People expanded the functions a computer could provide to its owner. People began to use computers for communication, creative purposes, research, and entertainment.

The Internet is a vast global system that links computer networks. People began taking to the Internet for government, commercial, educational, social, etc. purposes giving rise to digital media. By being able to connect with this growing amount of information, people were able to hear from multiple sources and to make it more personal by posting their own views'. Now publishing and blogging has become so easy that millions of people are able to post onto the internet creating a large amount of websites and information. As new people join the Internet, the amount of information viewed and provided expands.

How Digital Media affected News Media

During World War II, Massachusetts Institute of Technology began a project to develop a computer known as the Whirlwind. The Whirlwind was the first computer that operated in real time and used a monitor for visual purposes. Operating in real-time is a huge advantage that the Internet provided for digital news.

Newspapers are unable to compete with the speed that digital news releases their stories. Not only can the latest updates immediately be found online, but you can also view various articles to gain a better understanding and survey multiple points of view. This staggered the hold newspapers had over their communities and began to disrupt their monopoly. More sources for news sprouted up. Some question the reliability of sources on the Internet. A lot more personal opinions, amateur journalism, and biased articles can be found on the Internet. Blogs are an attractive form of digital media. They truly helped push consumer generated content throughout the Internet. Not only has the Internet allowed consumers to contribute to the news, they are also allowing them to personalize their news experience. A costumer does not have to buy a whole newspaper to read the select number of articles that interest them. Now they can go online and skip the other articles and skip the payment. Although newspapers have adapted to the rise of digital media by placing themselves online, being on the Internet does not guarantee the companies to make money back on lost business. According to the State of the News Media report, 75% of people are not willing to pay for online news content. They are more likely to go back to searching for free results. The report also states that 23% of people said that they would pay five dollars a month for unrestricted access to a local newspaper online. However, doubling the price a month drops the number by 5%.

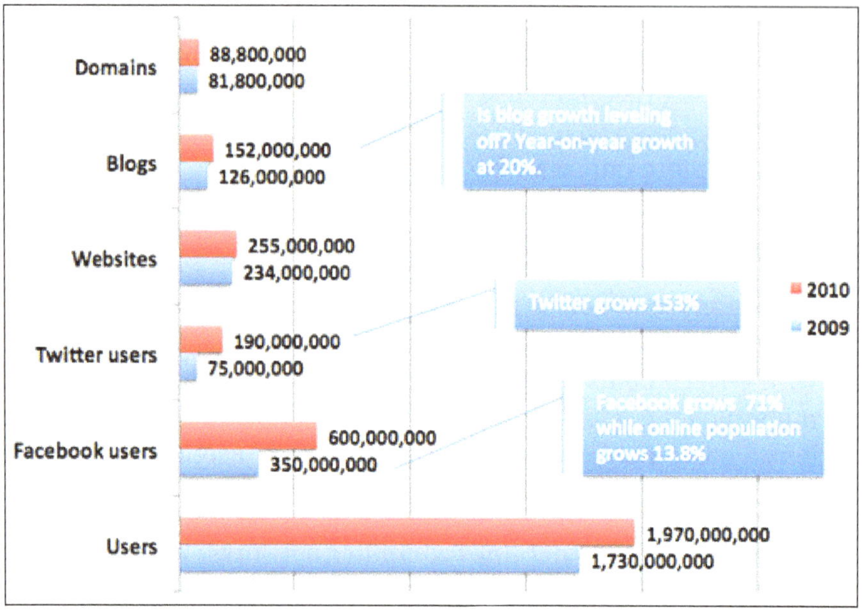

Mobile Devices and Digital Media

Internet use via mobile devices has made a large impact, especially over the most recent years. Mobile devices have played a large role in the digital media. A recent survey with Pew Internet and American Life Project states that 47% of Americans get a form of news from their mobile device. These usually include immediate search needs on the weather, addresses, traffic, etc. More people are also using their cell phones to send them updates from the Internet. Therefore, more people are using their cell phones for more than their original intended purposes. This has further broadened the ever growing field of digital technology. The numbers of people using mobile devices is doubling by the months.

How Digital Media affected the Entertainment Industry

Young adults are familiar with the rise of Napster in the late 1990's and how it affected the music industry and changed it forever. Music was, and still is, obtainable for free over the internet. The music industry has learned to benefit from the Internet and digital media, however it took some readjusting. Now sites can charge customers on sites like Napster so they can legally obtain the music they desire. Since digital media, it seems that i-tunes and downloading music has become more popular than purchasing CDs. Some up and coming bands attempt to use digital media to their benefit and realize that their material can be accessed by the world. They use the Internet as a tool in hopes of gaining a fan base.

The same goes for the movie industry. The movie industry has learned to cope with pirating by forming online accounts where people can purchase or rent movies instead of illegally downloading them. However, this does not mean that the movie industry has made the transition easily. The MPAA is battling against piracy constantly. The recent Writer's Strike was partially inspired by digital media. Writers demanded more compensation for Internet downloads, streaming, straight-to-Internet content, smart phones, and other on-demand online distribution methods. Despite all the battling that is going on, the movie industry still realizes the dawning of a new era.

The television industry has changed very similar to the movie industry. With devices like TiVo, television viewers can now fast forward through commercials. Television shows are being watched over the internet and various clips posted to sites.

The rise of digital media has also allowed people to communicate with others all over the world. Digital media has increased globalization by making communication with people from other parts of the world very easy. Video games can be played over the Internet with people from all over the world. For example, an online video game like World of Warcraft has over 10 million players. Some of the people that play WOW are from across the globe.

Books began appearing on the Internet for free. Writer's now have the option of placing their books online to be purchased or read through e-books. E-books are an electronic version of a printed book. Although the device to read the print may cost a lot more than the book itself, ordering more electric texts can be cheaper. It can be a lot more convenient than buying or borrowing a book. E-books also have the ability to translate text to other languages that the book is not published in.

Digital media has changed the flow of the entertainment industry permanently. With the rise of digital media, more and more people in the entertainment industry realize the importance of the Internet. Websites are made to advertise the show. A website may contain celebrity biographies, photo galleries, blogs, etc. The businesses refer to these sites also to monitor the feedback.

Last year the State of the News Media report predicted that 1,500 newsroom jobs would be lost at the end of the year making them 30% smaller than they were in the year 2000. This shows that digital media in the news continues to grow. Although traditional news media will most likely never be fully extinguished they will need to further adapt to the times. In order to make money, they will need to work with search engines to fight against news sites provided for free and rely more on advertising. Digital media has eliminated many cultural boundaries and will continue to do so as other less developed countries begin to become more reliant on technology. Digital media has provided instant communication between people all over the world. Different forms of digital media make this interaction easy and fun. Technology and the sharing of photographs on the Internet have found ways past language barriers. Thanks to digital media we are now entering a world that is culturally globalized.

Media Management

Media management is the practice of directing and controlling media related businesses and business functio includes management roles in the media industry, entertainment industry and media related teams in other ind Media management is a broad practice that can include the following areas:

Business Strategy

Developing strategies for media businesses to achieve goals such as revenue in a competitive and constrained For example, a strategy to adopt a new business model for a video game company based on the sales of virtual goods.

Media Strategy

Developing marketing communications strategies for businesses in any industry. For example, a media strategy launching a new high speed trains that involves media production, advertising, events, product showrooms and relationships with media representatives and influencers.

Marketing Communications

Managing the implementation of strategy in areas such as promotion, advertising, sales and branding. Public Relations Managing relationships with stakeholders and the media to share information and build your reputation. This focused on major communications such as press releases, product launches and investor events.

Social Media Management

Managing relationships with stakeholders through social media. This is often focused on promotion and manage feedback from customers and the public.

Media Analysis

Developing data and analysis of audiences and their use of media. This includes finding ways to reach a particular audience at a reasonable cost. Media analysis may also look at factors such as user intent and attention to disc reach an audience when they are most open to influence or ready to buy. Media Procurement Buying advertising to reach audiences. This includes automated processes such as buying digital advertising f exchange and processes of relationship building and negotiation. Media Technology Procuring, developing, operating and optimizing technologies for the production, delivery, management, buying and selling of media.

Media Production

Producing media such as films, music, video games, promotion videos and informational content. Media Distribution The distribution of media such as processes for distributing films to theatres. This may involve developing an distribution partnerships. Sales Management of media sales such as selling print ads in a magazine.

Talent Management

Managing the career of creative professionals such as actors, musicians and performing artists. This is a type acts to represent the interests of clients.

Media Measurement Measuring the objectives of a media organization or promotional effort.

Product Development

Developing media products and services. This may include innovation methods such as fail well whereby bra tried in small pilots that are allowed to fail cheaply and safely. Such methods of inexpensive experimentation common in the media industry long before they were adopted by other industries such as information technology.

Product Management

Managing media products through their entire lifecycle including planning, development, launch, improvement of-life. For example, a manager who is responsible for the revenue for a music streaming service who works sustains a large subscription base.

Licenses and Rights

Managing your licenses for other firm's media and enforcing your rights such as trademarks and copyright. Fo an entertainment company that uses artificial intelligence to recognize when its content has been uploaded wi permission to video sharing sites.

Legal and Regulatory

Developing and enforcing legal agreements with employees, partners and customers and ensuring compliance regulations. For example, a music company that manages complex legal agreements with a large number of a distribution partners.

Legal and Regulatory Developing and enforcing legal agreements with employees, partners and customers and ensuring compliance regulations. For example, a music company that manages complex legal agreements with a large number of a distribution partners.

Media Asset Management

Managing valuable digital assets and metadata. For example, a film production company that manages millio related to the master copies for films along with metadata such as credits, technical information and licensing details.

References

- What-is-electronic-media: skillmaker.edu.au, Retrieved 18 May, 2019
- Electronic-media: positivenegativeimpact.com, Retrieved 19 April, 2019
- Radios-digital-future: britannica.com, Retrieved 23 June, 2019
- What-Is-the-Difference-Between-AM-and-FM-Radio: progressive-concepts.com, Retrieved 18 July, 2019
- What-actually-is-the-difference-between-am-and-fm-radio: soundfly.com, Retrieved 15 March, 2019
- Corporate-structure-radio-station- 6067123: bizfluent.com, Retrieved 16 April, 2019
- Organizational-structure-tv-station- 5744951: careertrend.com, Retrieved 14 June, 2019
- Media-management: simplicable.com, Retrieved 16 July, 2019

2

Audience and Audience Research

Audience can be defined as masses of people with whom communication is performed through every medium. Clients in business, customers in market, members of an organization, etc. can be referred to as audience. The topics elaborated in this chapter will help in gaining a better perspective about audience research.

Audience

An audience is who you're communicating with through every medium; they're the spectators watching in the bleachers, metaphorically speaking. More importantly for businesses, an audience is a group of potential clients and customers. An audience isn't only helpful from a potential sales standpoint though, they also can help a brand immensely if the relationship is positively mutual. An engaged and enthusiastic audience can become a brand's biggest advocate.

Audience Development

Audience development is very much a buzz phrase in the content marketing and media space at the moment, but that doesn't mean people shouldn't take it seriously or think it will soon be a thing of the past. an official definition for it: "The term Audience Development describes activity which is undertaken specifically to meet the needs of existing and potential audiences and to help arts [and cultural] organisations to develop on-going relationships with audiences. It can include aspects of marketing, commissioning, programming, education, customer care and distribution."

Difference between Audience Development and Audience Engagement

Not only is audience development an integral part of content strategy, but so is audience engagement. But what exactly is the difference? Audience development happens before audience engagement. If you have nobody to engage with, you have no audience. Both should be ongoing, but development organically happens before the engagement. Audience development is what you do to find your audience, audience engagement is how you interact once you find them.

Find the Audience

Fortunately, in today's digital age finding an audience is a lot easier than it used to be. Through real-time commenting and social media, writers, marketers and content producers have better insight into who they're communicating with than ever before. A few general practices to follow include:

- Listen to who's commenting on your blog , social media and use keyword research to find what people are interested in.

- Surveys. It never hurts to just straight out ask your potential audience who they are and what they want.
- Social media. Leverage it to learn about the interests of who you're speaking to.

Audience Research

Audience research is a broad term that, in principle, denotes the systematic study of any → audience for any purpose. In practice, the term usually connotes efforts to describe and analyze patterns of media consumption, often for some commercial or administrative purpose. Such research became commonplace in the early twentieth century as new forms of mass media were introduced (e.g., film and radio) and those media became increasingly intertwined with the business of advertising and marketing. Contemporary audience research uses a wide range of theories and methods, which can be organized using the familiar labels of theoretical vs applied, quantitative vs qualitative, and, somewhat less conventionally, syndicated vs custom research.

Theoretical vs. Applied Audience Research

Theoretical audience research operates on two conceptual levels; micro and macro. The former tends to look at audiences from the "inside out," adopting the perspective of an individual audience member. Of theoretical interest are questions about what motivates media selections, what stimuli command attention, how media are used in everyday life, what meanings and pleasures are derived from use, and how people engage media as consumers and fans. The relevant bodies of theory run the gamut from the social scientific to the humanistic The latter, macro-level research tends to look at audiences from the "outside," in an attempt to understand their characteristics and behaviors in the aggregate. This perspective sees audiences as markets and publics and is often rooted in economics and marketing. Working at this level of analysis has allowed researchers to develop models or "laws" of audience.

Applied audience research provides information that can be acted upon by institutions and media industries. It is more prevalent than theoretical research, due primarily to the commercial character of most media systems. Since the early days of radio, advertisers have demanded surveys documenting the size and composition of the otherwise invisible audience. This gave rise to audience "ratings" research, which has become essential to the operation of advertiser-supported media throughout much of the world (→ Nielsen Ratings). Such data provide the basis for buying and selling audiences, and can be useful in supporting macro-level theoretical research. Commercial motives also drive a variety of research efforts measuring more "qualitative" aspects of the audience. These include surveys and various ethnographic methods designed to assess audience preferences, attitudes, lifestyles, and product usage. Foundations and nonprofit organizations may also do applied research to determine how media are used and whether they are meeting various social or instructional objectives. The producers of the children's television series Sesame Street, for example, have a long history of conducting evaluative research.

Quantitative vs. Qualitative Audience Research

Quantitative research methods are common in audience research (→ Quantitative Methodology).

The most prevalent is → survey research, which is based on some form of probability sampling. Audience ratings companies use surveys to estimate audience size and demographic composition for an ever growing number of media (e.g., radio, television, movies, video games, out-of-home, Internet, etc.). Other regularly scheduled surveys are used to provide syndicated reports that relate people's product purchases and personal characteristics to their media use, or assess their familiarity with and liking for various programs and celebrities (i.e., Q scores). One-of-a-kind surveys are often used to gauge media preferences, levels of engagement, opinions, and other administratively or theoretically useful information (→ Public Opinion Polling). Very large, nonrandom, samples or panels are also sometimes used to gather data. In fact, newer media technologies that produce a record of their use (e.g., server logs or digital cable boxes) offer the prospect of survey-like behavioral data based on a census rather than a sample (→ Rating Methods).

Quantitative audience research is not, however, confined to surveys. Media industries routinely measure the appeal of their offerings. Television and movie industries have long used a kind of theater-testing in which prospective viewers are recruited to watch a forthcoming film or pilot program. Respondents view the show in an auditorium and are asked to score various aspects of what they see – often in a near continuous manner that allows researchers to assess the ebb and flow of audience reactions. Such testing can help executives decide whether to go forward with a project, and if so, how to modify or promote it. Similar techniques have been used to measure people's reactions to political communication and candidate debates. True experiments are relatively uncommon in applied audience research, but have been, and continue to be, a staple of more academically oriented theoretical research; (→ Experiment, Field). Laboratory research sometimes features the use of physiological measures including eye movement, heart rate, and galvanic skin response (→ Experiment, Laboratory).

Although quantitative methods predominate, qualitative methods are increasingly popular in both applied and theoretical audience research (→ Qualitative Methodology). Sometimes labeled audience ethnographies, these techniques include focus groups, unstructured interviews, and participant observation (→ Ethnomethodology). Focus groups, in which a moderator guides a small number of recruits in a discussion, have long been a staple of marketers and programmers. The method has been used to develop products and ad campaigns, craft radio station formats, assess media personalities, and, in the case of more theoretical research, help determine how people "decode" or assign meaning to media texts. Similarly, in-depth → interviews and → observation have been used by both theorists and practitioners to understand the social uses of television, how people adapt to the introduction of digital video recorders (DVRs), and concurrent media use throughout the day.

Syndicated vs. Custom Audience Research

Syndicated audience research is a standardized research product that is sold to multiple subscribers. It plays an important role in media industries because its costs can be distributed across many buyers, and it provides a credible, "third party" accounting of audiences independent of the media or advertisers. The most visible form of syndicated research is audience ratings. Measurement companies in the US and much of the world record audience behaviors using a variety of techniques, some of which are quite expensive (→ People-Meter). These data are processed and packaged as different reports that constitute a "currency" used to buy and sell audiences.

Like many forms of information, producing such research has high "first copy" costs, and very low marginal costs. Moreover, the product is a → "public good." Once created, its supply is not diminished by consumption. These characteristics give the syndicators flexibility in pricing to attract additional business. They also make it difficult for new competitors to enter the market, since challengers will incur first-copy costs with uncertain prospects for displacing the competition and recovering those costs. Further, incumbent syndicators typically offer products that are the result of an ongoing negotiation between clients with disparate interests (e.g., advertisers and media). Their estimates reflect a compromise upon which all agree to conduct business, and their numbers become embedded in the routines of the affected industries. Even modest changes can upset the ecology of the system. Hence, in established industries it is not uncommon to see one syndicator emerge as the principle, quasi-official scorekeeper for the medium in question.

Custom research is tailor-made to suit the needs of a particular client. Media organizations often conduct research for their own internal consumption. Radio stations offering popular music formats will, for example, conduct "call-out" telephone surveys to assess the popularity of current hit songs. Alternatively, outside research firms and consultants are sometimes hired to gather data and make recommendations. Since these studies are designed to client specifications they can be quite useful internally, although for external consumption they lack the apparent objectivity of syndicated research.

Criticisms of Audience Research

Because of its central, and highly visible, role in the operation of media industries, syndicated research, and in particular audience ratings, has been the object of criticism. Generally, critics have one of three concerns: the accuracy of existing services, the need for different regimes of measurement, and more radical challenges to the entire enterprise of measurement.

In the US alone, billions of dollars in advertising are allocated in accordance with audience ratings. Programming is, in turn, cancelled, renewed, and cloned on the basis of those estimates. Increases in the sheer abundance and portability of electronic media, along with advertisers' desires to reach ever more narrowly defined target markets, has caused many in the industry to ask whether the current system is sufficiently accurate. While bigger, more representative samples and better behavioral measures always remain a possibility, they must be weighed against their costs. Quality is one of the factors upon which industry participants inevitably compromise.

A related concern addresses the appropriate object of measurement. The new media environment seems to invest audience members with ever greater control over what they see and when they see it. Advertisers worry that a simple count of "eyeballs" is no longer enough to guide their expenditures. As a result, there is growing interest in measuring the extent to which people are "engaged" with the media they consume. Such efforts are not new. "Qualitative ratings" have been used in western Europe and were briefly available in the US during the 1980s. The problem is reaching consensus on a useful definition of such factors, agreeing how to measure them, and finding clients willing to pay the price.

A much larger and more radical charge is that all commercially motivated audience research is part of an undesirable enterprise bent on colonizing and commodifying audiences (→ Audience Commodity). It is true that media industries often reduce people to one dimensional members of a target market, or assign them value on a "cost per thousand" basis. Whether the public is, on balance, harmed by this is debatable. While audience research inevitably fails to capture all the complexities of media consumption, the machinery of measurement has the virtue of making the audience manifest to institutions that desperately seek its attention.

Importance of Audience Research

Media development is often based on untested assumptions about the impact of media on governance. Local audience research can vastly improve the planning and effectiveness of media assistance projects.

When it comes to debating the field of media development, we can identify a significant lack of audience research – both in academia and in grey literature. We can detect the consequences of this gap for project design and policy making and also for broader efforts to integrate media into governance debates. So what about bringing back the audience?

Audience research here refers to two things: firstly, research measuring changing levels of media consumption amongst target audiences, and secondly, the (often qualitative) research which seeks to understand the complex, contingent and context-specific ways in which citizens make use of the media, both within governance processes and as part of their daily lives.

While the lack of evidence has been noted before, the extent of this gap has never been directly investigated.

An analysis of recently published scoping reviews of the relevant literature shows that:

- There is often an assumption that the media have a direct effect on audiences. The broader context or environment is seldom analyzed in depth. This instrumentalist view of the media is inaccurate, as the potential effects of different media on individuals are made up of complex combinations of long-term and short-term processes which are actively negotiated by audiences themselves and contingent upon both the contexts in which media are consumed and the broader lifeworld's of audiences. Put simply – we all respond differently to media content depending on our mood, knowledge, previous experiences, attention, trust, media habits and personal circumstances, amongst other things.

- Local audience research does not sufficiently differ in the content and scope of evidence from studies conducted in the Global North. There is also an absence of scholarship concerning how users actually engage with the media.
- The methodologies adopted for project evaluation in the field of media development focus on quick data gathering and finding success stories. This is problematic because it allows little room for a thorough examination of the uses of media by different audiences. Audience surveys conducted as part of an evaluation are often too small to ensure statistical significance, do not sufficiently target rural or poor audiences and focus only on reach and listenership. Of course, there are very good reasons why many media assistance evaluations adopt this approach, including a lack of time, planning and resources. The point here is not to criticize the evaluators but to point out that, as a result, project evaluations seldom produce robust evidence regarding what audiences actually do with media in relation to governance.
- Many manuals, guidelines and other types of practical media development literature include issues like mission and governance of a media house, management and staffing, infrastructure and finances and programming and community involvement but do not mention audience research as an integral element for performance assessment and improvement.
- The lack of reliable and accessible quantitative audience research data in many developing countries is a key element which has been widely neglected in international media assistance. Accurate quantitative audience research data for the transparency of media markets in the developing world is of crucial importance and a precondition for the financial sustainability of independent media houses.

In an era of evidence-based policy making, this is problematic for those wishing to raise the profile of media in debates about governance. Equally, for those seeking to design effective media development interventions, there is insufficient evidence to explain the precise ways in which, and circumstances under which, media may contribute to good governance (and vice versa).

This lack of detailed audience research is also important for challenging optimistic and universalizing normative ideals about the role that media should play in promoting good governance. The theory of 'media imperialism' was one of the dominant paradigms of development communication in the 1970s. It was claimed that, influenced by the dominance of mass media in more powerful countries, an exploitative capitalist and Western culture was spread to less powerful ones.

This theory rested, at least partly, on the assumption that Western ideology was carried by mainstream media and injected into the minds of non-Western audiences. The fallacy of this assumption was exposed by a number of audience studies which revealed the dynamics and complexities of the ways in which different audiences interpret content.

In the same way, audience research that focuses on the perspectives of ordinary citizens will likely expose and challenge the underlying assumptions within media development. Within the wider governance research agenda, for example, research which has adopted the perspective of citizens or end users has successfully challenged the traditional state-centric view of governance and instead highlighted the importance of hybrid and informal systems of governance.

De-centering the media. Most existing research into media development presupposes the importance of media in governance processes. Yet there may be circumstances in which the media's role is not important. Research has to be open to these possibilities.

Triangulation. Individuals are not always willing or able to offer an accurate and reliable account of their media habits when responding to surveys or as part of a focus group. Comparing data gathered from multiple contexts, over a period of time, is a useful way of increasing the credibility and validity of the results. Additional methods may include audience diaries and observational data.

Strengthening audience research capacities in developing countries. The establishment of independent audience research bodies (joint industry committees), the training of qualified audience researchers in developing countries and improved access to audience research data should become its own field of international media assistance.

Of course, generating research that takes into account even some of these issues will inevitably require a significant amount of resources. However, research has shown that rigorous audience research may refute various assumptions underlying media development projects and therefore contribute to significant improvements in project and program planning. In addition, supporting an independent and reliable audience research sector in developing countries would be an important step towards a transparent and sustainable media market in developing countries.

Social Media Analytics

Social media analytics is the practice of gathering data from social media websites and analyzing that data using social media analytics tools to make business decisions. The most common use of social media analytics is to mine customer sentiment to support marketing and customer service activities.

The first step in a social media intelligence initiative is to determine which business goals the data that is gathered and analyzed will benefit. Typical objectives include increasing revenues, reducing customer service costs, getting feedback on products and services, and improving public opinion of a particular product or business division.

Once the business goals have been identified, businesses should define key performance indicators (KPIs) to objectively evaluate the business analytics data.

Metrics to Track

Business metrics derived from social media analytics may include customer engagement, which could be measured by the number of followers for a Twitter account and number of retweets and mentions of a company's name. With social media monitoring, businesses can also look at how many people follow their presence on Facebook and the number of times people interact with their social profile by sharing or liking their posts.

More advanced types of social media analysis involve sentiment analytics. This practice involves sophisticated natural-language-processing machine learning algorithms parsing the text in a person›s social media post about a company to understand the meaning behind that person›s statement. These algorithms can create a quantified score of the public›s feelings toward a company based on social media interactions and give reports to management on how well the company interacts with customers.

Popular Tools

There are a number of types of social media analytics tools for analyzing unstructured data found in tweets and Facebook posts. In addition to text analysis, many enterprise-level social media analytics tools will harvest and store the data. Some of these tools come from niche players, while more traditional enterprise analytics software vendors offer packages dedicated to social media intelligence.

As more social media analytics rely on machine learning, popular open platforms like R, Python and TensorFlow serve as social media analytics tools.

Importance of Social Media Analytics

There is a tremendous amount of information in social media data. In decades past, enterprises paid market research companies to poll consumers and conduct focus groups to get the kind of information that consumers now willingly post to public social media platforms.

The problem is this information is in the form of free text and natural language, the kind of unstructured data that analytics algorithms have traditionally. But as machine learning and artificial intelligence have advanced, it's become easier for businesses to quantify in a scalable way the information in social media posts.

This allows enterprises to extract information about how the public perceives their brand, what kind of products consumers like and dislike and generally where markets are going. Social media analytics makes it possible for businesses to quantify all this without using less reliable polling and focus groups.

Social Media Intelligence is the closest term-cousin to Social Media Analytics. Social Intelligence represents the stack of technology solutions and methods used to monitor social media, including social conversations and emerging trends.

This intelligence is then analyzed and used to create meaningful content and make business decisions across many disciplines.

Social Media Listening is one of the terms most often confused with Social Media Analytics. But Social Listening applies to one specific aspect of Social Analytics: Learning about your audience.

The goal here is to uncover what they love, hate, and love to hate – as opposed to any assumptions you may have. It's about getting to know them as people, not just prospects.

For instance, if you want to know what people in Boston have to say about pizza, you can find out using a tool. From there, you can look for additional common ground to create audience segments to make your interactions more personal.

Social Media Monitoring is the second term most often confused for Social Media Analytics. It's also thought to be synonymous with Social Listening, but the two are very different.

Social Monitoring focuses on following social audiences to be alerted to spikes in activity that present either an opportunity you wouldn't want to miss, or a potential disaster you want to avoid. It's about seeing posts like this in time to respond and avoid a viral crisis.

Social Competitive Analysis is the process of investigating competitors of your brand and their audience. Because social media is such a transparent medium, Social Analytics Tools can be applied to brands beyond your own.

This gives you the advantage of seeing how they serve their customers, what consumers love or hate about them, and what new products or services they're offering.

This information allows you to save the day when things go wrong, or save your own budget by learning from competitors' mistakes. You'll also see what your shared audience gets excited about, so you can capitalize on fresh ideas you might never have had yourself.

Image Analytics is a new feature made possible by the evolution of Social Analytics technology. Image Analytics levels up text analysis by identifying scenes, facial expressions, geographical locations, brand logos and more in social images. This is especially useful when a brand is pictured, but not called out in social text.

As social users become increasingly visual, the ability to perform Image Analytics becomes more of a deal-breaker when researching Social Analytics Tools.

Social Media Sentiment Analysis

Social Sentiment is the tie-in that applies to all facets of your Social Analytics. Without it, you don't have any way of gauging why you've suddenly got 500K more "likes" or shares than usual. What if an uptick in activity isn't a good thing? The only way to know is through Sentiment Analysis.

This layer of Social Analytics uses Natural Language Processing (NLP) to understand whether social conversations are positive or negative, and to measure the strength of those emotions. This helps you triage responses so you don't waste energy on posts that don't matter, while ignoring posts that do.

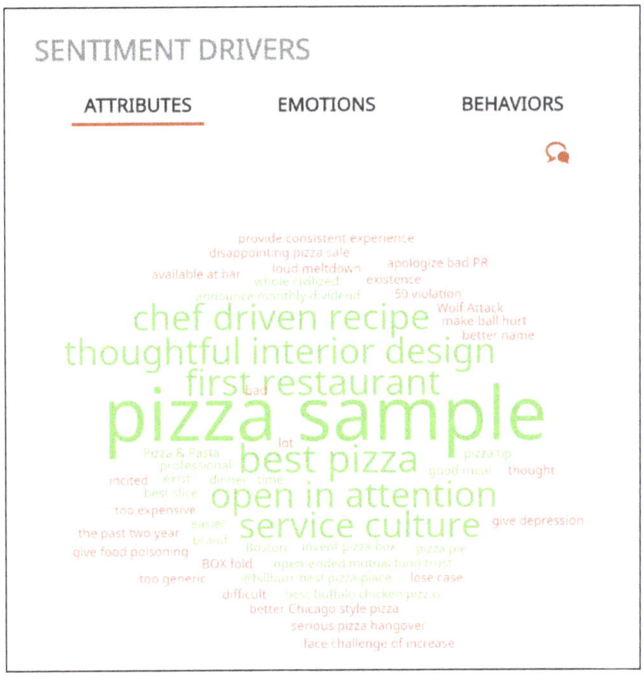

Customer Experience Analytics combines Social Listening insights with Voice of the Customer (VoC) verbatims like surveys, star ratings, net promoter scores, website feedback, chat messages, market research, and data from internal systems like call center, help center, and web support collected via CRM tools.

This additional data can be brought into your Social Analytics to give you a comprehensive understanding of your customers across all touchpoints.

Audience in Social Media

When it comes to online marketing and advertising, targeting right audiences is the key to success. This is because no online content will be having any influence unless you are able to pitch it to an appropriate audience. It doesn't matter how engaging or persuasive your content is.

If you are not able to find targeted and appropriate audience then your online business is useless. Here we will give you some tips to get the social media target audience.

How to Get Social Media Target Audience

It is not as easy as it looks to get the social media target audience. You have to follow and do certain things in which the audiences get influenced by your content.

Identify the Audience

Before you plan to search your audience, you have to decide that what type of audience you want. What will be the age group of the audiences? Do they have anything in similar?

These are some of the questions that you have to ask as they will give you a clear idea about who your audiences are going to be. you are doing social media services for large-brands, mid-size or small businesses then you have to help them to figure out their target audiences. One of the best ways is to ask some common question to your clients which will help you in identifying.

You can also check the social media channels and look where your audiences are spending their maximum time. In this way, you can get some idea about your social media target audience.

Take Survey of your Customers

It will not be helpful if you rely fully on the guide that is given above. Sometimes doing a survey of the customers will also help a lot.

Ask them everything that you need and know and see which social network they prefer the most. You can start with some of the following questions that are mentioned below:

- What is their favorite social media site?
- Do they read blogs regularly?
- How much time do they spend on social media?
- What are the kinds of people they follow in social media?

Find Out the Size of your Audiences

Facebook ads are not just for the promotion of your ads, they can also be helpful for finding out the size of your audience as well as some clear data about them. If you see that your target audience is quite large then it will be better if you start from the lower niche.

Try to narrow your audience as much as you can and look exact niches in which the potential buyers have an interest in. in the case of social media marketing, it can be the case of curation of the content, search engine marketing, advertising, and many others.

In any guide of marketing, you will find the same thing saying it is better to spend money on a small and engaged niche than spending it on the larger ones.

Find your Customers and Connect with Them

One crucial thing to keep in mind is that it is easy to upload the database of your email in almost any site of social media in order to find your customers. With the help of the Facebook Ads Manager, one can easily create a custom audience.

Now with the help of your CRM combining with the social media management software, you can reach out and get engaged with the social media target audience whenever you want to.

After you have created the custom audience, you can ask Facebook to create "lookalike audience". The lookalike audience is just as same as your valuable audiences. This means that Facebook will help you to put in front of more people who are just like your present audience.

Search Social Media Target Audience in Facebook Groups

If you are using Facebook like other people then you can go to the search bar and search for pages or groups that are matching to the interests of your customers.

However, if you have been providing the social media marketing services for more than two or three clients then it will be better you segment the audiences in a proper way so that you don't get confused.

Modify the Contents for your Audience

After you are done with the basics and finding your target audience, you can start to modify the contents according to their interest. Many times you will see that there are many complaints regarding the engagement of the posts. Here are some of the rules that you have to keep in mind:

- Not more than a single curated post in a week.
- Only two promotions in a week.
- There should be at least one engaging content in a single day.

So, is your page an engaging one? The audiences do not follow your page to buy your product every day. So, make sure you post content that is engaging as well as inspirational.

Utilize Hashtags Correctly

Hashtags are a fundamental part to rapidly grow a connected Social Media Target Audience base in a convenient and effective fashion. Utilizing hashtags will open your content to the new individuals who are not your followers.

All things considered, you need to realize that finding best hashtags for your business is vital for drawing in a crowd of people that will change over into more engagement, deals, and conversion later on.

In principle, it bodes well to utilize the most mainstream hashtags for the introduction – yet by and by, you won't get the long-term results. Beyond any doubt, hashtags like #love or #beauty have a huge number of posts, yet these nonexclusive hashtags will be pointless for your business if you do not get customers.

So, knowing the right tags and utilizing them will offer the real advantages to you.

Work with Social Media Influencers

Utilizing the correct influencers for your online image is the most outstanding amongst other approaches to rapidly grow a Social Media Target Audience base. It is always essential to use the privilege influencer who is well associated with your brand.

- You should never prefer influence just on their followers' count but upon their relevancy to your brand. It is important for you to ensure that your influencer bodes well for your brand image.

- It resembles local advertising and won't interfere with the browsing experience of your audiences. It also helps in SEO of your brand. It also builds brand awareness, plus it is affordable and offers higher returns on investments.

Some more broad tips to enable you to grow your Social Media Target Audience organically are:

Top Social Media Hacks to Increase Audience Base

- Use Videos,
- Be Consistent in Posting,
- Keep Interacting,
- Optimize Social Media images for all social networks,
- Schedule different tweets from your new blogs,
- Use Social Media Chatbot,
- Ask teams to pre-schedule Instagram Posts,
- Curate Slideshare Content,
- Create effective Call to Actions,
- Use Gifs in your Tweets, etc.

Use Social Media Tools to Automate Social Marketing

This is one of the most effective methods to optimize social media marketing in a more convenient fashion to generate Social Media Target Audience base. There are different tools that will alleviate your task of social media scheduling and management.

Utilizing tools will enable you to perform multiple tasks simultaneously that will increase your efficiency. Let us have a look at some of the social media marketing tools that you can use:

- HootSuite,
- HubSpot,
- MeetEdgar,
- TweetDeck,
- IFTTT,
- Buffer,
- Sprout Social,
- Raven,
- Social Flow.

References

- Audience-development-strategy, content-marketing: scripted.com, Retrieved 16 June, 2019
- The-significance-of-audience-research-in-media-development-19556460: dw.com, Retrieved 18 July, 2019
- What-is-social-media-analytics-why-is-it-important: netbase.com, Retrieved 17 May, 2019
- Reach-your-social-media-target-audience: marketing91.com, Retrieved 16 April, 2019
- Social-media-analytics: searchbusinessanalytics.techtarget.com, Retrieved 08 August, 2019

3

Media Channels for Content Distribution

Information stored in digital format is defined as digital content. This chapter delves into different ways in which digital content can be distributed such as, radio broadcasting, radio programming, television programming, broadcast syndication, paid promotion, etc., to provide an extensive understanding of the subject.

Creation of excellent content is just the beginning – it is the content distribution that helps your content get discovered, read and re shared, increasing the reach and the overall impact of your content. Content distribution is the process of promoting your content to specific, targeted individuals and communities where the likelihood of is increased. Any content creation effort will be worthless if newly developed content is not being timely distributed in multiple media formats through various channels! Content distribution have a lot of do with for your business. Because it's the collection of media elements that are being used in order to support the sales of products and services. There are 3 main types of content distribution channels – Owned, Earned, and Paid.

Owned Content Distribution Channel

It includes distributing content to media channels that your company owns and controls such as, your blog, email newsletter, social media channels, or microsite. The advantage of an owned content distribution channel is that marketers can distribute their content out to as many people as possible – you can rush to post more blog posts, more newsletters, etc. Let's have a look at how owned media platforms can be used for better content distribution:

Blog Posts

Make sure that the is consistent as consistency ensures the trust of users in your brand! Write about the topics that would prove to be of value to your audience. Consider experimenting with different content formats to have a better understanding of what works best for your target audience.

Landing Pages – They are dedicated standalone pages that can prove to be ultimate conversion tools for your campaigns. An optimized landing page omits many of the distractions found on blogs and traditional websites resulting in better conversions. Social media channels – Social media and content marketing are great companions! There exist a wide range of social networks that help you build brand awareness, perform market research, generate leads and build a relationship with customers. All that you are required to do is stay consistent on these social media channels, use a call to action in all your updates, upload high-quality images, and abide by your brand guidelines across all these channels.

Discussion Forums – They include platforms such as Reddit and Quora, that empower you to share information about topics related to your brand, product, and solutions. Users utilize these platforms to ask questions and hold discussions, allowing you to connect with them, answer their queries and build better relationships.

Earned Content Distribution Channel

It is hardest distribution channel to achieve and optimize as it involves the distribution of your content via third-parties. They can share the content in the form of press coverage, reposts, shares, or product reviews. Interchanging guest blog posts with notable brands is a standout amongst other earned media distribution strategy. It results in excellent quality backlinks as well as better user engagement as you can reach out to a broader audience.

Paid Content Distribution Channel

This is when brands explicitly pay to get their content in front of their audience through different paid promotion channels. I must say, money still talks money still talks! This form of distribution ensures placement and delivers eyeballs instantly to help achieve your objectives. A tremendous number of options are available to enable you to extend your reach and elevate engagement with your brand:

Search Engine Marketing – It is one of the most effective ways to grow your business in a competitive marketplace. It involves using search engines such as Google and Bing to elevate your promotions to your intended audiences. You can bid on keywords that users of 'Google and Bing' might enter in the search box while looking for specific products or services. Doing this shows up your promotions close by results for those search engines and give you the opportunity to motivate your visitors to sign up for your service or buy your products.

Social Media Ads – Social media networks also allows you to advertise your offers to your target audience employing paid advertisements. Facebook boosted posts, promoted tweets, Youtube ads, and updates are extraordinary methods to increase your content's reach much further, and do so much faster, by building paid promotional campaigns around your strongest content assets and special features. But what makes social media extremely suitable for paid promotion?

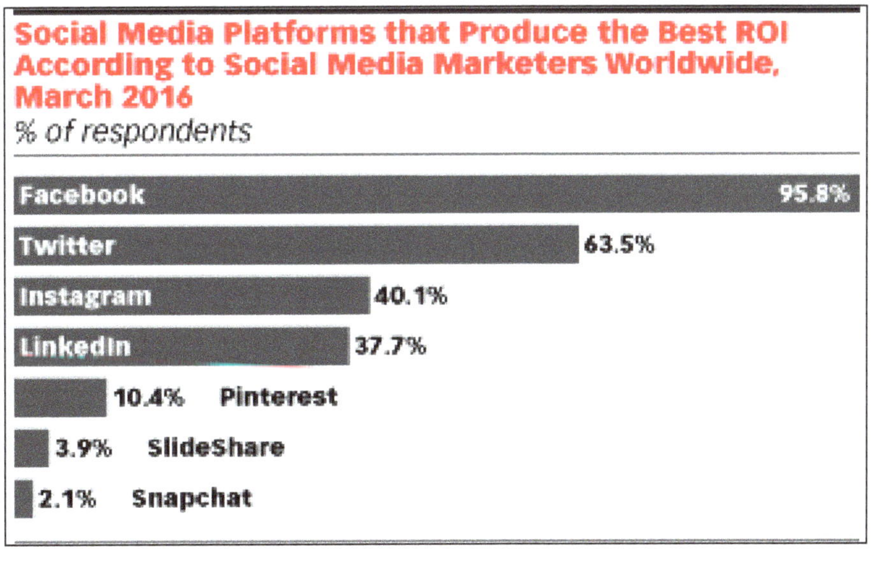

Social media is incredible at paid promotion as it provides you with fantastic targeting opportunities based on the following – demographics, interest, and behaviors. As per, Facebook produces the best ROI in social media platforms:

Native advertising – "Native advertising enables you to publish your content in the publications of online publishers. Your content will be totally "branded," however it will to a great extent match the look and feel of the of the platform on which it appears." Basically, native ads don't look like ads at all, i.e. they are non-problematic to the user's experience on a webpage. You can use networks like, and to run your native ads.

The success of your content marketing endeavors relies upon how effectively you distribute the content assets that you created and choose distribution channels that work for your brand and audience. To round out this talk, how about we compare the challenge of content distribution with a long-standing dilemma: If a tree falls in a forest, and nobody is around to hear, does it make a clamor? Similarly, if you publish your content, and nobody sees it, will it have an effect?

Content Distribution Network

A content distribution network also addressed as content delivery network plays a crucial role in the distribution of content. It comprises a large group of servers that are strategically placed across the globe to accelerate the delivery of rich media and web content to devices that are connected to the internet. These servers pull the assets that are static from the origin server and cache a copy of those assets empowering visitors to retrieve the data from the server that is closest. This helps to bridge the gap in distance between a visitor who is situated in Australia, while the origin server is situated in North Carolina, for instance:

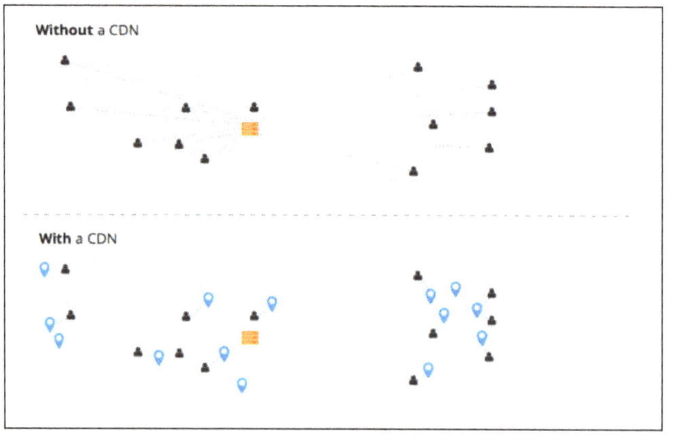

Distance plays a significant role in latency times. Thus having a dispersed bunch of servers that each hold cached content from your website could help to reduce latency and improve website performance. Other benefits of Content Distribution Networks are as follows:

- Enhances SEO.
- Less expensive than you may suspect.
- Traffic spike & downtime security.
- Increased security.

- Easy integration.
- Better user experience.

Writing a Distribution Plan

The accompanying will demonstrate to you generally accepted methods to make a compelling substance promoting circulation plan in five simple advances: There are chances that your content is losing all sense of direction in the crowd without a proper content distribution plan in place! If you want to perceive any positive results, effectively promote your content with the goal that your target audience come across it. It is believed by many marketers that you should spend . The following will show you how to create an effective content marketing distribution plan in 3 easy steps:

Research your Audience

The first step to creating an effective content marketing distribution plan is to create a buyer persona – a profile detailing your ideal customer based on market research.

You want to know as much as you can about your ideal audience. Find the answers to the following questions to ensure that you are sharing the content with the right people:

- How old are they?
- What do they do?
- What are their interests and hobbies?

You have to create and distribute with your buyer persona in mind, always. An excellent way to learn more about your audience is through Google Analytics. Pay attention to what content is performing better than the rest.

Create Specific Goals and KPIs

After creating the robust buyer personas, you'll want to set the key performance indicators and your goals. KPIs are precise measurements of performance that demonstrate to you how well your objectives are being met.

Think about the following:

- How many shares you'd like across each platform you distribute through?
- How much engagement do you anticipate from your audience?

Find answers to all the above questions and write the numbers down. Once you've noted them down, create a schedule for your content using a content calendar. Content calendars let you see weeks, months and perhaps years ahead with the goal that you can design your content distribution strategy accordingly.

The key is to optimizing your distribution strategy from the beginning to guarantee meaningful outcomes and meet your objectives.

Promote Content through various Channels

As said before, creating the content isn't sufficient. You have to promote your content to your target audience consistently.

Social media channels – You can post to different social media platforms that suit your audience. Suppose you're a wedding photographer trying to get a word about your recent wedding photoshoots, platforms like Facebook and Instagram might be great options for promotion while Pinterest and LinkedIn might not. Always keep your targeted buyer in mind when promoting. But sharing your content once and then forgetting about it won't get you the traffic you want. Remember the 80/20 rule? You've to be consistent if you want concrete results.

Social media management – These tools save you a great deal of time by allowing you to schedule what's going to get posted, when and how often. This lets you post at the most engaging times during the week since research shows that, generally, weekday afternoons are best.

Emails – Email advertising is fundamental in disseminating content. For each $1 spent on email advertising, there's a $38 ROI. If in case you already have an email list, email your supporters each time you publish new content. You can likewise add it to your newsletter if you have one.

Q and A platforms – Another method for getting your content saw is by advancing it through question and answer platforms. Quora and Reddit are incredible for content sharing and enable you to shape authentic associations with potential clients while naturally developing your supporters.

Content Aggregation

In its most straightforward form, content aggregation is the collection of information based on a common topic involving one or more related keywords. Aggregating other people's information conveniently augments your original content while providing a broader perspective. Benefits of content aggregation:

- Support of real-time information distribution.
- Low-cost approach.
- Expanded content offering.
- Associate your original content with influencers in your field.

Radio Broadcasting

Radio broadcasting refers to using radio waves to send signals to large groups of listeners. Early use of radio focused on using the technology as an alternative to the telegraph, but by the 1920s broadcast radio had taken off as a major telecommunications medium. Today, in addition to traditional AM and FM radio, there is also satellite radio, digital radio broadcasts and radio-style stations available through the internet.

Radio broadcasting is any use of radio waves to send messages to large groups of people. Typically radio is used to send audio signals such as talk or music programming. Radio stations broadcast at different frequencies, which are sometimes referred to as wavelengths, since the frequency of a radio wave and its wavelength are mathematically related. To pick up a radio broadcast, you must use a radio tuned to the right frequency.

There are commercial and nonprofit radio broadcasters in the United States and around the world, broadcasting on frequencies reserved for amplitude modulation, or AM, signals and frequency modulation, or FM, signals. FM is more widely used for music because it delivers better sound quality. Modern radio broadcasts include news, talk, sports, religious programming and wide varieties of musical styles. In the past, fictional dramas and comedies were often broadcast on the radio, but these have since largely moved to television and the internet.

Amateur and CB Radio

In the U.S., the Federal Communications Commission licenses radio broadcasters, and it's illegal to operate without a license. Stations that do so are known as pirate radio stations, and they risk legal trouble. Amateur radio operators, colloquially known as hams, are also licensed by the FCC, or the equivalent authority in other countries, and are allowed to use certain frequencies for amateur, noncommercial broadcasts.

Another set of frequencies are set aside for citizens band, or CB, radio. Anyone may broadcast on CB radio frequencies without a license, and the CB frequencies are sometimes used by long-distance truckers and drivers to communicate about road conditions. Some drivers have since switched to smart phone apps with a similar function.

New Styles of Broadcast Radio

In addition to AM and FM radio, there's also satellite radio, which uses a separate set of frequencies to beam signals from satellites in space to paying subscribers. Many cars come with satellite radio receivers and limited-time subscriptions, helping to boost the service's popularity.

Some broadcasters now broadcast digital radio signals, as well as traditional analog signals. These can deliver higher sound quality and additional information that can be displayed on a radio receiver.

Internet radio stations also exist. Though they're technically not using radio waves to reach listeners, they're often using similar formats to broadcast music, talk or sports. Radio also sees online competition from podcasts, which offer prerecorded programs that you can download or stream to listen to at your convenience.

Radio Programming

Commercial and BBC radio stations are all engaged in an unseemly scramble for the ears, attention and loyalty of the radio audience. They justify their existence and/or make their profits by attracting the largest possible numbers of listeners. Community radio stations should have a different attitude. As we have said before (and will say again) it is not our job to be popular. It is our job to be necessary.

But for all the importance of community involvement, training and other aspects of your social gain activities, it is the quality and nature of your broadcast output that will be noticed and hopefully appreciated by the vast majority of your wider community. While it is possible to run a community radio station by opening your doors to your community and letting things run their course, we believe that to get the maximum benefit it is necessary to have programming policies. These should guide you towards the type of radio programmes that your community wants and needs.

The word 'broadcast' literally means to scatter widely – to throw something out to the world. The overwhelming majority of radio stations don't throw their output randomly out at the world, but instead target it very specifically at a particular demographic – people of a particular age, type, social class etc. In media jargon, they don't broadcast, they narrowcast.

The reason for this is very simple – it is how you get the most listeners. People generally want to know what they are getting from their radio, they have a clear idea in their head of what types of music or speech they want to hear and that is what they will look for on their dial. If they keep hearing what they want to hear then they are unlikely to tune out. While there is a percentage of listeners who are open-minded, have very broad tastes or simply don't care much what they hear so long as there is a constant murmuring noise coming out of the box in the corner, they are considerably outnumbered by those who only want to hear a particular genre of pop or type of speech.

Some community radio stations have opted to narrowcast to a greater or lesser extent, to maximise their audience. Although this can apply to any area of programming, it is most clearly seen in different stations' approaches to their music playlist.

For example, in their 2005 community licence application, Stockport's Pure Radio specify a musical playlist of guitar-based pop and rock, judging that this is the single most popular style of music in their community and that it is poorly supplied by existing local radio his is an understandable approach, but not without its issues.

According to Pure's own research, 29% of Stockport's population prefer this type of music. If a large number of that 29% choose to tune in to Pure, the station could attract a very healthy listenership in numbers, but how healthy is it in other respects? The most ardent fans of rock music tend to be white males in their thirties and forties. So although the listening figures might be good, do they reflect the ranges of age, gender, ethnicity and social class in their community? Are the listeners it attracts the type of listeners with the most to gain from a community radio station? Does a rock-dominated output make volunteering at the station an attractive proposition for a teenage girl of Asian origin, or an isolated pensioner? It is vital that if a station chooses to concentrate on one genre in the daytime, it makes extra efforts to reach out to other sections of the community at other times, and ensures their social gain achievements are not restricted to fans of that particular genre – something Pure FM demonstrate admirably.

The alternative approach, designing your programming and schedules so that there is something in it for everyone is of course equally problematic. In attempting to be all things to all people it is possible to become nothing much to anyone. Finding ways of persuading some listeners to switch on without causing others to switch off is a difficult, but not impossible task. The variety found on community radio stations is one of our stronger selling points, and goes a long way towards demonstrating why we are fundamentally different to our commercial and BBC equivalents. When listeners are so accustomed to strictly formatted and playlisted radio stations, some can be shocked and alienated by what they hear. Thankfully others will be thrilled to find a station that is different to all the others.

Making yourself relevant in some way to every member of your community is a difficult challenge, but one that we feel community radio stations should at least attempt to tackle.

Understanding Listeners

Different communities have different tastes and different habits, but there are some broad rules that apply to radio listeners whoever and wherever they may be. Listeners behave differently at home, in their cars and at work.

At home most people tend to leave their radios tuned to the same station for days or weeks on end. They are often impressively loyal to their favourite station and refuse to listen to any others. However there are keen radio heads who will actively seek out programmes that are of interest to them. Many radio stations are aware of a different group of listeners in the daytime to evenings and overnight.

- In the car people constantly hop between channels without caring much which station they are listening to.
- At work people mostly want unobtrusive background music and undemanding chat that will not take up too much of their attention.

At different times of day there are different proportions of listeners at home, driving or working.

Key Times

- Breakfast - More people listen to the radio between 7am and 10am than at any other time of day. If you can attract listeners with your breakfast show then you should have a good chance of keeping them through the day. Your breakfast show presenters have the most important and prestigious job of all your broadcasters. Just what makes good breakfast radio is a highly debatable question however. There is a fine line between an energised and energising host, who puts smiles on faces and makes everyone glad to have got out of bed, and an irritating git who yells and giggles constantly. Finding the balance is never easy (as Radio 1's experiences over the years have proved – one listener's Chris Moyles is another's migraine) but bear in mind that the role should probably go to the most talented and popular presenters you have.

- Lunch time - Lunch time is another switch-on time for many listeners. As at breakfast time, they mostly don't want to be overly challenged or provoked over their sandwiches, so again a mainstream approach to your programming is probably desirable – light chat, popular tunes and a friendly attitude.
- Drive time - Although you may struggle to keep drivers tuned in for long, there are so many people listening to the radio in their cars between 4pm and 6pm that you can reach a lot of people and that is immensely important for your public profile. A good drive-time show should be a mix of the informative and the entertaining, and be designed with the listenership in mind. They will probably be listening closely to what you play and say, so there is some scope for thoughtful features and intelligent discussion, but bear in mind that listeners will be tuning in and out on a regular basis so keep everything short, snappy and varied.
- Evening and night-time – Later in the day listeners are more likely to be looking for programmes that reflect their specific tastes and interests. Listeners tend to be younger and fussier. They are also likely to be listeners who will not hear your station at other times of day. A broader range of specialist programming in the evenings will broaden your reach to your community.

This leaves plenty of hours free for the types of community programming (schools, community action, health and issues programming etc.) which make up such an important part of your role as a community radio station.

It is your task to ensure that this programming is as entertaining, fascinating and useful as possible to try to keep your listeners switched on and tuned in from morning to night. Try to avoid creating 'switch-off' points when your scheduling lurches suddenly from mainstream pop radio to death metal hour or a serious political debate (a station broadcasting in one main language would find the same effect by switching languages). Your scheduling should flow naturally and smoothly through the day and the week.

Community vs. Radio

The relative importance of community issues and radio production issues is a continual and healthy source of tension in community radio. Radio is a wonderfully democratic medium, a presenter and producer with the most basic equipment and minimal budget can sometimes make programmes as inspiring and polished as any BBC-produced, Sony Award-winning production. Assuming the talent is at your disposal, often the only obstacle is the time and effort required for training, education, research and preparation. Of course you want your broadcasts to sound as good and professional as possible. But never let that override your other commitments. There are three aspects to your programming at a community radio station:

- Quality of process – How much benefit is there to individuals and groups who are making these programmes?

- Quality of output – How good are the radio programmes you broadcast?
- Impact in the community – How valuable are these programmes to the wider community?

Occasionally you will make programmes that excel on all three criteria, but more often there will be some kind of pay-off between them. The volunteers who will gain most from making radio may not be the volunteers who will make the slickest broadcasts. Likewise the programmes with the greatest community impact may be presented by radio veterans who have learned as much as they will ever want to learn about creating radio and for whom 'self-improvement' is a non-issue.

At every community radio station there will be a slightly different attitude to the relative importance of each factor, and even within stations there will be enormous differences between shows.

Quality of Output

Of course you want your radio to sound as good as possible and to not care about quality altogether would be suicidal for a community radio station. Even the most sympathetic listeners have limited patience with endless stretches of dead air, whistling feedback, distortion, mumbling, shouting or any of the production disasters that can happen on air. But having said that, scrappy radio can sometimes be fantastic to listen to. Playing a record at the wrong speed or pressing the wrong CD button may be embarrassing for any radio DJ, but it never really did John Peel any harm. At a community radio station, where most listeners will be aware that presenters are amateur volunteers, audiences will be tolerant of and (to a point) amused by moments of chaos.

Authenticity is something that community radio has in bucket-loads and it expresses itself in many different ways. We always come back to that saying we first heard from Andy Kershaw – if we're faced with a programme where the production values might not be all that could be desired – would a listener say:

> 'For example, Panjabi MC's 'Mund.'

Anyone coming to community radio from commercial or BBC background will have a culture shock in store. Rather than highly trained professionals creating meticulously planned, researched and scripted programming, community radio volunteers are often thrown on air after only a few hours training and a brief chat about content. To a large extent they will learn on the job. They need space to make errors without an overzealous manager pulling them off the air.

Nevertheless there are some particular mistakes that are common and, in most cases, easily avoided with basic training:

- Dead air - Broadcasting silence is the worst thing a presenter can do. Listeners will quickly retune to another station. In our experience dead air is normally caused by a faulty automation system more commonly than a faulty human being, but some presenters do need reminding that long silences must be avoided.
- Quiet or loud voices - In the overwhelming majority of cases, when a presenter is speaking at the wrong volume it will be because he is not wearing headphones as he speaks. This makes it almost impossible to judge the volume of one's own voice – headphones off is a

mark of sloppiness and a vital discipline for any presenter – using your ears needs little training.

- Inappropriate talk - Radio presenters, almost by definition, love the sound of their own voices. Presenters should know what an appropriate amount of talk is between records or – in speech-based shows – between planned features. Another common mistake is for co-presenters to be so amused by the banter between themselves that they forget they are making radio and make inane, boring small talk about their private lives. Or get into a furious row with each other on air and shout personal abuse across the microphones. While this might occasionally make for great radio, in practice it is best avoided.

Presenters (particularly of specialist music shows) can easily forget their role as the presenter of your radio station, and think of themselves only as host on their show. They must commit themselves to station idents and other on-air branding. You can measure the ego of a presenter by counting the number of times they mention their own name compared to the name of the station. Also discourage presenters from talking over records (particularly vocal tracks). Even hip hop and garage MCs need to let the music breathe occasionally. Bear in mind that some listeners may love that tune and talking over it can be very annoying.

Impact in the Community

The impact you have will hopefully take many forms. Your mere existence should be of considerable value to many community groups and the people they serve. You should make a significant difference to the lives of many of your trainees and volunteers. But your programming should have additional value in its own right.

Of the four key mandatory gain requirements in the Community Radio Order 2004, three refer to partially or wholly to output:

- The provision of radio services to individuals who are otherwise underserved.
- The facilitation of discussion and expression of opinion.
- Promoting better understanding of the community.

The first places an obligation upon you to be as diverse as your community. 'Underserved' individuals can take many forms depending on the nature of your community, but in a complex inner city community it is likely to include some or all of the following:

- Members of ethnic minorities.
- Non-English speakers.
- Economically marginalised people.
- People marginalised by sexuality or identity.
- People with alternative lifestyles.
- People with disabilities.

- Those whose interests and hobbies are not represented on non BBC local and national radio.
- Those whose musical tastes are not represented on non BBC local and national radio.
- Or it can be as simple as people without a non BBC station local to them, which could apply in many rural communities.

The penultimate of these is, in terms of social gain, probably the least important on that list. Nobody ever lost their home or got beaten up for lack of a Throbbing Gristle record on the radio. However it will be number one priority for the vast majority of potential volunteers who approach your station.

The urge to play music is very strong, particularly among the young. But even if you have 50 people approaching you wanting to play hip hop for everyone who approaches you wanting to host a disabilities magazine show, that doesn't mean that hip hop is 50 times more important than a disabilities show. Of course you may also pick up more listeners with a non-stop banquet of whichever musical genre grabs the most attention in your area. But that should not detract from your obligations to the rest of the community.

You must balance your role as a facility – allowing people to make the radio they want to make, with your role as a provider – bringing radio to those who really need it.

Discussion and Opinion Shows

Generating discussion and expression of opinion is not usually a great problem for a community radio station. Usually they will take the form of:

- Studio discussion and interviews: One or more presenters plus one or more guests. Usually centred around a particular subject.
- Phone-ins: Usually one presenter and as many listeners as possible.
- Debates: Larger showpiece discussions which may combine studio and phone-in formats or even outside broadcasts.

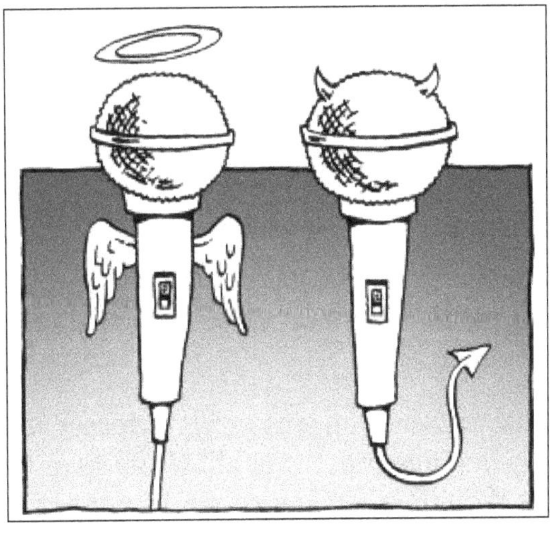

Call something a discussion show, and as soon as a presenter opens his or her mouth to speak, discussion begins. Your job is to make it as interesting as possible for the audience. Your listeners may want to hear about activities in the local area, news about health or education services and informative items about teenage pregnancy or gun crime, but they also want to hear some good music and be entertained. Community output will be unfamiliar to most people and may not immediately seem an attractive prospect. So concessions need to be made to their expectations and patience.

- Break up the discussion with music - Where appropriate use songs with a suitable or matching theme. And be wary of insensitive choices. Radio folklore is filled with tales of presenters saying things like: and we'll return to our discussion of traumatic adoption experiences right after the La Belle Époque classic, Black is Black, I Want My Baby Back."
- Make sure the presenter always has plenty of back-up questions or points of discussion in case conversation runs dry.
- Keep the topics moving along - If people are not interested in one topic, they may simply ignore it for a few minutes, but if the topic hasn't changed soon you will lose them. People will stay tuned for 30 minutes on six different subjects which they are not interested in, but won't stay tuned for 30 minutes about one subject which they are not interested in. People don't mind being bored too much, so long as they get regular variety in their boredom.
- Get different voices on air- One-to-one chat can rarely be sustained for more than five or ten minutes by any but the most skilled and fascinating interviewer and interviewee.
- Talk naturally and intelligently. Community radio offers a wonderful chance to talk to people as they want to be talked to, not yelled at by a hyperactive brat or patronised by an old Etonian.
- Research and brief your presenters on your guests, whether celebrities or not. There are few words more guaranteed to get an interview going badly than: 'So, it seems we have a new guest in the studio, who are you then?'
- Be ambitious with your invitations. Many celebrities, politicians, pop stars etc. are happy to be interviewed at a community radio station if they are in the area and have the time – sometimes because they want to help, often because they crave publicity.
- With high-profile interviewees, particularly political guests such as the local MP, invite questions from your listeners in advance and pick out the most interesting – crediting the listener of course.
- Be prepared to let interesting discussions run. Despite earlier warnings, use your common sense if studio guests are generating a captivating discussion. Give yourself some flexibility in your programme schedule.
- Above all, remember that a discussion is a two way process at least. The worst radio you can broadcast is a monotone monologue. Never allow guests or presenters to read from a page or bring anything more than the sketchiest notes into the studio.

- The presenter's role is to represent the listener, not to bang on about their hobby-horse, or keep putting their oar in for the sake of it.

Debates

Debates are a particular type of discussion show based around a single topic or theme. While most discussion shows will be non-confrontational – presenter and guests talking around a subject and conveying information – debates are centred on points of argument and dispute. Topics of debate are, by definition, controversial and so make great radio, but the OFCOM obligations for a radio station to be politically neutral must be your priority. A debate can be held in a studio, with a minimum of two guests holding opposing viewpoints and one presenter/chair who must strenuously strive to be impartial and fair to both sides of the argument. The best radio debates will usually have more than two guests and will also bring in points of view from listeners or, if the debate is an outside broadcast, the live audience.

Some useful tips for hosting a debate are:

- Debates take a lot of organization- Plan them with care. It's better to hold debates occasionally and well than it is to hold them often and badly.
- Get an experienced or well-trained chair- Authority and impartiality are crucial if a debate is not to descend into chaos. The chair needs the strength to tell some people to stop talking and the skill to encourage others to start. They should be well informed on the subject but know when to feign ignorance.
- Topics don't have to be local- You are promoting discussion in your community by talking about foreign policy or immigration just as much as by talking about the need for a new zebra crossing.
- If you are in a studio with only one phone line and the line gets busy, it's often better to have someone off air taking down the callers' points then reading them out. It gets many more people involved.
- Give out a number for SMS text messages, again to be read out,and of course via Twitter, Facebook and your social media platform of choice.
- You can host a public debate with only three microphones – one at the front table and two on 'walkabout' among the audience.
- Break up debates with the occasional record or interlude.
- Be prepared to clear the schedules. Sometimes the only time a showpiece debate can happen is in the evening, when your regular shows may have to step aside. Make sure all volunteers know this might happen to them some day.

Phone-ins

Many types of discussion shows can have input from telephone callers being put through to air, but the dedicated phone-in show is a different beast. It is one of the most popular radio formats in the world, and some commercial stations broadcast little or nothing else, 24 hours a day. They can be truly compulsive listening and they can sometimes be utterly awful. The key to a good phone-in show is the presenter. If he or she has charisma, wit, intelligence and a great radio manner, a phone-in show can be a huge success. Without those gifts the show is at the mercy of the callers, who are unlikely to be uniformly witty and wise.

Community radio volunteers will sometimes include one or two who fancy themselves as Howard Stern or other (mostly American) 'shock jocks' who entertain their listeners by engaging their callers in a battle of wit and rudeness, with the emphasis on humiliation and point-scoring rather than healthy discussion. This is not a particularly desirable format for community radio, partly because the volunteer is unlikely to have the skill to make such radio work, but also because such programmes are likely to prove corrosive to the relationship with your listeners.

Phone-in shows should ideally be:

- Friendly and non-aggressive – although a little controversy never hurts.
- Centred around a particular topic. Presenters sometimes think it will make great radio to just ask callers what they've been doing today and what's on their mind. It rarely does, and it can be harder to generate calls that way.
- Conducted through a switchboard, or at least a couple of lines. It is almost impossible to have a nicely flowing phone-in show through only one line. You need someone off air taking the calls and queuing people up.
- Hosted by a well-trained presenter. He or she needs particularly good training in legal issues and OFCOM codes, and be prepared to cut a caller off if they are about to, for example, commit libel or spout obscenities.

News

News is the one form of speech broadcasting which is separate to discussion. When you call something a news programme you take on particular responsibilities within the OFCOM code. Your news must be accurate and impartial, and it may not carry sponsorship. Note that there is a significant difference between discussion of the news (which can be as informal and flippant as you like) and actual news broadcasting which must be formal and under strict control. That's not to say it has to sound like the BBC, just be clear what's a news bulletin and what's not.

National and World News

Obviously a community radio station will not have the resources to run their own international news desk. Any pretence at doing so (for example by reading out stories from newspapers or the internet) is deceitful and may breach copyright (it can be a nice regular feature for breakfast presenters to discuss 'what the papers say', but don't brand it as your 'news' spot.). In practice, if a community station wants to run full news broadcasts they must beg, buy or borrow them from elsewhere. The principle options are:

- BBC - If you have a good relationship with your local BBC station, they may be willing to let you carry their news broadcasts – providing your station doesn't carry any spot advertising.

This can have the great advantage of bringing local news with it. Keep an eye on the CMA website for news of how this relationship has been formalised across the BBC.

- Independent Radio News - The default choice for most commercial stations, it is more chatty and showbiz-based than the BBC. You can get this through a Sky Digital box and it is often possible to get permission to broadcast in return for carrying some national advertisements.

Community News

Carrying national news may please your listeners (although not all) but it plays no part in your social gain objectives. Community news will do. But be warned: if you brand a programme or item as 'community news' then you must assume the same authority, impartiality and accuracy is required as would be required of a national BBC bulletin. The producers and presenters of community news must be made aware of basic journalistic standards and be especially aware of libel and contempt law.

While you may have roving reporters bringing you hot scoops from the street, in practice your community news is likely to be generated by your partner organisations within the community, especially schools, religious organisations, campaign groups etc. If you can persuade them to give you regular updates on their activities, that in itself can generate enough material for a snappy daily news spot or longer weekly show. Be wary of overscheduling community news however, chances are there won't be all that much of interest happening every hour even in the most vibrant and populous communities.

Programme Sharing

While of course you will be responsible for generating most of your output yourself, the wider community radio sector offers a useful source of sometimes superb programmes. Full shows or shorter items can be borrowed from or shared with other community stations through these sources:

- The Community Media Association developed a network – GetMedia – that will allow you to pull down whole shows or clips from the web and broadcast them direct. This of course also offers a prestigious opportunity for your own volunteers to have their best work shared around the country.
- The Radio Bank – the Government's source of material, particularly around health & safety issues and public health. Other health and social service agencies sometimes make special items for free broadcast.
- Collaboration on very occasional special broadcasts with neighbouring community stations. But don't do it too often – OFCOM are obliged to enforce diversity on the airwaves.
- Podcasting may also prove to be a fascinating source of grass roots opinion form across the world.

In your OFCOM application you have to be clear how much shared material you're using. As a proportion of the total it should be negligible – you are expected to be generating your own material

– but used carefully, shared programmes can give real depth to your scheduling. And don't worry if suddenly you go over the allocation in your license application – Ofcom wont fuss if its marginal and if it's more, tell them about it and why you feel it enhances your output.

Music Programming

Music vs. Speech

In your application to OFCOM you are obliged to specify what proportion of your output will be speech and what proportion music. There are wide variations in what community licence applicants specify, but typically they promise a balance of around 70% music to 30% speech. That leaves plenty of time for all your discussion and the promotion of your community but enough music programming to attract a healthy audience. Once you have made your promise to OFCOM, nobody will count up the minutes, but they will refer back to your promise with each annual report, so if you initially promise 80% speech then arbitrarily decide to begin broadcasting 80% music, serious questions will be asked.

In setting your ratio of speech to music, it's worth bearing in mind that in very general terms the more music you play, the younger your listenership will be. Older people tend to prefer speech broadcasts, younger people prefer music (although Angel Radio in Havant and the Isle of Wight would beg to differ on this point). In our view the best community radio is a hybrid of speech and music rather than, for example, only hosting speech in the daytime and only playing music at night.

One factor to bare in mind is that speech is generally more resource hungry – the time it takes to make any well-constructed hour of speech far exceeds the same programme length of music. So don't just make your planned ratio what you want it to be – be sure that you can deliver.

Playlists

The music you play will alter the audience you pick up, so think carefully about what the typical playlist at your station will be . If you want it to reflect your whole community, it will probably have to be quite varied. At ALL FM, for example, the playlist was divided between 'Gold' (classics), 'Community' (representing the full range of nationalities and ethnic origins in the area) and 'Choice' (current hits plus the presenter's or listeners' picks). But if you are trying to keep large numbers of listeners in the daytime you need to find some consistency and routine. By concentrating much of the non-Western music in specialist shows (which will pick up healthy audiences in their own right) it is possible to have a varied and lively daytime playlist which is mainstream enough not to alienate listeners but still incorporates the occasional African, West Indian, Asian or Irish tune, for example, giving the station a unique and we hope attractive musical identity. When you consider that the most listened to radio station in the country, BBC Radio 2, has a musical policy which is in its own way even more eclectic than that (comfortably spanning Oasis or Doves at one end and Lionel Richie or Frank Sinatra at the other), this is unlikely to be too much of a stretch for listeners, once they get used to it anyhow.

It is up to you how authoritarian you want to be with regard to your playlist. Many BBC and commercial radio stations will prescribe exactly which records presenters must play, or give them a very narrow list to choose from. This is certainly the easiest way to ensure the music played at your station matches your policies and give the listener a consistent station sound. But it is likely to lead to frustration for presenters and listeners alike. The best approach is to have a small number of station favourites from the current hits at any given time and encourage the presenters to play them regularly between their own choices. You might choose these records because:

- They are by a local artist.
- They are part of a local scene.
- They are popular records with your listeners.
- They are by an artist who has supported your station.
- They fit perfectly with your station identity.
- They have a message or spirit which is in keeping with your station ethos.
- They have been pressed upon you by your volunteers – who may have their ear closer to the ground than you.
- They have a 'killer hook' – that melody that won't get out of your skull.
- They simply sound great to you.

It is important that the person picking out records for a daytime show has a good ear for a tune. If you have an otherwise brilliant presenter with the musical taste of a dung beetle, you may have to diplomatically steer them towards a more suitable selection. If ever there was a place to leave your ego at the door, music programming is it – you choose for the station not yourself. Getting the flow of music right is important too, you wouldn't normally want to crash straight from Chris de Burgh into Motorhead, but if you want to keep fans of both tuned in, you will have to find space for each somewhere in the schedule. Take some chances too; in community radio you do have the editorial leeway to give a tune that you are convinced will grow on the audience the time to do that growing. The shareholders won't be there telling you to clear your desk for trying to broaden music horizons. That said, for every daring tune play a safe one.

A good tip for increasing daytime presenter's 'buy in' to the playlist is to involve them in its construction.

Specialist Shows

In the vast majority of cases, the presenters of specialist music shows will have complete control over their playlist. The role of the station is not to choose the right music but to find the right presenters. You want people who:

- Are willing to learn radio skills as well as turn up and play records.
- Are willing to contribute their time to the station, beyond turning up and playing.
- Have a genuine passion for their musical speciality. If someone only has 50 records they will soon begin to repeat themselves or wander off their remit.

- Will link you to local music and club scenes. This is good for your reputation and profile and will help attract celebrity guests.

But specialist presenters often bring their own problems. These include:

- DJs who forget they are on the radio- Many specialist DJs have a club background and the concept of talking into a mic or playing station idents, jingles or ads is alien to them. You should agree how many consecutive records they can play before back-announcing the names of records, repeating the station name, frequency, phone number etc. There's also a very different dynamic to a 'club mix' than to a radio playlist. A radio presenter is unlikely to have the time to build though ten tracks to an immaculate peak that has the punters bouncing off the ceiling and your listeners are more likely to be sober than those in a club. So select your radio tunes to stand on their own, at normal volume and to appeal to the un-intoxicated.

- DJs who forget they are in public- For some specialist presenters there might be little in the way of instant feedback, so the only people she knows are listening are a small group of friends. This is dangerous because it is easy to slip into in-jokes and bad broadcasting habits, including a dismissive attitude towards the OFCOM code. Don't spy on your broadcasters, but listen in to all your specialist shows occasionally and a casual mention of your attentiveness ("Hi it's me, just wanted to say the show sounded great last night") is a useful preventive/supportive measure.

- Presenters who don't feel part of the family- If a volunteer only comes into the station on Mondays at midnight and sees nobody else, he may feel alienated from the rest of the team. He may have un-addressed needs and feel unsupported, or he may be more slapdash with station rules and property. Have some form of regular supervision session with all your volunteers. Attendance at station meetings and social gatherings should be strongly encouraged.

- A community radio station could easily have 50 or even 100 different specialist music shows on a weekly, fortnightly or monthly rotation. That is a fantastic opportunity to put unlikely things on the air (as London's Resonance FM demonstrate on an hourly basis) so there is no excuse for predictable programming. If there's a fan of Himalayan nose flute music among your volunteers then let him have a monthly show. You might be surprised how many other nose flute fans there are out there. Specialist shows are a fantastic way of reaching out to sections of the community who would not normally be interested in your station, and a handful of flagship specialist shows can work wonders for a community radio station's reputation. Use them well and they will form one of your strongest hands.

- Community radio stations are obliged to open the airwaves to members of the community. As a general rule, the more people you get on air, the harder it will be to keep the quality high simply because the training, support and most importantly broadcasting experience you can offer will be more thinly spread. Wide access will mean more people have a stake in your station and more will have friends, neighbours or family involved – but on the other hand you may keep fewer regular listeners as specialist audiences often take time to grow. There is no perfect balance: some stations may have a 'come hither come all' policy where the broadcasting hours are allocated as widely as is practically possible. Others will have daily presenters on flagship shows and weekly spots elsewhere, meaning as few as 20 or 30 volunteers could dominate the schedule. There are some scheduling tactics and tricks that will help you find the right balance for your station.

Rotating Schedules

- You don't need to give everyone their own show. Give newer volunteers a role on another programme – co-presenting with a regular host or presenting short features or segments within magazine shows.
- Don't put new recruits in high-profile time-slots (Breakfast, Drivetime etc). It's not fair on them or the listeners. The potential switch-off points (for example after the Breakfast or Lunchtime shows) should be treated with caution too.
- Encourage DJ double acts and teams.
- Your specialist music shows can double (or quadruple) up on one time slot, so you may have four different heavy metal shows but the listener won't really notice or care. Metal fans will learn that they can always tune in between 10pm and midnight on a Wednesday and hear their favourite sounds.

The easiest way to increase your access is to rotate your schedules regularly. If there is a large demand for access to your station you are morally obliged to accommodate that demand. A schedule rotation is not the same as a schedule shuffle. It unfortunately means telling some or even all of your volunteer presenters that they cannot continue with their show (at least for a certain time) because someone else needs their timeslot. Just how you do it doesn't really matter, but it is crucial that the volunteers know exactly where they stand, and they do not think that they personally are being victimised because suddenly they are taken off the air. That means making sure everyone knows what the rules are for schedule rotation, and that you don't break them. Volunteers must understand that there is more demand than there is availability, so a show on community radio is a privilege not a right. Either of the following approaches is reasonable:

- Running rotation. Whenever someone starts a new show they are given a fixed term (perhaps 6 months or a year) after which they will automatically finish.
- Preset rescheduling points. Once or twice a year you throw out the entire schedule and start again with a new one.

Whichever approach you take, it is unlikely that you will have such a constant stream of brilliant, ready-trained new volunteers that you can regularly take all the old faces out and bring only new faces in. In practice you will probably want to give some of your existing volunteers different shows or timeslots; keep others where they are; and drop some of your less successful shows and volunteers who have shown less commitment and application. You will also find that redrawing the schedules is a frustrating and time-consuming process, trying to fit different shows into timeslots that suit everyone, like pieces in a three-dimensional jigsaw. You really won't want to do it more than once or twice a year.

Probably the best approach to a total reschedule is an application system, where every existing or potential volunteer presenter is required to apply or re-apply for a show. Let them know what grounds you are deciding on. They may include:

- Demand- If you have a long queue of experienced and talented volunteers all desperate to present your Breakfast show or a Saturday night hip hop show, then it is not fair to let just one hog that spot forever. But if only one volunteer is keen to present between 1am and 3am on a Tuesday, then it is pointless to take her off.
- Dedication- The process of making community radio is more important than the output. If a presenter reaches a certain level of competence then loses interest in training and self-improvement, it is reasonable to prefer another presenter who may be less competent now, but is showing real dedication and progress.
- Commitment- It is entirely fair to reward commitment to your station. If a volunteer is willing to mentor other volunteers, come in to make tea, wash dishes, attend meetings, do some filing .or lock up at 3 am it is entirely reasonable to take that into consideration when handing out the shows. It can make a significant difference to the amount of help you get from your volunteers too.
- Behaviour- If you have had regular problems with a presenter not turning up say, or smoking in the studio or being abusive to staff and other volunteers, of course you can take that into consideration. It is a good incentive for good behaviour.
- Representation- You will want as many different sections of your community as possible to be represented on air. If you have only one or two disabled applicants, you will probably want to consider that in your decisions. Likewise ethnic minorities, sexualities, music types etc.
- Ability- Last, and probably also least, is how good the presenter is at making radio. It is often not fair to judge on quality, partly because it is subjective and your opinion might be coloured by your personal relationship with the presenter, but more because it is unfair on newcomers who haven't had the same experiences. For all that, we'd be dishonest if we didn't acknowledge that some shows could be just too good to lose.

After your decisions are made, you should make clear exactly why your decisions have been reached, especially with those who have not been given a show. An appeals procedure must be in place if a volunteer feels unfairly treated. Unsuccessful applicants should be given every opportunity to keep training and volunteering off air (or as part of another programme team), and be given the greatest possible amount of support and guidance towards making a successful application next time round.

Station Branding

Giving your station output a recognisable brand identity is a great way of bonding with your listeners, improving the station's image, team-building and helping the flow and coherency of your programming. It is also relatively cheap and easy to do.

Many presenters, particularly in marginal timeslots, may not think of their shows as being one small part in a larger picture, but as a self-contained bubble. They may not mention your station name and frequency at all, and never think of playing a station jingle or trailer for another show. This is an abuse of your hospitality as station facilitators. While any mention of branding can induce anti-corporate revulsion in some community activists and volunteers, it's a simple fact that your station will develop a public image and identity whether you like it or not. Branding is one way in which you can steer and shape that to your own ends and the benefit of your community. And if they're still not listening a gentle reminder that more listeners for the station means more listeners for their show too should do the trick.

Ways you can improve your on-air branding include:

- Regular name/frequency checks. It is vital that listeners know what station and frequency they are listening to, or they might not be able to find you next time (it is also an OFCOM regulation). There is nothing simpler for a presenter than saying 'you're listening to Anytown FM on 96.2' every timCommon features and style to your jingles. It is very useful to have a single slogan or catchphrase that goes on every sting, trailer or jingle. Likewise there should be some common features to all your jingles, whether it's the same five note melody singing 'Anytown FM' at the beginning or end, or just a simple musical chord or sound effect. Your individual shows should make their own jingles, but give them one or two small elements to incorporate. Or use 'donut' jingles where the beginning and end remain unchanged and the volunteer can change the 'filling.'
- Make a varied range of jingles available for different times of day and different types of show – but all must be instantly recognisable as an 'Anytown FM' jingle.
- Keep stressing what it is you do. Casual listeners or those who find you by accident on the dial need to be told regularly that you are a community station, making radio by, for and from this community. It will change their appreciation of what they are hearing.
- Collect celebrity station idents whenever you do an interview or have a special guest. 'Hello, I'm Judy Finnegan. You are listening to Anytown FM on 96.2.' Instant Tinseltown glamour. Or something.

Cross Trailing and Promoting the Station

Like branding, cross trailing and promotion is easily ignored by volunteers and forgotten about by busy managers. With a vast body of volunteers who rarely see each other or interact, they'll often turn up, do a show and go home. But a radio station has endless opportunity to promote and advertise itself. You want listeners who find your station through a late-night music show to be attracted back the next evening and the morning after. Cross trailing is the best way to sell yourself to your listeners.

The programming manager must insist that volunteers understand that one of their principle duties – even one of the criteria for keeping their show – is promoting other shows on the schedule and other activities at the station.

You should expect your presenters to:

- Listen to the station in their own time. Otherwise they won't know what they are talking about.

- Refer to the shows before and after theirs. It is simple good manners for presenters to thank and credit the show that has just preceded them when they come on air. More importantly they should encourage listeners to stay tuned for the show after. If a presenter arrives at the studio 30 minutes before his show, he should immediately pop into the studio and say what is coming up on the next show.
- Refer to shows elsewhere in the schedule. If a daytime presenter plays a rock tune, it's worth saying 'if you liked that tune check out The Riff Raff Rock Show on Wednesday at midnight.' Or playing a trailer for that show.
- Talk about the station. If presenters are short of things to say, chatting about other programmes or the community activities of the station is the best use of that airtime. Have a clipboard or noticeboard in the studio with suitable announcements and news.
- Play community announcements and adverts. Presenters have received a wonderful gift of a radio show. It is the least they can do to devote a few moments to the things that keep the station afloat.

Types of Radio Programme

There are plenty of online radio programs that you could fit into 24 hours of broadcasting:

Chart Shows

Chart shows are a classic program type that you can add to your line up. Music chart shows are a countdown of the top-rated songs for the week or the month. You could create a chart of your own based on audience opinion and listener stats, or opt to broadcast a more well-known chart, such as a Billboard chart.

Entertainment Programs

Entertainment segments can provide some light fun to your online radio programming. These shows can include stand-up comedy clips, funny reviews, call-in quizzes, and fun competitions for your listeners. These segments could serve as an entertaining change of pace between music and talk segments.

Late Night

In online radio, late-night programming is incredibly flexible. Late evenings usually have fewer listeners tuning in, which could be a great time to debut new DJs who are still finding their groove. Late-night programs are often music-centric, though It often depends on a station's late-night listener stats.

Live Shows

Live online radio programs are broadcast in real time. There are plenty of options when it comes to live shows – be it talk, an interview, or live-event coverage. Broadcasting live is a fantastic way to engage your listeners in real-time events, by taking live calls, and allowing shout-outs, and more.

Morning Wake-up Shows

The Morning Show is another staple in the world of radio. This is your chance to help your listeners wake up and get pumped for the day ahead. For area-specific stations, morning programs are a great opportunity to cover recent events, news, traffic, and weather, to prepare your listeners for the day.

Music Shows/Genre Specific Programming

Music shows are just that – cantered on music. The average online radio music program may consist of an hour or two of nothing but great tunes. Music shows can be specific to a genre (disco, country), a decade (70's, 80's), or even a theme (movie soundtracks, workout music, etc.).

News and Weather

News and Weather segments are a great way of sharing useful information with your listeners. You can cover current events, weather, and exciting news stories on a local or global scale.

Radio Dramas

While the term "Radio Drama" might seem a bit outdated, many of these appear as podcasts today. Radio Dramas refers to programming that consists of stories, comedies, musicals, and more, that rely on dialogue and sound effects to tell a story. Radio dramas, depending on your demographic, remain a great way of entertaining your listeners every once in a while.

Request Shows/Call-in Shows

Request shows are an excellent way of engaging your listeners and enabling them to feel like they are a part of the show. These are usually live online radio shows that allow listeners to share real-time opinions or make live, on-air requests and shout-outs.

Specialty Shows

Specialty shows are a fantastic way of breaking from regular programming or long blocks of music.

These types of shows can cover fun and interesting topics such as travel, technology, history, or celebrity news. These segments can cover a fun new destination once a week (travel), the latest and greatest tech (technology), interesting figures from history, and more.

Sport Programs

Sports programs cover the latest in sports related to news, athletes, game coverage, and more. Online radio sports programs can also include live coverage of sporting events.

Talk Shows/Talk Radio

Talk radio typically consists of radio hosts discussing current affairs or events. These discussions may occasionally include special guest interviews and listener opinions. Talk shows could provide a relevant and informative break from music radio.

Television Programming

While the television set and the radio receiver are considered to be "hardware," programming is the essential "software" that actually tempts people to use these devices. The primary function of the station or network is to provide programming content that will appeal to some segment of the audience. The ability of a station to reach its desired audience will determine its success. Its programming mission and strategy are critical to its viability. As such, programming is the most visible and most vital commodity of television.

Programming Sources

There are some basic programming strategies that are common to both radio and television. A station or network must analyze the audiences that is available during a given time of day, examine its own schedule as well as that of the competition, determine the budget and revenues that are available for that time, and—with its ultimate goals in mind—make programming decisions. The programming day is broken into several day-parts, which (in the eastern time zone) are early morning (6:00 A.M. to 9:00 A.M.); daytime (9:00 A.M. to 4:00 P.M.); early fringe (4:00 P.M. to 6:00 P.M.); early evening (6:00 P.M. to 7:00 P.M.); prime access (7:00 P.M. to 8:00 P.M.); prime time (8:00 P.M. to 11:00 P.M.); late fringe (11:00 P.M. to 11:35 P.M.); late night (11:35 P.M. to 2:05 A.M.); and overnight (2:05 A.M. to 6:00 A.M.). The general manager, program director, and/or sales manager must determine the best type of program that is available for a given daypart and determine the source of the program. There are five primary sources for programming: network-fed, syndicator-delivered, independently produced, locally produced and in-house, and paid programming.

Network-fed Programming

In the earliest days of radio broadcasting, each station produced all of its own content locally. However, the production effort and programming costs were too great for most stations to bear this. Between 1923 and 1928, stations banded together to receive programming from a single, originating station. This innovative practice of networking decreased the production effort and spread the programming costs over a number of stations. Stations that affiliated with the networks (e.g., NBC and CBS) had the option of carrying local programming or the network-fed shows. This basic model is still alive and well in the broadcast television industry.

Local television stations are generally affiliated with one of the broadcast networks. Broadcast networks include ABC, CBS, NBC, Fox, WB, UPN, Pax TV, Univision, and Telemundo. An affiliated station, or affiliate, can choose to carry the programming that is fed by its network. The affiliate's agreement to broadcast the network program is a clearance, and the affiliate's decision not to broadcast a program is a preemption.

Upon clearing the show, the station airs both the show and all commercials that are sold by the network. The local station makes money on the arrangement by selling local commercial time during breaks in the network feed. These breaks are referred to as "availabilities." Generally, broadcast networks do not feed programming twenty-four hours a day. When the local station has no network feed available or decides to preempt network programming, it relies on one of the remaining sources of programming. The most common source in this situation is program syndication.

Syndicator-delivered Programming

A syndicator is a company that makes contractual arrangements to place programs or movies on television stations and cable networks. Syndicators make a wide variety of programming available to each broadcast market and to cable networks. The shows range from *Oprah Winfrey* to *The Flintstones* to individual college football games. Station and cable network executives are usually responsible for examining the syndicated programming options and for conducting negotiations to obtain the rights to the programs that are best suited to their needs. Some negotiations occur at the annual National Association of Television Programming Executives convention. It is a "shopping mall" of syndicated programming options, and it is attended by syndicators and television executives.

The three most common types of syndicated packages are referred to as "first run," "off network," and "feature film packages." Feature film packages are groups of movies that are put together by a syndicator and offered to a local station. The local station negotiates the number of runs it gets for each film title, the amount of money that it may have to pay for airing the movies, and the dates and dayparts in which the film may air. Feature film packages may come with a mixture of box office hits and critical mis-fires. The station must determine the best way to use the titles to meet its programming goals.

Off-network programming refers to episodes of series that have previously played on a broadcast or cable outlets. Local stations negotiate with syndicators for episodes of series ranging from The Andy Griffith Show to Buffy, the Vampire Slayer. For the majority of successful network sitcoms and dramas, syndication is their major source of revenue. This is not surprising when one considers that off-network contractual agreements are made at virtually every television station in the United States and in many international stations and networks as well. Some successful series such as Cheers, Home Improvement, and Seinfeld have each generated hundreds of millions of dollars in syndication sales.

First-run programs are those series that have had no previous network exposure. The majority of syndicated fare is considered first run. Included in the category of first-run series are talk shows such as Oprah Winfrey and Jerry Springer, court shows including Judge Judy and Divorce Court, game shows such as Wheel of Fortune and Jeopardy!, news/entertainment series including Entertainment Tonight and Inside Edition, and entertainment series including Xena, Warrior Princess and Hercules, the Legendary Journeys. Stations and cable networks contract with companies such as Paramount, King World, and Studios USA for the rights to syndicated series. Contractual negotiations for all syndicated programs fall into one of the following three categories: barter, cash, and cash-plus-barter.

The contract in barter syndication is the simplest. A station contracts for the rights to air a series or special. The station pays nothing for the program but must run all of the commercials that are sold by the syndicator. A one-hour program may contain fourteen minutes of commercial time or "inventory." The syndicator makes its money by selling about half of the commercial inventory in the show. The station makes its money by selling the remaining minutes of commercial availabilities in the show. Although economical, the station sacrifices a great deal of commercial inventory time in such arrangements. Barter programs are usually scheduled by frugal stations and in the less desirable time slots of a channel.

The contract for off-network series and some new programming is handled on a cash basis. In such cases, the station receives the series, as well as the entire commercial inventory, for a stated length of time. It attempts to turn a profit on the contract by selling advertisements. Cash deals can either be long-term contracts to run older series or short-term contracts to cover newer series with fewer numbers of episodes.

The most lucrative arrangement for the syndicator is one in which it can sell commercial inventory within a series and receive further compensation from individual stations. Such contractual agreements are called cash-plus-barter, or cash-plus. The station or network pays a cash license fee and must air the commercials that are sold by the syndicator. Unlike the barter deal in which the station is generally left with just half of the commercial inventory, cash-plus contracts leave the station with the majority of the commercial inventory. The station must attempt to recoup its investment by selling the remaining commercial availabilities. Though the cash-plus appears to be the worst value for the buyer, almost every successful daily syndicated series is sold on a cash-plus basis. This includes Oprah Winfrey, Wheel of Fortune, and Entertainment Tonight.

Independently Produced Programming

An independently produced program is one in which a station or network makes an exclusive contract with an outside producer to deliver a series, telefilm, or special. Though rare in local television programming, it is a standard operating procedure for networks. Networks make series and film commitments to producers such as Steven Bochco and Marcy Carsey and Tom Werner for a portion of their prime-time programming. They agree to a set amount for a project and determine the number of episodes to be delivered. The networks attempt to make their investment back through commercial sales.

Locally Produced and In-house Programming

In the early days of television, locally produced television shows ranged from children's programs to sports to news programs. Since that time, however, local productions in television have largely been limited to newscasts that air in the early morning, early evening, and late fringe time periods. Local newscasts can be the most profitable programs of a station, and they are used to establish an identity in the station's local community. Because of the heavy reliance on network and syndicated fare, some stations are returning to the concept of regularly scheduled local programs in an attempt to regain the notion of localism. Despite their relative rarity, local productions can be the most important programs of a station because they connect the station to its core audience.

For the major television networks and many cable networks, in-house programming is commonplace. NBC produces the *Today Show*, the *Tonight Show*, and others on a daily basis. The cable network E produces *Talk Soup*, *Mysteries & Scandals*, and many other series and specials. The networks can air these shows whenever they wish and can syndicate them for added revenues.

Paid Programming

Another source of material for television outlets is that of paid programming. There are three types of paid programming: program-length commercials (i.e., infomercials), paid religion, and program-length political advertisements. In each type, the station or network sells an entire block of time to an entity in exchange for a cash payment. Through paid programs, the station lowers its programming costs and does not have to concern itself with selling commercial time. Paid programs are economically sound, but they generally deliver poor ratings and can interrupt the station's regular flow of programming. The use of any program source, including paid programming, is largely dependent on the goals of a station.

Programming Goals

Every broadcaster—commercial or noncommercial—must fulfil at least one goal: to serve the "public interest" as mandated by the Federal Communications Commission (FCC). To stay viable, broadcast licensees and networks watch their profit and loss statements closely. However, not everyone›s programming goal is to be number one in the ratings. For the majority of stations and networks, this is unrealistic. Each broadcaster must have a set of specifically worded goals to see if it is meeting the needs of the public and the owner. These programming goals may include one or more of the following concepts: reaching a stated target audience, conserving programming resources, creating a positioning statement, branding of programming, and integrating technology.

Reaching a Stated Target Audience

Targeting the "mass audience" and striving for the top spot in the market or nation may be the goal of a station or network. Given the dizzying array of program options, most stations prefer to focus on a subset of the television audience. Stations that are affiliated with Univision and Telemundo (the Spanish-language networks) attempt to reach a significant portion of the local Hispanic audience. Other stations, such as ESPN, work to become the top sports source in the market. With that goal in mind, the station will combine live sporting events and shows that cater to the sports-minded audience. The notion of targeting specific audiences has long been associated with the magazine industry, with local and national radio, and with cable television. Since the 1980s, as programming options have continued to grow, targeting audiences has been refined and expanded to become the norm for all forms of television.

Conserving Programming Resources

Some stations or networks will sacrifice ratings to avoid the risk that is associated with high programming costs. These outlets have conserved programming costs by accepting barter programs, airing reruns, and allowing paid programming instead of pursuing superior programming alternatives that would involve a higher cost. As the concept of reaching a "mass audience" becomes less probable other than for major events (e.g., the Super Bowl), stations and networks will continue to lower programming risks by being very choosy in the area of high-budget programs and by relying on modest-to low-budget programs, reruns, and local and in-house productions.

Creating a Positioning Statement

A positioning statement is a one-or two-sentence description that distinguishes one business from another. In broadcasting, radio broadcasters have used positioning to help audience members make a link between the statement and the programming that is carried by the station. A statement such as "All Oldies, All the Time" can explain one's programming goal in a memorable manner. In television, the increased number of cable networks has encouraged both local stations and cable networks to adopt positioning statements. In cable, Lifetime uses "The Network for Women." In local television, "Family First" stations may make programming decisions to limit on-screen violence and offensive language, while a "Watch and Win" station may use promotional contests to call attention to its program lineup. As was the case in the magazine and radio industries, increased television outlets will result in more stations adopting program-based positioning statements.

Branding of Programming

Branding is a concept in which a show or, moreover, a block of shows is given its own unique identity. ABC uses this concept with its "TGIF" Friday night of situation comedies. This concept allows a network to target a specific audience for a portion of the day and to focus attention on that group of shows.

Integrating Technology

Stations and networks often use technological innovations to call attention to their programming, especially news and weather on local stations. Stations that are the first to adopt and actively promote digital technology, high-definition transmission, active Internet programming, and interactive television options are promoting their programs through technology. High-definition Monday Night Football games, Internet communities that are devoted to popular television shows, and interactive play-at-home versions of television games are just some of the concepts that have been successful. The convergence of digital television, Internet applications, and interactivity will be the fastest-growing area of television in the early part of the twenty-first century.

Audience Measurement

The Nielsen television ratings m erasure the percentage of the television audience that is watching a particular program. Most of commercial television's best programming and first-run episodes of series are shown during the major ratings periods called the "sweeps." The sweeps months of

November, February, May, and July, are the only months that Nielsen gathers audience da ta for the entire nation. Families are selected to take part in the ratings process and fill out diaries about each show that is watched in the household for a stated ratings period. Nielsen tabulates the results both for the local stations that buy the ratings information and for the national networks.

Ratings data is also collected on a daily basis. For the national ratings estimates, five thousand selected households are sampled every day, and the results are published the next day. This quantitative data, known in the industry as the "overnights," is made possible because of the "People Meter" technology. The meter attaches to the television and sends instantaneous viewership data. These meters are also used in most of the fifty largest U.S. television markets and provide stations with daily statistics. As a result of this instant ratings data, stations and networks can quickly assess which programs are living up to expectations and which ones should be moved to a different time period or eliminated from their schedules altogether. The ratings information has a direct effect on what programming the audience sees—or does not see—on its television set.

Though programming maneuvers are made based primarily on the ratings numbers, the programmer also uses qualitative information. Viewers have mounted successful write-in campaigns to save quality programs and to have offensive programming either changed or removed from the schedule. Overwhelming critical praise of shows can also sway a programmer toward keeping an underperforming show on the schedule. Research departments often obtain information from test audiences (i.e., focus groups) that screen or pre-screen television programs. A focus group may give the program producers critical insights concerning program elements that may need adjusting. Viewers, therefore, have a direct and indirect effect on the programming process from development to ultimate success or failure.

Types of TV Programme

TV shows fall into two basic types: scripted or unscripted. Each of these categories has many distinct sub-groups. Programs made for television are either created on film or recorded to tape via digital cameras.

Unscripted TV Shows

Examples of unscripted television shows are sporting events, game shows, reality shows and news. However, unless they are broadcast live, these "unscripted" TV shows are manipulated and edited to fit a particular running time and a predetermined outcome. Reality shows make up the broadest group and can include talk shows (for example "The Tonight Show," "The View"); newsmagazines ("60 Minutes,""Dateline NBC;" "Nightline"); game shows ("Who Wants to be a Millionaire," "Are You Smarter Than a Fifth Grader"); reality competitions ("American Idol," "Survivor," "The Amazing Race"); how-to shows ("The Barefoot Contessa," "This Old House"); awards shows (for "The Academy Awards," "The Grammys"); commentary ("The O'Reilly Factor," "Hardball") and specialized reality programming such as "Extreme Makeover" and "Ice Road Truckers.".

The large number of specialized channels available to viewers who subscribe to cable television or satellite services has dramatically increased the number of unscripted programs available. This rapid proliferation of unscripted TV shows is due in part to the fact that they are cheaper to produce than scripted shows and can be put together in a relatively short amount of time.

Scripted TV Shows

Scripted TV shows account for the remainder of TV programming. They can take the form of documentaries ("48 Hours"); made-for-TV movies or miniseries ("Lonesome Dove"); situation comedies ("30 Rock," "Hung"); dramas ("Lost," "CSI") and variety shows ("Saturday Night Live").

Daytime Drama - TV Soap Opera

A particular type of popular daytime TV show which owes it roots to the early days of radio is the serialized soap opera seen Monday through Friday. Unlike most scripted dramas, soap operas are rarely ever rerun or syndicated. Their increasingly sensationalized story lines deal with such subjects as incest, amnesia and past life.

Types of TV Show Production

Television shows can be produced live, live-to-tape or on film. Each has a distinctive look.

It is hard to mistake a scripted program for an unscripted one. However some cross-over can occur in the documentary and variety show category. Some situation comedies, and documentaries and all variety shows are recorded-to-tape with (digital) television cameras.

Most if not all dramas as well as some comedies are produced on film.

New Media - webisodes

Webisodes are a new type of TV show being produced initially for the Internet. While not strictly falling into the "broadcast" category, some of these webisodes have crossed over into broadcast venues. These programs are usually run five minutes and deal with serialized story lines. They are posted on sites such as YouTube and Hulu. Some can get massive exposure. It is theorized that in the coming years a great deal of programming will be created as webisodes for people with little time, short attention spans and a proclivity to "channel surf."

Broadcast Syndication

Broadcasting syndication is the license to broadcast television programs and radio programs by multiple television stations and radio stations, without going through a broadcast network. It is common in the United States where broadcast programming is scheduled by television networks with local independent affiliates. Syndication is less of a practice in the rest of the world, as most countries have centralized networks or television stations without local affiliates; although less common, shows can be syndicated internationally. The three main types of syndication are "first-run syndication", which is programming that is broadcast for the first time as a syndicated show and is made specifically to sell directly into syndication; "off-network syndication", which is the licensing of a program that was originally run on network TV or in some cases, first-run syndication (colloquially called a "rerun"); and "public broadcasting syndication".

Types

First-run Syndication

In first-run syndication, a program is broadcast for the first time as a syndicated show and is made specifically to sell directly into syndication (not any one particular network), or at least first so offered in a given country (programs originally created and broadcast outside the US, first presented on a network in their country of origin, have often been syndicated in the US and in some other countries).

Off-network Syndication

In off-network syndication, a program that originally aired on network television (or, in some cases, first-run syndication) is licensed for broadcast on another network. Reruns are usually found on stations affiliated with smaller networks like Fox or the CW, especially since these networks broadcast one less hour of prime time network programming than the Big Three television networks and far less network-provided daytime television (only one hour for the CW, none at all for Fox). A show usually enters off-network syndication when it has built up about four seasons› worth or between 80 and 100 episodes, though for some genres the number could be as low as 65. Successful shows in syndication can cover production costs and make a profit, even if the first run of the show was not profitable.

Public Broadcasting Syndication

This type of syndication has arisen in the U.S. as a parallel service to member stations of the Public Broadcasting Service (PBS) and the handful of independent public broadcasting stations. This form of syndication more closely resembles the news agency model, where nominally competing networks share resources and rebroadcast each other›s programs. For example, National Public Radio (NPR) stations commonly air the Public Radio Exchange's *This American Life*, which may contain stories produced by NPR journalists.

When syndicating a show, the production company, or a distribution company called a syndicator, attempts to license the show to one station in each media market or area, or to a commonly owned station group, within the country and internationally. If successful, this can be lucrative, but the syndicator may only be able to license the show in a small percentage of the markets. Syndication differs from licensing the show to a television network. Once a network picks up a show, it is usually guaranteed to run on most or all the network's affiliates on the same day of the week and at the same time (in a given time zone, in countries where this is a concern). Some production companies create their shows and license them to networks at a loss, at least at first, hoping that the series will succeed and that eventual off-network syndication will turn a profit for the show. A syndicated program is licensed to stations for "cash" (the stations purchase the rights to insert some or all of the advertisements at their level); given to stations for access to airtime (wherein the syndicators get the advertising revenue); or the combination of both. The trade of program for airtime is called "barter."

In the United States (as a result of continued relaxation of station ownership regulations since the 1970s), syndicated programs are usually licensed to stations on a group level, with multiple stations owned and operated by the same broadcasting group carrying the program in different markets (except in areas where another station holds the market rights to the program) – making it increasingly more efficient for syndicators to gain widespread national clearances for their programs. Many syndicated programs are traditionally sold first to one of five "key" station groups (ABC Owned Television Stations, NBC Owned Television Stations, CBS Television Stations, Fox Television Stations and Tribune Broadcasting), allowing their programs to gain clearances in the largest U.S. TV markets (such as New York City, Los Angeles, Chicago and Philadelphia, where all five aforementioned groups each own stations), before striking deals with other major and smaller station owners. Shows airing in first-run syndication that are carried primarily by an owned-and-operated station of a network may sometimes be incorrectly referenced as a network program, especially if said network›s syndication wing distributes the program, regardless to its distribution to stations of varying network affiliations and despite the fact it is not part of an individual network›s base schedule.

Since the early 2000s, some programs being proposed for national distribution in first-run syndication have been test marketed on a selected number of or all stations owned by certain major station group, allowing the distributor to determine whether a national roll-out is feasible based on the ratings accrued in the selected markets where the program is being aired.

While market penetration can vary widely and revenues can be unreliable, the producers often enjoy more content freedom in the absence of network's standards and practices departments; frequently, some innovative ideas are explored by first-run syndicated programming which the networks are leery of giving airtime to. Meanwhile, top-rated syndicated shows in the United States usually have a domestic market reach as high as 98%. Very often, series› that are aired in syndication have reduced running times. For example, a standard American sitcom runs 22 minutes, but in syndication it may be reduced to 20 minutes to make room for more commercials.

Syndication can take the form of either weekly or daily syndication. Game shows, some "tabloid" and entertainment news shows, and talk shows are broadcast daily on weekdays, while most other first-run syndicated shows are broadcast on a weekly basis and are usually aired on weekends only. Big discussion occurred in the 1990s and 2000s about whether previously aired episodes of a show could become syndicated while new episodes of it continued to air on its original network. There had been much opposition to this idea and it was generally viewed to lead to the death of the show. However, licensing a program for syndication actually resulted in the increased popularity for shows that remained in production. A prime example is *Law & Order*.

Influence on Television Schedules

In earlier times, independent stations thrived on syndicated programming, including some venerable and quite profitable stations such as KMSP-TV in the Minneapolis-St. Paul market. With the loosening of FCC regulations and the creation of new additional broadcast networks (such as Fox, The CW, MyNetworkTV and Ion Television), most of these independents have joined one or another of these or smaller (religious or low-budget) networks.

In other cases, like those of KCAL-TV in Los Angeles, KMCI-TV in Lawrence-Kansas City and WMLW-TV in Racine-Milwaukee, those independent stations are used to complement their network-affiliated sister station (respectively in the mentioned cases, KCBS-TV, KSHB-TV and

WDJT-TV) by allowing a duopoly control of more syndicated programming than would be possible on one station (and to spread it throughout the schedule of the two stations, often several times a day), or to air news programming in times unavailable on the larger network station, along with fulfilling network and syndicated programming commitments, which allows popular or network programming to be moved to the independent stations due to breaking news or sports commitments without the traditional inconvenience of a late night or weekend airing of the pre-empted show. A duopoly of a network-affiliated and independent station also allows a network station to move a low-rated syndicated program to their sister independent station to stem revenue losses.

Off-network Syndication

Off-network syndication occurs when a network television series is syndicated in packages containing some or all episodes, and sold to as many television stations and markets as possible to be used in local programming timeslots. In this manner, sitcoms are preferred and more successful because they are less serialized, and can be run non-sequentially, which is more beneficial and less costly for the station. In the United States, local stations now rarely broadcast reruns of prime-time dramas (or simply air them primarily on weekends); instead, they usually air on basic cable channels, which may air each episode 30 to 60 times.

Syndication rights typically last for six consecutive showings of a series within three to five years; if a program continues to perform well enough in broadcast or cable syndication during the initial cycle, television stations or cable networks can opt to renew an off-network program for an additional cycle.

Syndication has been known to spur the popularity of a series that only experienced moderate success during its network run. The best known example of this is the original *Star Trek* series, which ran for three seasons on NBC from 1966 to 1969, gaining only modest ratings, but became a worldwide phenomenon after it entered off-network syndication. Its success in syndication led to the *Star Trek* film series, *Star Trek: The Next Generation*, and the later versions in the franchise.

It is common for long-running series to have early seasons syndicated while the series itself is still in first-run network production. In order to differentiate between new and rebroadcast content, until the 1980s it was not uncommon for series to be syndicated under a different title than that used in their original broadcast run. Examples include *Bonanza* (which was syndicated as *Ponderosa*), *Gunsmoke* (as *Marshall Dillon*, a title still used to differentiate reruns from the early, half-hour and black-and-white episodes of the show from the later one-hour color episodes), *Emergency!* (as *Emergency One*), *Ironside* (as The Raymond Burr Show), Hawaii Five-O (as McGarrett), M*A*S*H (as M*A*S*H 4077th), Marcus Welby, M.D. (as Robert Young, Family Doctor), CHiPs (as CHiPs Patrol), and Happy Days (as Happy Days Again).

Syndication of older episodes can also increase exposure for a television show that is still airing first-run network episodes. In the case of the CBS sitcom *The Big Bang Theory*, its syndication, particularly on TBS, is one of the reasons attributed for a rise in first-run ratings for its sixth season. The sixth-season episode "The Bakersfield Expedition", for example, was the first episode of that series to attract 20 million viewers.

Strip/Daily Syndication

Off-network syndication can take several forms. The most common form is known as strip syndication or daily syndication, when episodes of a television series are shown daily five times a week in the same time slot. In the 1960s and 1970s, independent stations with no news departments began viewing strip syndication as a necessary means of obtaining effective counterprogramming to the local news programs airing on network affiliates. Typically, this means that enough episodes must exist (88 episodes, or four seasons, is the usual minimum, though many syndicators prefer a fully rounded 100 episodes) to allow for continual strip syndication to take place over the course of several months, without episodes being repeated. However, there are exceptions, such as the 65-episode block (common in children's programming), which allows for a 13-week cycle of daily showings, so there will only be four repeats in a year.

In some cases, more than one episode is shown daily. Half-hour sitcoms are sometimes syndicated in groups of two or four episodes, taking up one or two hours of broadcast time. If a series is not strip syndicated, it may be aired once a week, instead of five times a week. This allows shows with fewer episodes to last long in syndication, but it also may mean viewers will tire of waiting a week for the next episode of a show they have already seen and stop watching. More often, hour-long dramas in their first several runs in syndication are offered weekly; sitcoms are more likely to get stripped. In recent years, there has been something of a trend toward showing two consecutive episodes of a program on Saturday and Sunday nights after prime time (generally following the local news). This pattern has been particularly prominent for shows which are still in production but have run long enough to have many previous episodes available.

As with commercial stations, not all the airtime nor all the perceived audience are met by the productions offered U.S. public-broadcasting stations by PBS; additionally, there are some independent public television stations in the U.S. which take no programming from that (somewhat) decentralized network. As a result, there are several syndicators of programming for the non-profit stations, several of which are descendants of the regional station groups which combined some, not all, of their functions into the creation of PBS in 1969. American Public Television (APT) is the largest of these, nearly matched by the National Educational Telecommunications Association (NETA); similarly, the now defunct Continental Program Marketing was another of the syndicator-descendants (of the Northeastern, Southeastern, and Rocky Mountain educational networks, respectively) of the pre-PBS era. Among the other notable organizations in the U.S. are Westlink Satellite Operations (based at Albuquerque›s KNME), BBC Worldwide Americas (which often works with other distributors and individual stations, since it has no satellite access of its own in the U.S.), Deutsche Welle, Executive Program Services, the Program Resource Group and PBS's Long Island, New York member station WLIW, which is (with the arguable exception of KNME) the most prolific contributor of any individual station of syndicated programming, most obviously the *BBC World News*, *Doctor Who* and *Monty Python›s Flying Circus* in the U.S.

Off-network syndication in its various forms, including Internet, international and traditional direct-to-station sales, constitute roughly half of an individual television program's overall revenue stream, with the other half taken up by advertising.

Types of Deals

Cash deals are when a distributor offers a syndicated program to the highest bidder. A cash plus deal is when the distributor retains advertising space to offset some of the cost for the program. The station gets the program for a little less in exchange for some ad space for the producer.

Barter deals are usually for new untested shows or older shows. In this type of deal, distributors get a fraction of the advertisement revenue in exchange for their program. For example, in a 7/5 deal the producer gets seven minutes of advertising time, leaving five minutes for the station to insert local as well as national advertisements.

Radio Syndication

Radio syndication generally works the same way as television syndication, except that radio stations usually are not organized into strict affiliate-only networks. Radio networks generally are only distributors of radio shows, and individual stations (though often owned by large conglomerates) decide which shows to carry from a wide variety of networks and independent radio providers. As a result, radio networks such as WestwoodOne or Premiere Networks, despite their influence in broadcasting, are not as recognized among the general public as television networks like CBS or ABC (many of these distributors ally themselves with television networks; WestwoodOne, for instance, is allied with NBC, while Premiere is allied with Fox). Some examples of widely syndicated commercial broadcasting music programs include weekly countdowns like Rick Dees' Weekly Top 40, the American Top 40, American Country Countdown with Kix Brooks, Canada's Top 20 Countdown, the Canadian Hit 30 Countdown and the nightly program, Delilah, heard on many U.S. stations.

Syndication is particularly popular in talk radio. While syndicated music shows (with the exception of some evening and overnight shows such as *Delilah* mentioned above) tend to air once a week and are mostly recorded, most popular talk radio programs are syndicated daily and are broadcast live. Also, with relatively few 24-hour live talk radio networks (though this, in recent times, has been changing), most radio stations are free to assemble their own lineup of talk show hosts as they so choose. Examples of syndicated talk programs are Premiere Networks' *The Bob & Tom Show*, Dial Global's *The Jim Bohannon Show*, and the self-syndicated *The Dave Ramsey Show* (more recently, talk networks such as Talk Radio Network have been marketing and packaging all-day lineups, marking a departure from the syndication model; as such, popular shows such as Cumulus Media Networks' *The Savage Nation* and Premiere›s *The Rush Limbaugh Show* now air as part of a broader network lineup in many markets, particularly on Premiere owned-and-operated stations, though they continue to be syndicated to non-network stations as well). Talk syndication tends to be more prevalent because voice tracking, a practice used by many music stations to have disc jockeys host multiple supposedly local shows at once, is not feasible with live talk radio.

National Public Radio, Public Radio International, and American Public Media all sell programming to local member stations in the U.S., most of which are subsidized through the Corporation for Public Broadcasting but operated by private nonprofit organizations, universities, state or local governments. This is in contrast to centralized public radio networks in other countries (such as Canada›s CBC, Australia's ABC and the United Kingdom›s BBC) that own and operate all of their stations as arms of the national government and run them as a strict network (from 1948 to

2013, the United States had a strict anti-propaganda law, the Smith–Mundt Act, that prohibited broadcasting government-owned networks such as Voice of America to American audiences. The law was mostly repealed in 2013, but distribution of VOA or other federally produced radio programming is still rare). Two independently produced, non-commercial syndicated programs, heard on hundreds of community radio and indie radio stations, are *Alternative Radio* and *Democracy Now!*. Some (in fact, most) radio programs are also offered on a barter system usually at no charge to the radio station. The system is used for live programming or preproduced programs and include a mixture of ad time sold by the program producer as well as time set aside for the radio station to sell.

Before radio networks matured in the United States, some early radio shows were reproduced on transcription disks and mailed to individual stations. An example of syndication using this method was RadiOzark Enterprises, Inc. based in Springfield, Missouri, co-owned with KWTO. The Assembly of God, with national headquarters in Springfield, sponsored a half-hour program on the station called *Sermons in Song*. RadiOzark began transcribing the show for other stations in the 1940s, and eventually 200 stations carried the program. The company later produced country music programs starring among others, Smiley Burnette, George Morgan, Bill Ring and Tennessee Ernie Ford (260 15-minute episodes of *The Tennessee Ernie Show* were distributed), and more than 1,200 U.S. and Canadian stations aired the programs. Many syndicated radio programs were distributed through the U.S. mail or another delivery service, although the medium changed as technology developed, going from transcription disks to phonograph records, tape recordings, cassette tapes and eventually CDs. Many smaller weekend programs still use this method to this day, though with the rise of the Internet, many stations have since opted to distribute programs via CD-quality MP3s through FTP downloads.

It was not until the advent of satellite communications in the 1980s that live syndication became popular (though it could be transmitted through network lines, it was not particularly common because of cost, network congestion and quality issues). Since then, most syndicated radio programs are distributed using satellite subcarrier audio technology. Shortly after satellite networks such as RKO, Transtar and SMN began, the Fairness Doctrine was repealed, which is credited with helping Rush Limbaugh become the first national talk radio superstar. At the same time, the FCC began issuing more FM radio licenses to suburban and rural areas in the late 1980s, which allowed more room for music stations on the FM dial; radio formats such as country music that were traditionally AM fixtures even after most pop and rock music moved to FM were now moving to FM as well, leaving much more room for talk formats on the AM dial. As the 1990s went on, Dr. Laura and Howard Stern began their national shows, rising to become national icons. The Telecommunications Act of 1996, which led to significant concentration of media ownership, facilitated the rapid deployment of both existing and new syndicated programs in the late 1990s, putting syndication on par with, and eventually surpassing, the network radio format.

After the September 11, 2001 terrorist attacks, syndicated talk radio saw a notably rapid rise in popularity, as networks rushed new national shows into syndication to meet the demand for discussion of national issues. Many of these, such as Laura Ingraham, Bill O'Reilly, Sean Hannity and Glenn Beck, were mostly supportive of the actions of the Republican-led government; a few others, such as Alex Jones, were openly critical of the government's actions and motives. After the Democrats took control in the late 2000s, the gap between the two styles narrowed due to the mutual opposition of both camps to the government›s actions, which allowed Jones greater clearance on stations.

In contrast to conservative talk radio, which has predominantly been driven by syndication, progressive talk radio has almost always been a network-driven model. The incompatibility of conservative and progressive ideologies and the lack of syndicated progressive hosts required solutions that could produce all-day programming to individual stations. It was not until Air America Radio launched in 2004 that progressive talk would become viable; though it failed several years later, Dial Global now carries a network slate that is carried on most progressive talk stations. Sports radio is likewise mostly a network phenomenon, partially because the irregular nature of sports pre-emptions makes having a full-time network to be able to cut into and join in progress at any time highly convenient. Syndicated radio is not as popular in other parts of the world. Canada has a few independently syndicated shows, but the bulk of syndicated content there comes from the United States, and the sum total of syndicated programming is far less than most American stations, as Canadian stations rely more heavily on local content. Most other countries still follow the network radio model.

International Syndication

Syndication also applies to international markets. Same language countries often syndicate programs to each other – such as programs from the United Kingdom being syndicated to Australia and vice versa. Another example would be programs from the United Kingdom, Mexico, Brazil, and Argentina being syndicated to local television stations in the United States, and programs from the United States being syndicated elsewhere in the world. One of the best-known internationally syndicated television series has been *The Muppet Show*, which was produced by Grade's English ITV franchise company ATV at Elstree Studios in Hertfordshire, and was shown around the world, including the United States, where it aired in syndication (including the owned-and-operated stations of CBS), and Canada, where CBC Television aired the show. The 1970s was a time when many British comedies, including *The Benny Hill Show* and *Monty Python›s Flying Circus* were syndicated to the United States and worldwide. Many soaps and long-running series are also successfully syndicated around the globe.

The television show *CSI* earned $1.6 million per episode in its first cycle in cable syndication. There were many different versions of the show making it an international success. It was already popular in the U.S., so becoming a success internationally as well as within the U.S. made syndication sensible. Whether a series is produced in the U.S. or not is based on the economic value and potential viability of its sales internationally with the possibility of syndication.

Economic factors that influence production outside the U.S. play a major role in deciding if a television show will be syndicated, internally and internationally. International syndication has sustained a growing of prosperity and monetary value amongst the distributors who sell to them. Due to a rise in competition, syndicators have upheld high standards for different countries to buy the rights to distribute shows. During the 1990s poor ratings were common amongst syndicated shows, but distributors still made it possible for international competition to happen and buy U.S. shows. Colombian, Brazilian, Mexican and Venezuelan telenovelas are programmed throughout the Portuguese and Spanish-speaking world, and in many parts of India, China and Europe, while Turkish television drama is broadcast in the Balkans, some other European countries, Western and Central Asia and North Africa.

Regional Syndication

There are three key reasons why a radio station will decide to pick up a syndicated show – the program is unique and has difficult to replicate content, has a decent ratings track record or offers a celebrity host. New developing radio programs are generally able to claim one of these attributes, but not all three. Regional syndication attempts to replace these benchmark attributes with other benefits that are generally recognized by the industry as also being important. Given the financial downturn within the industry, the need for quality cost effective locally relevant programming is greater than ever before. Programs that offer regionally specific content while providing the economic benefits of syndication can be especially appealing to potential affiliates. Regional syndication can also be more attractive to area advertisers who share a common regional trading area versus assembling a radio network of stations that hopscotch across the United States.

Paid Promotion

Paid advertising is any kind of advertising that you have to pay for, versus owned or earned advertising.

With paid advertising, marketers pay the owner of ad space in exchange for use of that space. The price paid for the ad space is often settled through a bidding process between marketers and the ad space owner.

There are several categories, including pay-per-click (PPC), pay-per-impression (PPI), and display ads.

Efficient marketing campaigns capitalize on all channels for advertising. Although paid advertising costs more than owned or earned advertising, paid forms are an effective way to expose your company's name to a large audience.

Paid ads are usually displayed to users on the sides, tops, or bottoms of web pages. Marketers can pay more to have their ads featured on more popular websites to increase traffic.

The different categories of paid ads — PPC, PPI, and display ads — allow marketers to further customize their campaigns. The growing popularity of social media has recently turned sites such as Facebook and LinkedIn into effective platforms for paid ads.

References

- Content-distribution: robertkatai.com, Retrieved 19 June, 2019
- Definition-of-radio-broadcasting: techwalla.com, Retrieved 14 May, 2019
- Programming, on-air: communityradiotoolkit.net, Retrieved 20 June, 2019
- Different-types-online-radio-programs: spacial.com, Retrieved 15 April, 2019
- Types-of-tv-shows- 12197904: itstillworks.com, Retrieved 17 March, 2019
- Paid-advertising, marketing-dictionary: trackmaven.com, Retrieved 14 February, 2019

4

Digital Advertising and Marketing

Advertising and marketing are of the publicity strategies used by firms and organizations to reach their target audience. The diverse applications of advertising and marketing such as digital advertising and marketing; video, email and radio marketing, cinema and television advertising, digital billboards, paid media, etc. have been thoroughly discussed in this chapter.

Digital Advertising

Digital advertising is a targeted, data-driven advertising strategy for reaching consumers in every stage of the buying funnel and moving them from one stage of the buying funnel to the next. From awareness to purchase, you can use digital media advertising (and online ad channels like Google) to drive revenue.

How is Digital Advertising different from Traditional Advertising

Like traditional advertising, it promotes your business, products, and services to generate brand awareness, sales, and more. It leverages digital, rather than traditional channels, however. Instead of billboards and magazines, your ads appear on Google, Facebook, YouTube, and more.

Online advertising also comes with a massive amount of data. You can track the performance of your campaigns in real-time, for example. In addition, you can learn about the demographics, interests, and habits of the people viewing and interacting with your ads.

In comparison, traditional advertising delivers the bare minimum when it comes to data. You don't have immediate insight into your campaign's performance. A billboard, for example, may provide your team with almost zero data.

That's why digital advertising often seems like a smart alternative to traditional advertising.

Why use Digital Advertising?

Companies use digital advertising for a variety of reasons, including:

- Increasing brand awareness.
- Improving product sales.
- Generating qualified leads.
- Driving repeat purchases.

What motivates businesses to use online digital advertising, however, comes its range of advantages. When you use digital advertising, you provide your company with a measurable and cost-effective strategy that drives the kind of results you want.

A few of the most mentioned benefits of digital advertising include:

Digital Advertising Reaches your Target Audience

Purchase a billboard, and you can hope that your target audience not only sees it but also acts on it. There are zero guarantees, though, especially when you're targeting drivers inside and outside your target audience.

A digital ad campaign, however, is the exact opposite.

With digital advertising, you're reaching (and directing your ad spend) towards the people with actual interest in your business. Using targeting options like location, interests, and behavior, you can ensure your ads focus on the people that matter most to your business.

Not to mention, with online digital advertising, you're reaching people when they want to be reached.

Instead of trying to get their attention on the highway, you're connecting with them when they're searching for your business or researching products in your industry. Digital advertising pulls people to your company versus pushing them towards it.

Digital Advertising Provides Measurable Results

Whether it's offline or online, you want to track your advertising initiatives.

Otherwise, how can you prove that your strategy worked?

Luckily, it's easy to track and monitor your online digital advertising efforts. Digital ad platforms, like Google Ads, often monitor your campaigns for you. Just log into your account and view your data. You can even export it into reporting tools like Google Data Studio for review.

Digital ad campaign data not only helps your team show the results of your strategy but also find opportunities for improvement. For example, if you have a low-performing ad, you could brainstorm new copy, images, and more to increase its performance.

Digital Advertising Supports Every Ad Budget

Whether you're operating a small business or massive enterprise, you can use digital advertising.

Compared to traditional advertising, online digital advertising allows your business to create a budget. You don't have to fulfil specific budget requirements to launch a billboard or air a television commercial. Instead, you decide what you'll spend (and what you'll pay) for your ads.

Many online advertising platforms also prevent pay-to-win schemes.

A company, for example, can't place a higher bid to earn the best ad placement. They also need to deliver a relevant ad and excellent user experience. This bidding model allows all businesses to achieve excellent ad placements without bidding an obscene amount.

Digital Advertising Offers Options when it Comes to Strategy

No matter your business, you want options when it comes to advertising, whether offline or online.

With digital advertising, you have options. You can launch ads on Google, Facebook, or YouTube. Not to mention, you can choose between text, image, and video ads. Plus, you can customize your ads with advanced targeting options, including remarketing.

Your company can also use online digital advertising for a variety of goals, including:

- Building brand awareness.
- Driving product sales.
- Increasing contact requests.

All these options provide your team with flexibility and versatility when it comes to advertising.

Digital Advertising Delivers Instant Results

When your company adopts digital media advertising, you can expect results instantly.

As soon as you launch your paid campaigns, you can start receiving clicks, orders, phone calls, and more. You can also track and associate each of these actions with your campaigns. With that kind of tracking, your company can easily see the impact of digital advertising on your business and its bottom line.

In comparison, online marketing can take longer to see results.

If you use a strategy like content marketing, for example, it could take several months before you see traffic increases, new leads, or product purchases. That's why many businesses will use digital marketing strategies in coordination with online advertising ones.

How does Online Digital Advertising Work

Compared to traditional advertising, online digital advertising works in an unusual way.

With traditional advertising, your business generally pays a provider, like a billboard company, upfront. That's not the case with digital advertising. When you use digital advertising, you only pay when a user completes a desired action on your ad.

This action can range from clicking on your ad to viewing your ad.

For example, you may launch an ad campaign with a cost-per-click (CPC) of $2.00. This means you're willing to pay $2.00 for every click on your ad. You might pay less, however, due to the auction algorithms of different platforms, like Google and Facebook.

If you partner with an advertising agency, the payment process is somewhat different.

You pay an upfront management fee, for example, which covers the costs of developing and managing your strategy. Your company also sets aside a designated ad spend, which is what you pay ad platforms, like Google, to deliver or show your ads.

When you use digital advertising, you can also use advanced targeting methods to reach your target audience. These targeting features go beyond the capabilities of traditional marketing which forces your business to target people in and outside of your target market.

A few of the most common targeting options in digital advertising include:

- Keywords: With keyword targeting, you can reach people who search keywords and phrases related to your business. As an example, a flower shop may target phrases like, "florist for wedding."
- Interests: With interest targeting, advertising platforms like Google Ads and Facebook allow your business to reach users past on their past behavior. For example, your ads can appear for shoppers with an interest in hiking and camping.
- Demographics: With demographic targeting, you can reach consumers based on their demographic information, like their age, location, and even parental status. A daycare center may target parents between the ages of 25-34, for instance.
- Remarketing: With remarketing, your business can target users that visited your site. Your ad campaign, for example, may show ads to people who not only looked at your service page but also match the demographics of your target market.

Like traditional advertising, however, digital advertising requires research and planning. Before you launch your campaign, for example, you need to determine your advertising goals, strategy, budget, and more.

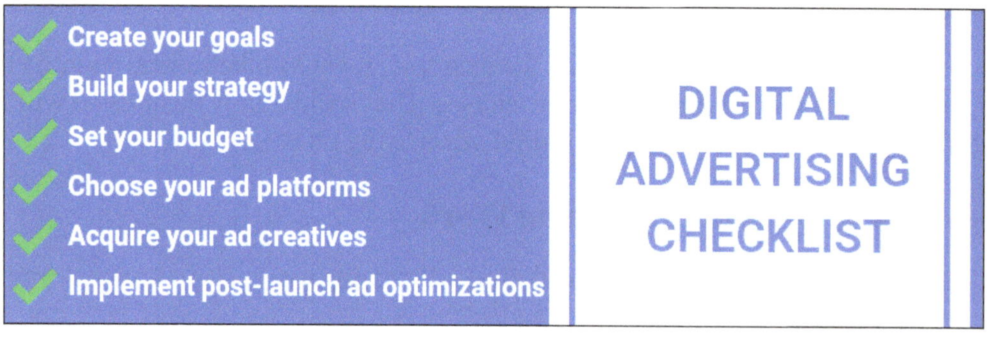

In most cases, launching an online digital advertising campaign includes the following checklist:

- Create your goals.
- Build your strategy.
- Set your budget.
- Choose your ad platforms.

- Acquire your ad creatives, like copy and media.
- Implement post-launch ad optimizations.

This approach is significantly different from traditional advertising. With digital advertising, your team can continue to optimize and improve your campaign, even after it launches. In comparison, your company only has one chance to nail your traditional advertising campaign.

Definitive Bidding Models in Digital Advertising

Before exploring the different types of digital advertising ads, it's helpful to understand the different bidding models available with online digital advertising. That way, you can choose the best option for your business and its campaigns.

The four most common bidding models in digital advertising include:

Cost-per-click (CPC)

With CPC, your business pays every time someone clicks on your ad. For marketers, CPC is a go-to choice because you're paying someone to interact, rather than view your ad. A click also brings users to your site (or another dedicated landing page), which can motivate them to convert.

A variety of advertising platforms use CPC, including:

- Google Ads,
- Bing Ads,
- Facebook,
- Instagram,
- Twitter.

Cost-per-thousand-impressions (CPM)

With CPM, your company pays when your ad earns 1000 impressions or views. While CPM is excellent for building brand awareness for well-known brands, like Coca-Cola or Pepsi, it's not cost-effective for small-to-midsize businesses (SMBs). A view doesn't translate to the kind of actions you want, like purchases.

Like CPC, CPM is available on several advertising platforms, including:

- Google Ads,
- Bing Ads,
- Facebook,
- Instagram,
- YouTube.

Cost-per-lead (CPL)

With CPL, your business pays every time your ad generates a new lead. If you're a business-to-business (B2B) company, this bidding option can work well. It's essential, however, to develop an ad that targets high-quality users as you don't want to pay for low-quality leads.

A few examples of advertising platforms that offer CPL include Google Ads and Facebook.

Cost-per-action (CPA)

With CPA, your company pays when a user completes a desired action. This action includes a variety of conversions, from signing up for an email newsletter to purchasing a specific product. Companies often use this bidding option on social media but can take advantage of it on other channels, like search.

A couple common advertising platforms for CPA include Facebook and Instagram.

How much does Online Digital Advertising Cost

Like traditional advertising, your company can spend as much as you like on digital advertising.

On average, however, SMBs dedicate $9000 to $10,000 per month to online digital advertising. That translates to an annual investment of $100,000 to $120,000 per year. While your business may spend more or less, this amount can serve as a point of reference for your team.

If you're pitching company decision-makers on digital advertising, create a potential budget. This hypothetical budget should include a breakdown of your costs, which can range from your monthly ad spend to your advertising tech.

How to Create a Successful Digital Advertising Campaign

For your digital advertising campaign to succeed, you want to follow these industry-best practices:

Make your Offer Compelling

While your business knows what makes your product or service amazing, your target audience doesn't. Use your ads to showcase the unique benefits of your goods. It's also essential for your team to convey these advantages in a way that resonates with your market.

As an example, if you're a landscaping company, you need to ask what your audience wants from a landscaper. Do they want non-intrusive service, one-of-a-kind gardens, or something else? Research your audience online to determine what they're looking for in a landscaper.

You can also promote savings, like a free quote, to make your offer even more compelling.

Write some Killer AD Copy

If you want users to interact with your ads, whether across search, social media, or video, write some snappy ad copy. As many ad providers, like Google, maintain character limits on ad copy, you need short, yet compelling text to hook your audience.

Appeal to your audience's interests, needs, and pain points to create successful ad copy and creatives

Even if you're investing in display ads, it's essential for your team to develop ad creatives that grab your audience's attention. You can use a compelling offer or emotional appeal to get users to watch your video or click on your ad.

Appeal to your audience's interests, needs, and pain points to create successful ad copy and creatives.

Get Custom Creatives

A lot of businesses decide to build creatives for digital advertising in-house. If you're a company with an in-house team of designers and videographers, this move makes sense. Otherwise, it's a decision that can cost your business money.

While you may pay more upfront for graphics and videos from professionals, custom creatives can help the long-term performance of your ad. They show your company's professionalism and quality, which can serve as trust signals for users in your target audience.

Invest in top-notch creatives upfront to get the most from your digital advertising strategy.

Target the Dream Client

Companies often start with a broad target audience with online digital advertising. This approach can result in a ton of ad clicks and even conversions, but rarely achieve your overall goal of working with your ideal client or shopper.

That's why your business should focus your ads on your dream customer. With digital advertising, your company can access advanced target options, which can help your team reach the consumers you want. While you may see fewer clicks and conversions, you will notice an increase in customer quality.

Plus, this approach saves your business money as you're only paying for the users that matter.

Digital Marketing

Digital marketing is the use of the internet, mobile devices, social media, search engines, and other channels to reach consumers. Some marketing experts consider digital marketing to be an entirely new endeavor that requires a new way of approaching customers and new ways of understanding how customers behave compared to traditional marketing.

Digital marketing targets a specific segment of the customer base and is interactive. Digital marketing is on the rise and includes search result ads, email ads and promoted tweets – anything that incorporates marketing with customer feedback or a two-way interaction between the company and customer.

Internet (a.k.a. online) marketing differs from digital marketing. Internet marketing is advertising that is solely on the Internet, whereas digital marketing can take place over the telephone, on a subway platform, in a video game or via a smartphone app.

In the parlance of digital marketing, advertisers are commonly referred to as sources, while members of the targeted ads are commonly called receivers. Sources frequently target highly specific, well-defined receivers. For example, after extending the late-night hours of many of its locations, McDonald's needed to get the word out. It targeted shift workers and travelers with digital ads, because the company knew that these people made up a large segment of its late night business. McDonald's encouraged them to download a new Restaurant Finder app, targeting them with ads placed at ATMs and gas stations, as well as on websites that it new its customers frequented at night.

Digital Marketing Channels:

- Website Marketing: A website is the centerpiece of all digital marketing activities. Alone, it is a very powerful channel, but it's also the medium needed to execute a variety of online marketing campaigns. A website should represent a brand, product and services in a clear and memorable way. It should be fast, mobile friendly, and easy to use.
- Pay-per-click (PPC) Advertising: PPC advertising enables you to reach internet users on a number of digital platforms through paid ads. You can setup PPC campaigns on Google, Bing, Linkendin, Twitter, Pinterest, or Facebook and show your ads to people searching for terms related to your products or services. PPC campaigns can segment users based on their demographic characteristics (age, gender etc) or even their particular interests or location. The most popular PPC platforms are Google Ads and Facebook.
- Content Marketing: The goal of a content marketing is to reach potential customers through the use of content. Content is usually published on a website and then promoted through social media, email marketing, SEO, or even PPC campaigns. The tools of content marketing include: blogs, ebooks, online courses, infographics, podcasts, and webinars.
- Email Marketing: Email marketing is still one of the most effective digital marketing channels. Many people confuse email marketing with spam email messages we all receive per day, but that's not what email marketing is all about. Email marketing is the medium to get in touch with your potential customers or the people interested in your brand. Many digital marketers use all other digital marketing channels to add leads to their email lists and then, through email marketing, they create customer acquisition funnels to turn those leads into customers.
- Social Media Marketing: The primary goal of a social media marketing campaign is brand awareness and establishing social trust but as you go deeper into social media marketing, you can use it to get leads or even as a direct sales channel.
- Affiliate Marketing: Affiliate marketing is one of the oldest forms of marketing, and the

internet has brought new life to this old stand-by. With affiliate marketing, you promote other people's products, and you get a commission every time you make a sale or introduce a lead. Many well-known companies like Amazon have affiliate programs that pay out millions of dollars per month to websites that sell their products.

- Video Marketing: YouTube has become the second most popular search engine and a lot of users are turning to YouTube before they make a buying decision, to learn something or just to relax. There are several video marketing platforms, including Facebook Videos, Instagram, Vimeo to use to run a video marketing campaign. Companies find the most success with video by integrating it with SEO, content marketing, and social media marketing campaigns.
- SMS Messaging: Political parties and candidates use SMS messages to send positive information about their candidates and negative messages about their opponents.

Digital marketing poses special challenges for its purveyors. Digital channels are proliferating rapidly, and digital marketers have to keep up with how these channels work, how they're used by receivers and how to use these channels to effectively market things. In addition, it's becoming more difficult to capture receivers' attention, because receivers are increasingly inundated with competing ads. Digital marketers also find it challenging to analyze the vast troves of data they capture and then exploit this information in new marketing efforts.

The challenge of capturing and using data effectively highlights that digital marketing requires a new approach to marketing based on a new understanding of consumer behavior. For example, it may require a company to analyze new forms of consumer behavior, such as likes on Facebook and tweets on Twitter.

Types of Digital Marketing

Content Marketing

Content marketing is a type of digital marketing that focuses on creating and distributing content for a target audience. The content aims at being valuable, relevant, and (ideally) consistent. Its ultimate goal is to drive a profitable customer action.

Example of content marketing

- relevant and helpful blog posts
- educational videos on the topic

Example of traditional marketing

Offline advertising that people are less likely to pay attention to

The crucial part here is "*valuable*" and "*relevant*". This is what tells content marketing apart from traditional spammy advertising. The target audience should want to seek the content out and consume it.

In the broader sense, content marketing is part of every other digital marketing activity, be it social media marketing, SEO, or email marketing. Quality content should be the core of every other marketing activity you pursue.

Some examples of content marketing include: blog posts, videos, podcasts, infographics, white papers, case studies, ebooks.

Search Engine Optimization (SEO)

SEO, or Search Engine Optimization, is the process of getting quality traffic from free, or organic, search results on the search engines (like Google and Bing).

It's important that the traffic you drive to your website is relevant to your industry. If you manage to attract a high volume of visitors searching for Macintosh computers while what you actually do is selling raincoats, the traffic will do you no good.

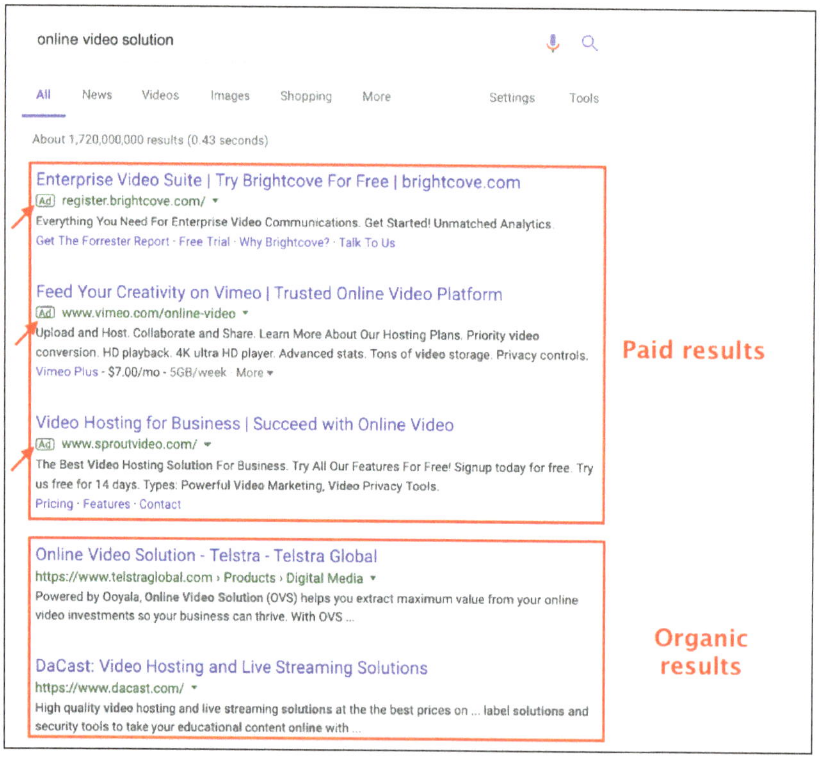

SEO is one of the most important types of digital marketing. By optimizing your content for search engines, you can increase a steady stream of relevant traffic that will only grow over time. Without search engine optimization, people simply won't be able to find you on the Internet.

Some optimization techniques include: researching relevant keywords and including them into your website copy, optimizing your website titles, description and loading speed, building relevant backlinks.

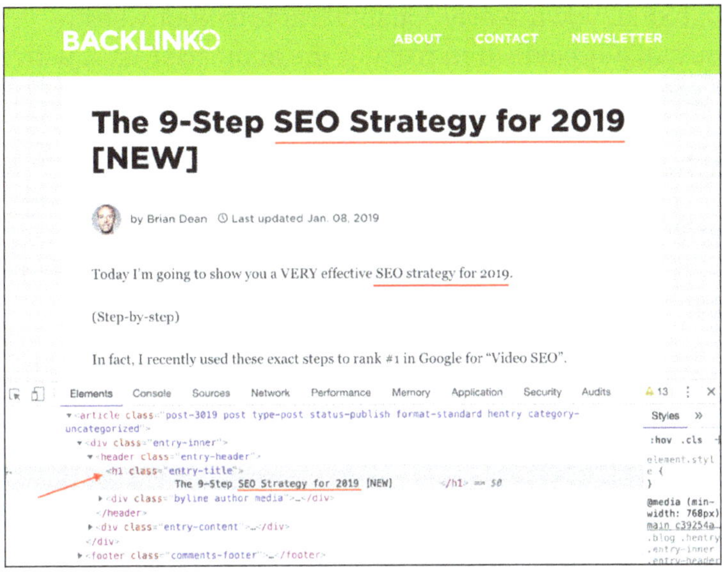

Notice how Brian Dean of Backlinko optimizes the blog post for the keyword "SEO strategy for 2019" by including it in the H1 title and the first paragraph.

Search Engine Marketing (SEM)

Initially, the term *"search engine marketing"* was used as an umbrella term for the process of gaining both paid and free search traffic. Over time, the industry switched to using the term "SEM", or Search Engine Marketing, solely for paid activities.So, what does this type of digital marketing mean?

Search engine marketing refers to a form of digital marketing that aims at increasing the visibility of a website in search engines by using paid methods. In other words, it's the ads you put out there on Google AdWords and Bing Ads.

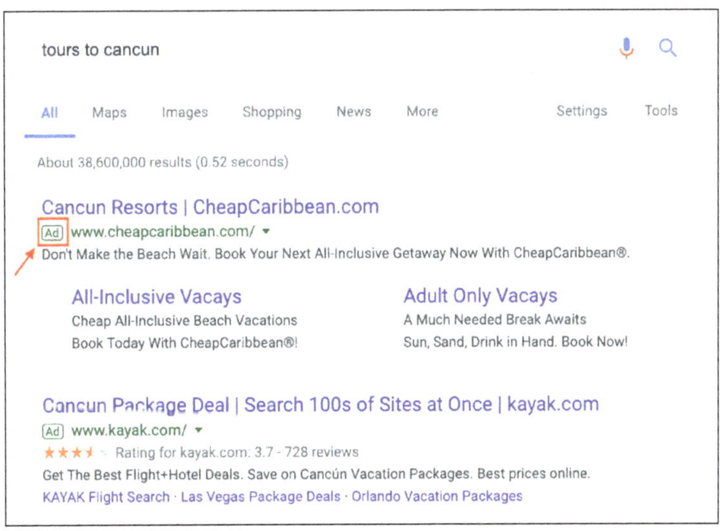

You can recognize paid search results in Google by the little sign "Ad" at the beginning of the URL. Also, Google puts these pages first in the search results.

By combining SEO and SEM, you can drive quality traffic to your website. With the help of search engine marketing, you can put yourself in front of the audience that is actively searching for services and brands like yours.

Social Media Marketing (SMM)

Simply put, social media marketing refers to the process of using social media platforms to attract traffic and attention. By using social media, you can increase exposure and build meaningful relationships with your customers.

While everybody can benefit from SMM as a type of digital marketing, B2C and SaaS companies tend to get the most out of it. Social media marketing is all about listening to what your customers have to say, engaging in the conversation, and sharing valuable content.

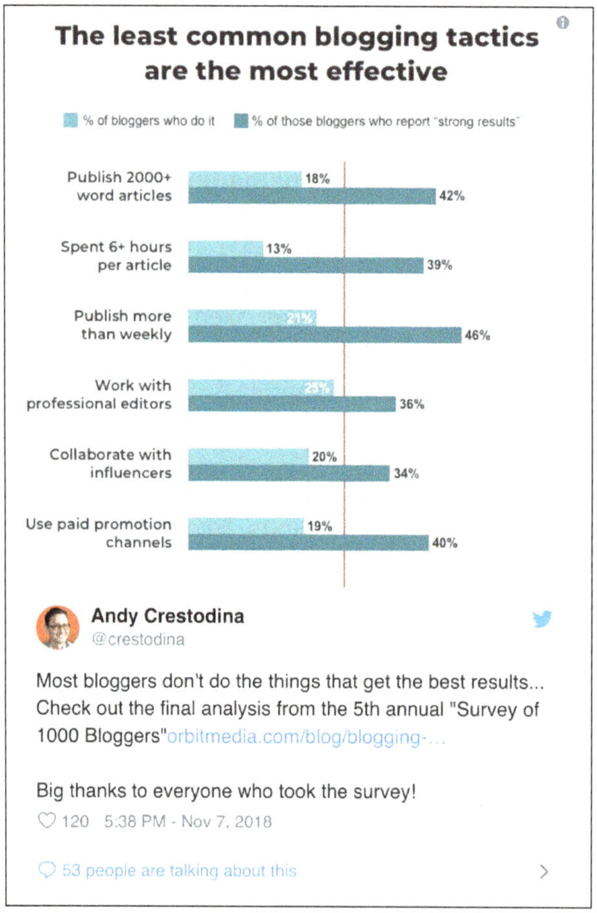

An example of a tweet from Andy Cristiana of Orbit media. Notice how he attracts attention by sharing valuable information (info graphic), drives traffic to his website by posting the link and evokes discussion.

Together, content marketing, SEO, and social media marketing constitute what is called "inbound marketing". It is a marketing methodology that aims at attracting, engaging, and delighting leads. Some goals of inbound marketing include attracting users' attention, driving relevant traffic to the website, and converting it into happy customers.

Pay-per-click Advertising (PPC)

Pay-per-click is a model of advertising where marketers pay a fee every time people click on their ad. Basically, it's the process of buying visits to your site, as opposed to getting them organically via SEO or other types of digital marketing.

PPC is one of the types of paid search. It's similar to SEM (search engine marketing) but can also include display advertising (cost-per-click based), and affiliate advertising.

Affiliate Marketing

Affiliate marketing is one of the popular ways people make money online these days. If your affiliate program is successful, you might earn quite a decent passive income.

Basically, affiliate marketing is a type of digital marketing where a person partners up with other businesses in order to receive a commission for the traffic s/he generates for this business. Imagine this: you put a link to an external website on your own blog or website. Every time a user proceeds to this external website and makes a purchase, you receive a commission.

This marketing strategy might work especially well for bloggers, since they can write different types of articles on the given topic and naturally include affiliate links.

Email Marketing

Email marketing is one of the most popular types of digital marketing. To put it shortly, it's the use of email for promoting one's products or services.

If you go a little deeper, email marketing might also refer to building relationships with your customers. Ideally, emails you send out to your clients should not only speak *at* them but also encourage meaningful interaction with your brand.

Notice how the guys from Buffer start a meaningful conversation by asking their readers' opinion in their emails.

There are many things that contribute to the success of your email marketing strategy, from the content you create to the time you send your emails. One thing is certain, though: email marketing is far from being dead and should definitely be part of your overall digital marketing.

Instant Messaging Marketing

Instant messengers are the latest communication trend. There are 1.5 billion people globally using WhatsApp on a monthly basis, followed by Facebook Messenger and WeChat. If you want to be where your audience is, enter instant messaging marketing.

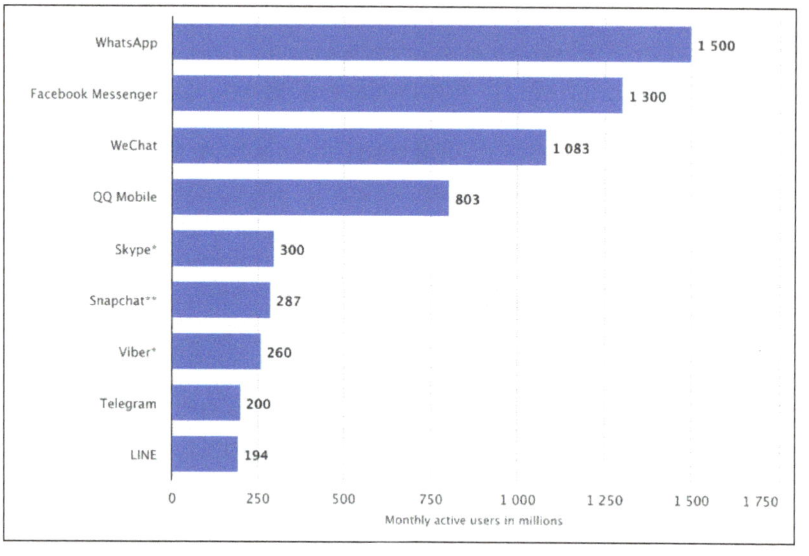

Most popular global messenger apps, based on the number of monthly users.

This type of digital marketing exploded over the last couple of years. People are much more likely to trust the information sent via a messenger (as if it comes from a good friend) than email or SMS that are vulnerable to spam.

An example of messages from a marketing consultant Matthew Barby sent via a Facebook.

There are different ways how you can proceed with instant messaging marketing, from using them for customer support to updating your users about new posts on your blog.

Radio Advertising

While considered "old-fashioned" by some, radio advertising might still be a powerful medium, especially for B2C companies and local businesses. In the US alone, radio advertisements account for 7.8% of total media expenditures.

Radio advertising is also relatively cheap, as you don't need to produce fancy visuals: you solely rely on your customers' imagination.

Just like with any other type of digital marketing, to create successful radio advertising strategy, you have to know your target audience. In addition to that, create a great script, hire a professional voice talent for the job, and get your timing right.

Television Advertising

With the general population spending over 4.5 hours a day in from of the TV, it's still one of the most popular medium types. It reaches people faster than, say, newspapers or radio. Due to the powerful effect video has on humans, it might also be very effective.

Television advertising is expensive, and coming up with a great and engaging ad might be a daunting task, too. TV ads work great for FMCG products, clothing brands, cars, medicine, and food.

Electronic Media Advertising

Initiating with the print media to electronic media, the journey has been amazing and worth applaud. As today new advertising mediums, electronic media has built its own base where every firm or sole proprietor wishes to market its stuff for earning name and fame.TV, which is now the member of household, is one of the best illustrations of electronic media. In every stage of the day it's involving with us. Whether an individual is enjoying daily movies, soaps operas, the news, football commentaries or anything, advertisements are all around. Even if we wish to see them or not, they surely enter our lives anyhow.

Why to use any Electronic Media?

The reason to use electronic media can be for many valid reasons, one of the reasons is using it to show off your skills and anything special from businesses to stuffs and so on. Electronic media is an economic way to connect to one another, either by using of media appliances and networks or social media resources like Television or Internet these are some common techniques to use Electronic media to your benefit. There are wide range of Electronic medias to broadcast variety of contrasting things like marketing and promotions. Different Electronic media types are listed below:

- Television,
- Radio,

- Internet,
- Online Shops.

About Television and Radio

The Internet and electronic communications (also known as computer mediated communications or CMC) do not simply mean new communication tools; it means new techniques to communicate. Today the firm interacts with its various elements differently; associates, board members, clients, partners and others, based on the property of message, the aims to achieve and the strengths and weaknesses of the available media; fax machines, telephones, printings, voice-mail etc. The broadcasting field is and has been experiencing essential changes. There are extra jobs available off-camera and the off-microphone than on-air areas. On-air job competition is higher, while the initial pay is lower. Initial areas are particularly observed at small town local production efficiency, rather than networks.

About Internet Media

Careers in electronic media, radio-television and broadcasting comprise broadcasting station manager, film and tape librarian, broadcasting director, community relations director, film editor, the unit manager, director of news, news writer, transmitting engineer, sales coordinator of advertising technical director, traffic and continuity expert, media buyer, marketplace researcher, announcer, actor, disc jockey, the news anchor, writer of comedy , PR manager, casting director, the producer, business manager, account administrator, floor manager and the talk show host. Communication courses that supplement career in electronic media and radio-television broadcasting: oral communication, print communication, public speaking, inter-personal communication, introducing to mass communication, studio and field development, media researching, media criticism, marketing, media law, interviewing, and acting.

About Online Shops

Online shopping is a type of electronic commerce enabling clients to directly buy goods or services from a seller from the Internet using a browser. Clients find a stuff of interest by visiting the retailer website directly or by looking among numerous vendors by shopping search engine, displaying the same product's availability and costing at different e-retailers. According to 2016, clients can shop online using a range of various computers and appliances, including desktop PCs, laptops, tablet PCs and smart-phones.

How Well to Select your Electronic Media

Well, this is based on the type of business you own and if you wish to make use of Electronic media advertising or not, mostly all business use Electronic media in some or the other way to attract new or more clients, simply say you select to advertise using Facebook which is a fundamental Electronic media facility helping to your benefit, businesses normally use the "check-in" technique where if you check in their store they will provide you something in return, either a discount or any points on a membership card, this produces more client flow to the store and in turn enables more profit to be generated.

Electronic Media's Impact on Business Operation

Electronic media is a technique for the business to be heard of; but not just heard, experience too. As your Business turns its own entity online, you own a brand and that brand has a face, if organized well it is sure to increase profits. If not then your business may fight to get back up from the base with many other rivalries.

Although the term "Electronic Media" is generally connected with content recorded on a storage media, recordings are not needed for live broadcasting and electronic networking. Any equipment applied in the electronic communication procedure (television, radio, telephone, desktop PC, game console, handheld applicants) might also be considered as electronic media. Also two more terminologies are used for electronic media: Broadcasting, Media. They are used to conduct or sent details through the use of several Electronic media devices or the wide world of mass communication through Electronic media.

Video Marketing

Video marketing can be used for everything from building customer rapport, to promoting your brand, services or products. Additionally, video marketing can serve as a medium to present how-to's, promote customer testimonials, live-stream events and deliver viral (entertaining) content.

How Video Marketing Works

On the surface, the *how* of video marketing is pretty simple: Your brand creates videos that, in some way or another, promote your company, drive sales, raise awareness of your products or services, or engage your customers. In practice, it's a little more complicated. Like many of your marketing efforts, video marketing is data driven, so you'll want to monitor various metrics and track customer engagement.

To develop your video marketing strategy, you'll want to:

- Allocate resources: You're going to need to designate some budget for video – at the least, decent equipment, good editing software, and a video marketing guru (or, better, team) – as well as time to create it.
- Tell your stories: Storytelling has never been as important as it is in video, so get brainstorming: What stories do you want to tell? How will you tell them?
- Engage: It's not enough to simply tell your stories; you must engage your audience while you do so. How will you make your stories interesting? What will hook your audience?
- Keep it short: There's no set length for marketing videos (although there are recommendations), but the general rule is that shorter is better. Be ruthless with your editing. Cut, cut, cut out everything extraneous. Attention spans are short, so make the best of what you get.
- Publish: Publish your videos far and wide – embedded in your website, uploaded to Google-owned YouTube, and on all your social media channels. Then, promote, promote, promote.
- Analyze: Track metrics and stats, to determine which videos do the best – and why.

Examples of Video Marketing

Video marketing is all over the Internet. Look no further than your favorite brands, your Facebook, your YouTube homepage, and there it is: successful video marketing that has found its way to your eyes.

Benefits of Video Marketing

The benefits of video marketing are many. Let's begin with the easily quantifiable: statistics, numbers, and data.

Video helps you connect with your audience. Today, so much of a company's marketing efforts are designed to help build trust. Video is the bridge that links what you say to who you really are, allowing customers to peer behind the curtain and get to know your brand.

- Video is an SEO gold mine, helping build backlinks to your site, boosting likes and shares (which can effect search rankings), and driving traffic to your site. And let's not forget that YouTube is owned by Google, so be sure to post your videos to YT and tag, tag, tag with keywords/key phrases.
- Videos boost information retention. If your customers hear something only, they're likely to retain about 10% of that information three days later; by contrast, if what they hear is accompanied by relevant imagery, they'll retain an average 65% of that information three days later.
- In 2017, video content will account for an estimated 74% of all online traffic. Your customers love video. Would-be customers also love video, which means good video marketing can attract new visitors.

- Email subject lines that include the word "video" see a 19% increase in open rates, and a 65% boost in click-through.
- Four times as many customers would prefer to watch a product video, than read a product description.
- Do you like money? Then consider this: after watching a video, customers are 64-85% more likely to make a purchase.

Challenges of Video Marketing

Once upon a time, cost was a serious challenge to video marketing: The cost of equipment, editing software and, from an end-user's perspective, the data cost of consuming online video.

Today, those challenges are mostly in the rear-view mirror. Yes, you still need some budget – good equipment, editing software and a delivery platform are more affordable than they once were, but they're not free – and you do need a marketing team with experience in video, but these are all surmountable obstacles.

In fact, the biggest challenges of video marketing in 2017 are strategic: How to build a solid and effective video marketing strategy, how to create content that people want to consume, and how to create engaging videos that get shared. Additionally, video content marketers need to have a solid understanding of metrics, and how they indicate a video's success and areas for improvement.

Email Marketing

Email marketing is a kind of internet marketing that occurs when a company sends promotional messages or materials to groups of people by email. Usually, these messages contain advertisements, commercial messages, sales solicitation or donation, or a call for business.

Any kind of email with the said content can be considered email marketing and their purpose is to acquire new customers, build or enhance a company's relationship with their current customers, and for the customers consider a repeat business with them to develop trust, loyalty, or to give them awareness about their brand.

For email marketing to work, a marketer must know the deliverability of an email. Deliverability is defined as the way an email marketer measures the success of their email campaign reaching a subscriber's inbox. It doesn't only distinguish if the email is an existing one, but also if the internet service provider of the email's owner throttles the income of high volumes of messages, if the email sends several messages with the same content to spam, and similar problems. One such tool that email marketers can use to measure the deliverability of emails is G-Lock Apps.

Email marketers carry out their email campaigns by using different types of emails.

The first one is a transactional email. These emails arrive at a customer's inbox once they've done business with a merchant. These emails are what guide the customer through their purchase of a product or service, or to complete or confirm a transaction they made with the sender. An example of these transactional messages are purchase order or return confirmations, order statuses, and electronic or email receipts.

The second one is a direct email. The purposes of these emails is solely to present promotional material such as announcements, special offers, discounts, or maybe a glimpse of a product catalog available online.

The third is the 'Welcome!' emails. These emails are what customers receive when they sign up for a mailing list. This is what starts the establishment of trust with the customer, the enhancement of the brand, and to show the credibility of a company.

The last is the newsletter emails. The purpose of these emails is to give customers the gist of products a company has on a regular basis. However, a marketer has to know what the goal of the newsletter is, such as an increase in social sharing, strengthen the image of the brand, or maybe nurture the company's relationship with an existing customer.

There are both advantages and disadvantages to using email marketing in comparison to traditional advertising mail.

Advantages

Email marketing is popular with companies for the following reasons:

- An exact return on investment can be tracked. It has been proven to be high when done properly. Email marketing is often reported as second only to search marketing as the most effective marketing tactic.
- Compared to traditional mail, email marketing is cheaper and faster than traditional mail. Traditional mail requires time for producing the artwork, printing, addressing, and mailing.
- Email provides a cost-effective method to test a variety of marketing content. This includes visual creative, marketing copy and multimedia assets. The data gathered by testing in the email channel can then be used across all channels of both print and digital marketing campaigns.
- Advertisers can reach substantial numbers of email subscribers who chose to receive email communications on subjects of interest to them.
- If compared to standard email, direct email marketing produces higher response rate and higher average order value for e-commerce business.

Disadvantages

- The mail can be classified as spam. People's inboxes get inundated with email, both solicited and unsolicited. Many servers have filters in place to cut down the amount of unwanted emails. People can also further adjust their email filters to their own tastes. This could result to the email to land in a spam folder and never get viewed.
- Email marketing requires constant tweaking to keep the subscribers engaged. The marketer

must work to maintain a level of engagement to keep the reader from unsubscribing. Another thing to work on is to carefully craft the email marketing to look exactly the marketer envisioned it.

Businesses use email marketing as an affordable and effective advertising tool.

Radio Advertising

Choosing the right radio stations from the many that are available to you isn't as difficult as it may seem at first. Radio divides its audiences into age ranges (18 - 34, 18 - 49, 25 - 54, 45+ and so on) and gender (female, male and adults-choose adults if your customers are evenly split between male and female). Each radio station delivers a very specific audience, so once you know the age and gender of your target customers, you can zoom in on stations that serve those people.

When you're approached by any of the many radio sales representatives who'll find you-and trust me, they'll find you--ask for each station's primary demographic. If it matches your target customer, request a media sales kit. Whatever you do, don't reveal your demographic needs before you get that information. These sales reps are working under great pressure to meet budgets and they can be very persuasive. They'll find a way, no matter how convoluted, to make your demographic match theirs if you tell them first.

Frequency is very important when considering an advertising schedule on radio. Listeners tune in and out, change stations, and are often engaged in some other activity while the radio is on, so your message needs to appear often if they're going to hear it. Listeners of country and talk formats tend to stay with the same station for longer periods of time than other listeners who flip through channels constantly, so you need to run fewer commercials to reach those "settled" listeners than you need to run for the flippers.

But don't run a schedule with fewer than 18 commercials-and preferably 24 or more-in one week. And don't advertise for one or two weeks and then stop. People need time to get used to hearing your business name, particularly if you're new, and then they need to hear what your business is all about.

Decide what you want your schedule to do for your business. Is it a maintenance schedule used as a reminder to people who already know a lot about you? If so, you'll run a small number of commercials over a long period of time. Are you running a weekend sale? Then you want a large number of spots to run in a very short period of time. Are you brand new and building awareness of your business name of what you do there? Then you need to run a heftier schedule consistently. Building name recognition and getting people used to hearing about you, let alone getting them to come in, takes a concerted effort on your part.

If you can't afford more than one station, choose that single station carefully and buy as much time as you can afford to nail that audience. Then, when you can afford more, add another station--don't just switch stations and abandon the first audience. The idea is to keep current customers while you're rounding up new ones.

The first quarter of the year is probably the best time to negotiate a favorable contact rate or take advantage of special programs designed to bring much-needed business into radio stations (after business owners have just finished blowing their budgets on the holidays). But remember, no matter how good any deal sounds, it's a waste of money if it's not offered by a station that reaches your audience.

When it comes to the length of your commercials, you might think about using a 60-second commercial and then adding in some 15-second spots to boost your frequency. This helps you get the most bang for your buck when it comes to your budget. Note: If you need to, you should be able to change your commercials frequently at no charge.

Your radio message needs to be clear because listeners want to know one thing: "What's in it for me?" Ask your sales rep to help you write and time the message, but when it's done, pretend you're the listener and see if each line answers that question. If it doesn't, get rid of it. For example:

The listener asks:	Commercial answer line:
"What's in it for me?"	"XYZ Wallpaper Depot is family-owned."
"What's in it for me?"	"We've been in business since 1912."
"What's in it for me?"	"You can save 30 percent on all in-stock wallpaper."

People don't care if your business is family-owned or if it's been around since before their grandmother was born-that's important to you. They want to know the information in line three.

Radio is a good place to ask about trade advertising, where you pay for your commercial schedule partly with cash and partly with products or services from your business. All stations need prizes for on-air giveaways, as well as office products and furniture, station vehicles and service for those vehicles, cleaning services, and much more to keep their own operations going, and they're more than willing to trade those out for advertising. This can be a huge help to an entrepreneur concerned about the cost of advertising.

Radio advertising might be seen as old-fashioned especially with the rise of the internet and other types of media and that their audience has decreased. This is not the case, however. Commercial radio has a reach of more than 16 million Australians every week. 17 hours of the week are spent listening to the radio with the majority of it at home (49%) and in the car (32%).

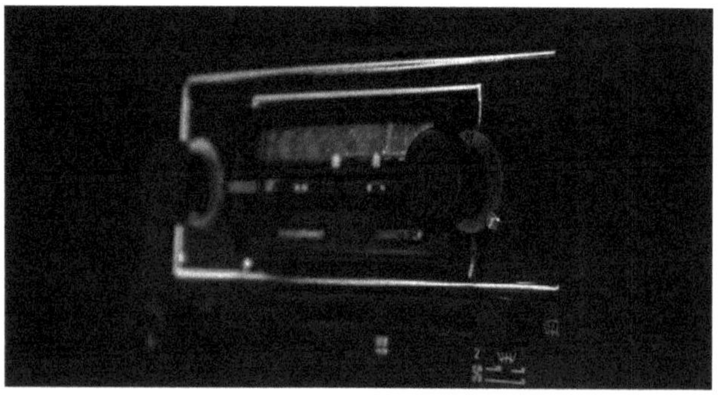

Selective Targeting

Radio station already targets specific demographics and market segments. Therefore, by choosing which station to broadcast with, you can lock into your potential customers and increase the frequency of delivering your message. At the same time think about all the advantages and disadvantages of radio advertising in your selected radio.

Increased Frequency

Advertising works with frequency and reaching your audience repeatedly. Radio is the perfect medium for this, being able to expose your ad to the audience repeatedly to build awareness. Also due to the loyalty of people listening to the same station, you are able to impact the same people more often.

More Memorable

Compared to written advertisement, sound is more effectively stored in memory. In addition, there is the ability to instil emotion and also allows listeners to use their imagination to create their own image of the product/service.

Cost Effective

Radio advertising has significantly fewer costs compared to other types of media. Television and print ads can go up to hundreds of thousands including costs for video equipment, studio time, actors, models. Radios ads require fewer resources while being able to reach the same target audience that a television spot would have resulted in.

Time Efficiency

Lead times with print and television ads can be very long, especially with planning and may take up to a year for the ad to run. In contrast, producing a radio spot can occur between two to three weeks. Another advantage of this is the ability to adapt and react quickly to changing market conditions.

Measurable Results

You can track results quickly and accurately compared to television where it may take months for measurable results or print media which can be even more difficult to track. Results for radio ads can be analysed on a daily basis, and if the message is not working in a week or two, a new radio spot can replace it efficiently as mentioned above. With the widespread access people have to radio, even indirectly through shopping centres and supermarkets, radio continues to have a big presence in the advertising industry. Small businesses should continue to consider it as a top medium to advertise their product/services as the advantages over other resources remain strong.

Cinema Advertising

Cinema advertising shouldn't be confused with movie trailers – the "coming attractions" that immediately precede the main feature. Movie ads come before the trailers, and they have been a presence in theaters since the first one opened in 1902.

This means that your parents or grandparents probably have fond memories of movie ads, too, if only for their comedic value. In the early days, movie ad montages were put together somewhat haphazardly, sometimes with slides appearing upside down or with sketchy lines blocking an advertiser's phone number.

Some enterprising business owners tried to overcome these obstacles by engaging viewers with trivia questions that flashed on the screen. Some companies lobbied for better quality control. And others may have suffered the indignity in silence. After all, as Film Journal says: "Mostly, local companies wanted to part of the magic of the movies."

The same sentiment lingers today, as sure as the aroma of popcorn still wafts into theaters. But computer and digital technology have advanced so much that the production quality of the advertisements can rival the quality of the feature presentation. And some people would argue: consumers' expectations have helped raise this bar.

As Americans acclimated to TV – and TV commercials – the length of cinema ads began to mirror their length. Today, cinema advertisements usually run from between 15 and 30 seconds – long enough for a small business to make an impression.

Benefits of Cinema Advertising

If you haven't had the pleasure of meeting with someone who sells cinema ads, you may want to prepare yourself for the distinct possibility of hearing how Americans love movies and, perhaps even more intensely, *the movie-going experience.*

They have a point. Aside from newly released movies that you can see only in a theater, there is no doubt that watching a movie in a theater offers some distinct advantages over watching the same movie on even a jumbo screen at home. A theater offers:

- A wall-to-wall, ceiling-to-floor screen.
- Surround sound.
- Pitch darkness.
- The intensified emotional reaction of viewing a movie with a group, during which time a mildly amusing scene can become laugh-out-loud funny while somewhat sad scenes can become tear-jerkers.

Even a cynical small-business owner might be hard-pressed to disagree with these realities. But still. *Tell me about the benefits of the actual advertising,* you might say, *not the experience.*

At this point, you might also hear that the advantages of a movie theater and that the advantages of movie theater advertising are intrinsically linked. The synergistic relationship is similar to that of newspapers and magazines in that people gravitate to newspapers and magazines because they can hold the paper in their hands, thumbing through the pages. These readers enjoy the experience that these media provide.

As you mull the logic of this argument, consider the other distinctive advantages of movie theater advertising:

- A movie theater supplies a generally captive audience. People paid for their ticket and they want to be there. The images on the screen don't have to compete with most people's No. 1 distraction: their phones. Most theaters ask customers to turn off their phones before the cinema ads begin to roll.

- A movie theater is truly one of the "last frontiers" in terms of offering an advertiser an uncluttered media environment in which to present a message. Sitting in a movie theater may be one of those few times during the week when people are *not* working on a laptop or tablet and are looking at their phone while a radio or TV plays in the background. Even people who have grown impatient with commercials cannot fast-forward over cinema ads or rely on an ad blocker to obstruct them.
- "Silence is golden" in movie theaters as soon as the house lights go down and the ads start to roll. Talking over a commercial in a movie theater, unlike at home, can be considered rude behavior.
- A movie theater offers the small-business owner a targeted demographic group, meaning people who live, within a 10-mile radius of the theater. Narrow the demographic group even further by realizing that most movie-goers are between the ages of 16 and 44.
- A movie theater offers an enviable forum in which to initiate some crossover marketing or promotional activities. For example, you can hand out product samples or corporate keepsakes in the lobby before the movie begins. Or you can say goodbye to movie-goers as they leave, handing them discounts or coupons for your business.

Do People actually Watch Cinema Advertisements?

Advertising provides no guarantees, but an assurance that you can expect some return on investment, known as ROI, from cinema advertising would go a long way.

Keep in mind, however, that researchers_ *know*_ that asking people if they actually watch cinema ads is much like asking people if they take the time to read the newspaper they have delivered, either to their in-box or their mailbox, every day. Since they›re paying for the product, respondents often feel compelled to say that yes indeed, they›re riveted, alright.

In other words, the results of any research, study or report should be read with a grain of salt. One industry report, "The Bigger Picture," is quoted often and widely. Conducted by Hall & Partners for Digital Cinema Media, it found that:

- "Cinema is working in a very different way to any other media, with ads watched in the cinema being processed by the brain more consciously, proving a much more powerful and emotionally engaging medium for brands."

The company arrived at this conclusion, Marketing Director Zoe Jones said, because:

- "Cinema advertising is eight times more effective at making your brand stand out from the crowd than television. If you show people an unbranded still from an ad, three times as many cinemagoers will actually recall which brand it is for, when compared with TV viewers. Cinema audiences are four times more likely to be emotionally engaged than a television audience, and those exposed to ads in the cinema are twice as likely to recall a brand compared to TV."

Credit the "experience factor" of the movie-going experience, Jones said: "You still can't beat the big screen for sheer impact and scale."

How much does Cinema Advertising Cost Compared to other Methods?

Your marketing team should compile a detailed analysis of how much it costs to advertise in all the mediums that seem well matched to the customers you wish to reach. A comparison with cinema advertising rates will be more straightforward, and less frustrating, with these numbers in hand.

Like other forms of advertising, cinema advertising rates vary, based on:

- The length of the ad: 15, 30 or 60 seconds. *The number of theaters the ad will appear in.* The number of screens within those theaters the ads will appear on.
- The duration of the advertising campaign.

"Ad buys typically include all the screens in a single movie theater, but can also include certain screens to reduce movie ad costs," Blue Line Media says.

Still, keep in mind that some theater chains require a "minimum buy," meaning a minimum number of theaters (or screens) that will showcase your ads. Furthermore, ad rates may change without notice, though once you've signed a contract, you should be safe from unexpected rate increases.

Think in terms of ballpark figures, until a member of your marketing team can confirm the rates at your favorite movie theater. To run an ad for four weeks, Blue Line Media says to expect to pay:

- Between $1,000 and $2,000 per theater for a 15-second spot. Between $2,000 and $3,000 per theater for a 30-second spot. Between $3,000 and $4,000 per theater for a 60-second spot.

Effective Type of Cinema Advertisement

Cinema advertising may strike you as so "out of the box," so different from other, more conventional advertising methods that you may be tempted to create an advertisement that is equally outside of the norm.

This would violate one of the steadfast rules of advertising: be true to your brand and your image. Start with your logo and corporate colors, and then reproduce them to a T. Look at your print ads for inspiration, and then use some of the same language. Review your online ads and perhaps incorporate some of the same images. And if you rely on TV or radio advertising, get some of the same actors involved.

If you want to create an effective cinema advertisement, create one that provides symmetry with your other advertising initiatives. Symmetry will help you build brand awareness among new customers while also solidifying your image with people who already know you. In this case, symmetry can be a *happy* conspiracy, just as you may have suspected all along.

Television Advertising

While national TV advertising is usually out of an entrepreneur's price range, advertising on local stations and on cable television can be surprisingly affordable. And really, it's not so hard to buy TV schedules. Why? Because no matter what demographic your audience falls into, you can find appropriate programming on any one of the networks. Every station reaches every audience daily, with schedules that include cartoons, celebrity, talk, sports, soaps, news, movies, reality and prime time programs.

Like all forms of advertising, there are different price ranges within the TV medium. Locally, you can pick up a 30-second commercial slot in a show like Oprah for an average of $90 to $300 (but check your local affiliate because prices fluctuate), or get into a noon to 4 p.m. soaps rotation with the same commercial for $150 to $300, again depending on your location and also the time of the year. You'll pay anywhere from $200 to $1,500 per 30-second commercial for local news at noon, 5 to 6 p.m., 6 to 7 p.m., sometimes 10 p.m., and 11 p.m.; the most expensive time is usually 6 to 7 p.m. The best thing to do is check with your sales reps for a list of programs that fit your needs at the time you want to advertise. Nationally, you can expect to pay double the local rate. If you're in a situation to be able to buy nationally, find a media buying service or an ad agency that will do your buying for you on a commission basis.

Prime-time commercials are going to be pricey even locally, but audiences can be huge for popular shows. And here's an insider's tip: When rerun time rolls around, refuse to pay the full price for your commercials in any time slot. Many reps won't volunteer the lower rate-you have to let them know you won't pay the same amount for reruns and then stick to your guns. Programming like Good Morning America, Today Show, local and national news, and soaps never have reruns and are always a good bet because the audience stays true all year long.

This is the one form of advertising that can include actual bidding when push comes to shove. When someone wants the time slot you've already purchased, they'll offer more-and bump you out. You always have the opportunity to up the price you're willing to pay, of course, but many businesses can't afford to get into that kind of bidding war. When is that most likely to happen? The fourth quarter of the year is when lots of inventory is snatched up by holiday ads. And anytime a hot political race-either local or national-is going on, you can be sure the competition for time slots will increase. Unfortunately, these are also the times when small and midsized businesses really need coverage but get shut out.

While some large businesses are starting to use more 60-second commercials to try and cut through the clutter, the length of choice for most commercials is still 30 seconds. In most markets, you have the ability to run a combination of ads-that is, you can mix 10-second or 15-second ads in with your 30-second spots, which allows you to increase the number of times your ad is seen without the higher cost of paying for all 30-second ads. The reason it's important to increase your frequency this way is because the number of times your current and potential customers see your ad is directly related to whether they react to it. But don't think you can really increase your frequency if you run all your commercials in the shorter lengths, because they're only meant to be reminders-they're not long enough to provide the critical information a 30-second ad can hold. Their best use is to bolster your regular commercials and increase retention of your longer message.

One good way to capture a lot of people watching at a particular time is to run an ad during the 6 to 7 p.m. or 11 p.m. news on all your local news stations on the same day. That delivers your message to just about everyone watching the news at that time.

What's the best time to buy TV time? The first and second quarters of the year, with the first quarter being the best for negotiating discounts. Sales reps are scrambling to make their budgets when advertisers are trying to recover from their holiday expenditures. Deals will be made! Don't hesitate to compare prices from station to station or among comparable programs. As long as you're choosing programming that suits your audience, it doesn't matter if your commercials are scattered over different networks. Negotiate your little heart out, and if you know you have the budget, go ahead and settle into an annual contract. This can mean running a certain amount of commercials every week or just agreeing to run a certain number of commercials during a 12-month period without having to know exactly when you'll run them at the time you sign the contract.

Types of Television Advertising

Broadly, there are two types of advertising namely, sponsored programmes and announcements.

Programme or Sponsored Programme

It is a type of telecast where a story, play, a film is sponsored by the advertiser who pays for the time. He takes advantage of this and advertises his product or service.

The merits of sponsored programmes are:

- It builds an image for the advertising house and its products.
- The programme can be designed to fit the sponsor and his product.

Announcement

Announcement is a kind of telecast which is presented to the audience between the sponsored programme and the station break. Here, the advertiser pays only for the duration of advertisement, as he is not paying for the sponsored period. Majority of the advertisers go in for this type.

The advantages of announcements are:

- It is very economical.
- It is most flexible.
- It is effective for advertisements that are brief. These television commercials can be of 10,15, 20 and 30 seconds duration.

Advantages of Advertising in Television

- Ability to create deep Impact: Television is a perfect synchronization of sound, sight, motion and colour. It successfully catches the viewers' attention. It is an ideal medium to exhibit products, including its demonstration. Colour advertisements present the products in their true original form. T.V. commercial very nearly replaces personal selling.

- It is selective and flexible: Like radio and newspapers, T.V. is a highly flexible and a selective medium. It can be used locally, regionally and nationally. The advertisers are free to choose the time slots and the nature of message to the viewers through sponsored programmes and announcements.
- It is a mass communication media: It is a mass medium where an entire family is exposed to it, perhaps for several hours a day. So, television advertising is considered a platform for gaining popularity for a product.
- Helps Distributors and dealers: A TV campaign of a product or a service is appreciated by dealers and local merchants. T.V. has more prestige and glamour than any other media. That is why, wholesalers and retailers of a product are very impressed by TV advertising in view of its immense popularity and try to stock more the products that are advertised in television.
- It is immensely Popular: The most striking feature of T.V. medium is its instantaneous transmission of sight, motion, sound and colour, irrespective of wherever an event took place in the world. Of all the media, TV is the closest to replicate the actual life conditions. It presents events as they are and as they happen. This offers limitless opportunity for advertising.

Disadvantages and Limitations of Advertising in Television

- It suffers a short life: The commercial message on T.V has a very short life. For a moment it is viewed and heard and the next moment it is gone. It does not remain as a part of household like a magazine or a calendar on the wall. If the prospects misses the commercial, the advertiser loses his opportunity. It warrants repeated relay of messages to have an appreciable impact on the target audience.
- It is very expensive: High cost of advertising on television is another serious limitation. In recent years, the rates have risen so much and it is weigher than that of newspapers, magazines, radio, and outdoor media. Hence, advertisements produced are very brief and up to the point, perhaps providing inadequate information. The high advertisement tariff of TV may be out of reach of small and medium-sized manufacturing units.
- Too many commercials: TV advertising suffers from over-crowding of too many commercials in a very short span of time. Both the advertisers and the viewers complain about it. This 'clutter' reduces the effectiveness of the commercials. The advertiser feels that he has spent a lot without much impact and the viewers feel that it is quite difficult to remember all advertisements, which they may not be in a position to recall.

Sponsorship

Marketing sponsorships present significant value beyond brand visibility and website traffic. Sophisticated marketers today are looking to get the most out of sponsorships, and one way to do so is utilizing the benefits of search engine optimization. In order to improve marketing sponsorships with SEO, you need to identify the different sponsorship types available and the key criteria necessary in analyzing SEO value.

Traditional Media – Print, TV, Radio

Sponsorships through traditional media typically come in the form of ad placements or live endorsements on programs (e.g., "This message is brought to you by"). While this can be a great way to drive users to your website, it contains little SEO value in itself.

Yet it is possible to leverage the power of site traffic to support your SEO initiatives. For instance, if you are offering prospects incentives for visiting your website via a sponsorship, give them the option to share the page they land on through methods such as social sharing buttons and email. Social shares can send "signals" back to search engines and present the opportunity for people to link back to your website through other sites like blogs and forums.

Advertorials

Advertorials can provide great SEO value when structured and implemented properly. There are important considerations when addressing the value of an advertorial.

- PageRank – Although Google may not put as much stock as they used to in PageRank, the value hasn't gone away completely. It's still one of the best ways to determine the power of outbound links on a particular website.

- Relevancy – Websites that link back to you are best when they are authoritative and relevant. When possible, utilize the SEO power of linking partners with content pertinent to your industry and products/services.

- Outbound Links – This is often an overlooked metric, but one that is growing in importance as Google updates their algorithms. A high volume of outbound links from a website can appear "spammy" to the search engines. If you're offered an advertorial and the page your content will reside on is filled with Google Adsense or links out to the other sponsors, it might be a good idea to pass.

Social Media Sponsorships

Social media sponsorships can carry SEO value, and their influence on SEO is likely to increase as social networks continue to expand. If you're offered a sponsored Tweet or Facebook post as part of a partnership, you should weigh the value in common sense metrics.

Does this company have a high volume of Twitter followers or Facebook fans? Perhaps more importantly, do they have a high engagement rate amongst their community members? If you decide to pursue a sponsorship that includes social media mentions, be sure to write the Tweet or Facebook post with SEO in mind.

Include product or service names you are focused on, as well as a link back to your website. Popularity is one of the most important signals sent to search engines from social networks. Ensure that your social media team is re-tweeting or sharing posts to drive the highest engagement possible.

Keep in mind that the search engines will read social signals and attribute these to your overall website popularity, but the value will wane if you don't continue to send these signals. Try to secure sponsorships that promote your brand through social media in a consistent manner.

Video Sponsorships

Video sponsorships typically come in the form of pre-roll or adjacent ad placements on video based social sites. Ad placements such as these can send traffic to your website, but they contain little SEO value beyond that- unless the video sponsorship opportunity is on a popular, high-traffic site like YouTube.

To get started, check with the potential partner to see if they will provide a permanent link for you within the video description. If possible, this link should be surrounded by a description of the page it is linking to (including 1 or 2 target keywords) as well as a link with a keyword-rich anchor text.

It's important to point out that links from social media sites such as YouTube are considered "no-follow," however; many of us in the SEO field believe that no-follow links from social are becoming more valuable, and like the aforementioned social media sponsorship example, will continue to grow in the future.

Directories/Sponsorship Listings

Many sponsorship packages will include a listing within a "Sponsors" section on the partner's website. These listing pages can act similar to directories, which today still present great SEO opportunity. There are a couple of critical considerations for pages such as these:

- PageRank – As mentioned in the advertorial section, check the PageRank of the website that will feature you in a dedicated sponsorship section- the higher, the better.
- Description and Links – Try to ensure you not only get featured on a sponsor page, but that you also have a bit of description and have a text link back to your website. Logos are typically an easy way to set up these pages. A link from a logo will carry some value, but you really want to seek out a text link and if possible, write a custom description of your business, products, etc. (with keyword focus).

In conclusion, sponsorships can carry significant SEO value when assessed and implemented properly. Each sponsorship opportunity is unique, and each implementation recommendation should be custom.

Digital Outdoor Advertising

The digital medium can bring many benefits to your outdoor ad campaign. The new format ads are not only flexible and cost-saving but can also be interactive, building a better brand-customer relationship. They can also be tailored specifically to the company's own needs, allowing for more creativity and effective marketing.

Digital Outdoor Advertising is more Flexible

The big advantage of going digital is dynamism. By using digital screens, you can choose the time and frequency of your ads, which is particularly useful if you're targeting a specific group. According to their habits and routines, you can maximise the efficiency of your campaign by displaying it at certain times of the day.

For example, if you sell stationery, you can choose to show your ad only around the hour parents pick up their kids from school. Similarly, if you're advertising your ice-cream parlour, you can choose to display the ad only after the temperature outside has reached a certain point. Clever, isn't it?

Digital Outdoor Advertising is Interactive

Digital ads try not to only catch people's attention, but to also build a link with them and engage them even further. Nowadays ads can incorporate touch screens, QR, NFC codes and the like that can make customers interact with product through their own mobile devices. They can also redirect them straight to social media accounts or the company's own website, thus creating a link between the brand and the customer and maintaining it even after the initial contact with the outdoor ad.

Digital Billboards

Digital billboards often feature up to six different adverts, which alternate during a single, 60-second period.

This means that your advert will be displayed for approximately 10 seconds every minute, minimising your long-term exposure and removing the sense of exclusivity associated with traditional billboard bookings.

This can also cause potential customers to miss out your messaging, while this lack of exposure also undermines the potential return on what is a significantly higher advertising spend.

You'll also be required to compete with five other brands and adverts in this scenario, which can cause significant issues. Although you won't be required to share advertising space with a direct competitor, it's important to note that a more eye-catching or memorable design could well put your brand in the shade.

Who should use Digital Billboards and what Alternatives are Available?

By now, you should have developed a basic insight into the benefits of digital billboard advertising, and the potential drawbacks of this channel.

Still, when choosing whether or not this medium is right for you, you'll need to consider the unique needs of your business and the main objectives of advertising in in the first place.

Given the cost of digital billboards, they're widely used for medium and larger-sized companies, particularly those with a more generous marketing spend. As we've touched on, they're also ideal for businesses looking to advertise time-sensitive or limited period promotions, as they can tailor their messaging and artwork to achieve the best possible results.

If you're promoting an aesthetically pleasing product or brand, you can also use the enhanced visuals of digital media to your advantage. The same principle applies if you're looking to advertise a particular outlet at night, as bright, neon lighting can be used to garner the attention of passing traffic.

If you're a smaller business or remain primarily focused on building brand awareness through increased exposure, however, you'll need to find an alternative to digital billboards. One of the most viable options exists in the form of paper format billboards, which can reduce marketing costs, optimise returns and drive a higher rate of assisted conversions within integrated campaigns.

They are Extremely Affordable

While the production and print costs associated with traditional billboards can hit your pocket, this is offset by the competitive price of long-term bookings in busy locations.

Not only this, but suppliers often cap production costs and charge a standard fee to clients, creating a transparent and relatively low price that is extremely appealing to small or start-up ventures (or firms that want to achieve superior value for money).

In simple terms, a two-week booking for a 48-sheet billboard can cost as little as £495 *including* production, making it more than 50% cheaper than a digital alternative. Many companies also heavily discount longer-term bookings, which is ideal if you're looking to build awareness around your burgeoning brand.

Not only this, but you won't want to share advertising space with other brands during this period, enabling your messaging to stand apart from the crowd and engage customers more effectively.

They Drive Assisted Conversions

If you're looking to use OOH media or billboards as part of an integrated marketing campaign, you'll need to be aware of assisted conversions.

This term refers to Google's measure of brand interactions that take place *before* the final click, with each one given a specific value as part of the customer's journey. With this type of data, businesses can measure the impact of each individual channel that they use, enabling to shape more effective and informed campaigns in the future.

Traditional billboards are great for driving assisted conversions, thanks to the levels of exposure, engagement and trust that they're able to provide. So not only will they help your brand to reach a broad and motivated target market, but they also drive increased levels of brand interaction online and through mobile.

So whether you're looking to drive local customers online or build traffic flows through a branded mobile app, traditional billboards are ideal for you.

They Drive Consistent Branding and Messaging

While having the ability to create flexible and changeable messaging is great, it can have negative connotations for burgeoning businesses.

New or startup firms must rely on consistent branding and messaging to build awareness, for example, and traditional billboards let them do this over a sustained period of time.

So long as your initial messaging is thought-through and concise, this will present a clearer proposition to your customers while also laying the foundations for increased brand recognition in the future.

Pros and Cons

Before we determine whether or not your business should use digital billboards and what viable alternatives are available, we need to consider the universal benefits and disadvantages associated with the channel.

This type of understanding is crucial, particularly if you're to make the most of this medium and realise its full potential.

They are Often Built in the Prime Locations

The demand for digital billboard advertising has increased significantly in recent times, and this trend is set to continue for the foreseeable future at least.

In fact, the global DOOH market is expected to grow at a compound annual growth rate of 12.6% over the course of the next six years, by which time it will be worth an impressive $8 billion.

As a result of this, digital billboards are increasingly being built in the busiest locations, meaning that customers are able to access more traffic and engage a larger audience within a relatively short space of time.

This may not always translate into the desired ROI on your marketing spend, but it certainly helps brands to raise awareness and increase recognition among their consumer base.

Better Chronological Targeting

If you are to optimise the reach and the engagement levels associated with your billboard, you'll need to target specific demographics as effectively as possible. Digital billboards can help in this respect, particularly when it comes to capturing the attention of customers at different times of the day.

Suppliers often allow you to air your advert as specific times, for example, as they usually host up to six different marketing messages at any one time.

Let's say that you own a bar, and are looking to promote a discount or a happy hour promotion. In this instance, there's little point in targeting morning commuters, as people are likely to be far more interested in this proposition once they're at the end of a long, gruelling day.

This enables you to optimise your spend and your potential return, while ensuring that you engage your target customers at the best possible time.

Reduced Production Costs and Real-time Artwork Changes

There's no doubt that this is typically cheaper than creating a digital ad.

However, the cost of *producing* a digital billboard is far more competitive, as there are no posters or materials such as paper required. You'll also save money by not having to print your ads, and this can help to optimise the profitability of your campaign.

It's fair to say that digital billboards are also a flexible and fluid advertising channel, and one that enables customers to make real-time adjustments. They can alter the artwork if necessary, while the messaging can also be tweaked to ensure that target audiences are engaged effectively as possible.

Any promotional offers being advertised can also be updated, which helps you to analyse your campaigns and correct elements that are not working.

Promote Multiple Messages as Part of a Larger Campaign

On a similar note, you can also vary your messaging across different digital ads as and when required.

For example, you may have launched two different products or services at the same time, each of which will have a specified target market. You can then alternate between relevant messages that promote each of these, leveraging different time slots to achieve the best possible results.

At the same time, you can vary the address across different messages, in order to direct customers to different stores in various locations.

This type of flexibility may seem like a small detail, but it can play a pivotal role in complex or integrated marketing campaigns.

Shorter Lead Times and Punchier Campaigns

Timing is everything in the world of advertising, particularly when looking to increase your brand's engagement levels or direct specific customer actions.

This is another tick in the box for digital billboards, as your finished ads can be sent directly to a screen and displayed within a matter of hours.

This mean that there are no print delays or design issues, which in some instances can create a two-week window between commissioning your advert and it's being displayed.

Digital billboard campaigns also tend to be shorter and more impactful, meaning that you don't necessarily need to book an advertising slot for two weeks. This is highly beneficial from a cost and profitability perspective, while it's ideal if you need to promote time-sensitive or limited offers to a local audience.

This increases efficiency and reduces wastage, while the striking visual nature of digital billboards is also sure to have a greater impact in the minds of consumers.

While these factors make a compelling argument for digital billboards, this channel is not without its disadvantages.

Counting the Cost of Digital Advertising

The most obvious downside of digital billboard advertising is its cost, with placements far more expensive than traditional paper ads or online messaging.

Even competitively priced DOOH placements can set you back £1,200, depending on the location that you choose and the size of the billboard (among other factors). This price will also increase significantly when looking to access prime locations, while increased demand may continue to drive prices upwards in the near-term.

For smaller firms, this could create a situation where the ad's location is compromised in order to save money, which could render your campaign far less effective.

The Issue with Message Transfers

We've already said that the real-time flexibility of digital billboards offers some benefits to businesses, but it can also create issues when it comes to engagement.

This is because the messaging on these ads is constantly changing and rotating, while you may also make subtle changes to your wording or artwork.

This means that some customers may miss out on a specific message as they go about their daily business, and this remains a significant risk with prominent roadside billboards.

You also run the risk of diluting your messaging and creating a convoluted proposition, and one that discourages customers from interacting further with the brand.

Paid Media

Paid media refers to external marketing efforts that involve a paid placement. Paid media includes PPC advertising, branded content, and display ads.

Paid media is an essential component of revenue growth and brand awareness for online businesses.

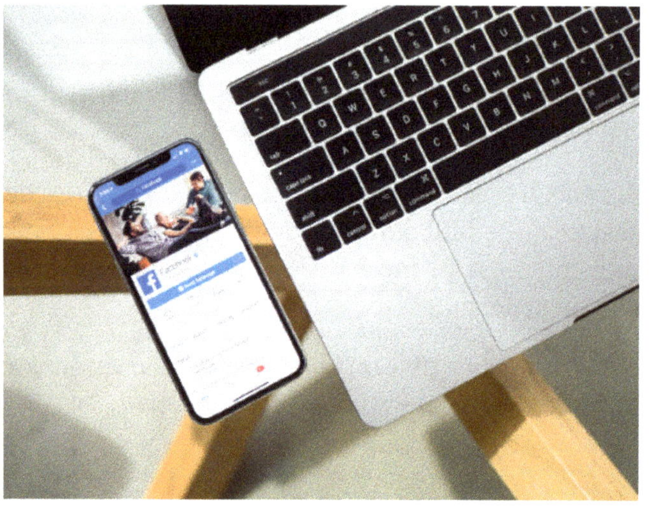

Types of Media: Paid, Earned and Owned

Owned media is a website, blog or other web entity that you control.

Earned or Organic media is content that organically travels across the web based on its popularity and inherent value, such as reviews and social media comments.

Paid media, on the other hand, is closer to traditional marketing, whereby you pay a third party to broadcast your message to other individuals.

Though it was once possible to firmly categorize all media as either paid, earned, or owned, the cross-channel marketing experience is blurring these lines.

For example — social media is technically earned media, but it allows for paid placements. This makes it a platform that supports varying strategies, techniques, and campaign types.

Why use Paid Media?

At first glance, paid media might appear archaic or and unnecessary.

After all, one of the strengths of web marketing and social media is that it allows you to avoid the typical pitfalls of paid advertising by exposing different users to your brand in new, different and engaging ways.

While this is true, paid media still has a valid usage and can work in tandem with earned & owned media to help an online business grow.

Paid media is one of the quickest ways to drive traffic.

Paid media is a good way of opening doors, even if just a crack, that would otherwise stay closed.

For some users, a promoted post or tweet will be their first exposure to your business or brand. Whether yours is a new venture, fresh on the scene or already well established, the opportunity to spread your brand as widely as possible should be a top goal.

Your content, even if paid for, will still potentially get clicks and perhaps even followers, leading to earned clicks in the future.

Additionally, the results of your paid content will be easier to track than organic content.

Social media typically provides statistics on how many Impressions, clicks and Leads your paid content receives while viewing the same information about organic content can be trickier.

Finally, just because content is promoted doesn't mean it's not valuable. As many social media experts will tell you, the ways of the Internet and social media are mysterious, and there's often no way to explain or predict why one piece of content becomes more popular than another.

Sometimes, it's just a matter of the moment.

Paid promotions can help ensure your content - whether a promotion for a big sale, an update on a charity or cause, or an informative video aimed at establishing you as a thought leader - gets picked up, shared around and goes to the right influencers.

Using Paid Media on Social Networks

Paid media takes various forms across different social media platforms.

Facebook

Chief among these platforms is Facebook, which over the years has gone from being one of the numerous social media options to becoming virtually synonymous with the term.

Facebook advertising offers a number of paid promotional options. The two most commonly used for E-Commerce are:

Carousel Ads

Carousel ads are swipeable ads that allow you to view multiple images or videos in a single ad space.

Facebook allows your creativity to flow by permitting you to showcase up to ten products within one ad, each with its own link. You can also add up to 10 videos in a carousel format.

This will allow you to tell a better story, showcase a larger range of products or display a more detailed description of your products.

On average, it's driving 30-50% lower cost-per-conversion than single-image link ads. Carousel ads help deliver a reduction in cost per lead and an increase in click-through rates.

If you are just setting up shop carousel ads are the way to go as you can select and design what you'd like to display.

According to Facebook, here are the latest requirements for a carousel ad.

Images

- 2-10 Images.
- Recommended format: JPG or PNG format.
- Image file size: Maximum of 30MB.
- Image resolution: 1080X1080.
- Text: 125 characters.
- Headline: 40 characters.
- Link Description: 20 characters.

Videos

- 2-10 Videos.
- Recommended format: MP4 or MOV.
- Image file size: Maximum of 30MB.
- Text: 125 characters.
- Headline: 40 characters.
- Link Description: 20 characters.

Dynamic Product Ads (DPA)

DPA's allow retailers to showcase exactly the same products or services their shoppers are interested in.

As and when a customer browses through your website, views a product, or adds to cart, facebook's pixels pick it up.

Facebook then showcases those products your customer has shown interest in.

Dynamic Product Ads reduces the workload of creating multiple ad units for every product/product line.

Dynamic product ads also get 3X the engagement than a normal Facebook ad.

You can get started with Dynamic Product Ads in 2 simple steps:

- Submit your product feed in an XML or CSV format to Facebook.
- Setup the Facebook pixel on your website. Configure when you want the pixel to fire i.e. add to cart, view Content, or purchase.

Facebook has the highest number of social media users, you can choose to take advantage of the site's more than 1 billion users and rich database of user data by paying for a Facebook ad.

Facebook lets online businesses target their ads based on metrics such as:

- Geographic locations, filtered by country, region, city or even postal/zip code.
- Age.
- Gender.
- Spoken languages.
- Interests, including sport, films and music.
- Behaviour, from where and how they shop to whether they're a house hunter.

This lets you tailor your product to the exact demographic of your typical customer. For instance, if you were a sports retailer based in a Spanish-speaking area of a city, you might choose to target an ad for basketball shoes to users aged 18-40 who speak Spanish and are interested in the sport.

Your ad will appear on their news feed like any other product.

You can do the same thing when it comes to boosting your posts. Choose how much you're willing to spend, pick an audience profile and your post will be sent out to many more people. This is especially useful if your business is running a promotion you want to let people know about.

Twitter

Twitter offers similar services like its promoted tweets, which act as regular tweets but are sent out to more people who may be interested in your business.

They will pop up on both timelines as well as at the top of relevant search results that users make.

Promoted tweets can be used both to raise awareness of your business and inform users of a particular event or action.

You can also pay to set up a promoted account, where Twitter will encourage users to follow your account.

Twitter's promoted posts can be used predominantly to achieve two major goals:

To drive a particular action:

- Promote content that you believe will stand out and use that to drive traffic to your website.
- Offer coupons and deals in the copy of your Tweets.
- Add a coupon or deal offering to your tweet.
- Lead generation cards are a powerful tool that you can use.

To drive awareness for your business:

- Use Twitter to publish long-form content.
- Spread brand awareness with the help of influencers ensure you get a larger reach.
- Design copies that help spread awareness around events and product launches.

Instagram

With more than 1 billion active users every month, Instagram is a great platform to advertise.

As Instagram is solely a visual medium make sure your creatives are strong.

Let's take a look at the four ways you can use Instagram to promote your ads:

Photo Ads

Photo ads allow you to promote your brand or product in a single image format. It's a simple method to showcase your products to your users.

Your ad can consist of one photo, an ad copy and a CTA.

Video Ads

Video ads are a far more interactive to photo ads. Each 60-second video can be uploaded in either landscape or square format.

In times to come video content will represent 74% of all internet traffic.

Carousel Ads

These swipeable ads help in reducing Cost per conversion by 69% in comparison to link ads.

Just like Facebook, Instagram allows you to display 10 images within a single ad space.

Story Ads

Instagram stories now allow you to promote your products to 300 million users daily. You may use alternative content to try out or experiment with story ads and complement your feed.

Like most ads on Instagram, you can use Facebook ads manager or power editor to launch your stories.

While creating ads on Instagram create high-quality images, HQ images reinforce trust in the consumers, inept images may cause a loss of trust in the customers and drive them away from your product.

A lack of effort in visual post reflects badly on a customer, he/she may hesitate from clicking on a link they cannot trust.

Just remember: With all of these things, it's not enough to pay to boost your content - the content itself must also be crafted well to succeed.

Remember, too, that all of this paid content will be labeled as such. You're not going to be tricking any users into clicks.

Additionally, Instagram added Shoppable instagram posts that allow buyers to add products to an ecommerce store directly from Instagram photos.

Instagram allows you to pay for photos or videos that will get promoted on user's feeds.

Influencer Marketing

A trend that is really picking up the pace, influencer marketing is a form of marketing in which a brand uses a social figure or a thought leader to inspire or promote your content to his followers.

A large number of brands have been investing in Influencer marketing, the industry scaled to $570 million on Instagram in 2016, alone.

Influencer marketing really helps you tap into an audience which otherwise would be hard to reach out to.

Here are the steps you could use to help build an influencer campaign:

- Identify key brand or product influencers.
- Create a marketing campaign directed for the influencers which help stand out.
- Understand the audience and make sure your campaigns are audience-centric.
- Create a secondary marketing campaign for the influencers to drive greater awareness to a larger set of target consumers.
- Track key metrics relating to reach, sales and brand awareness.

Paid content is one part of what should be a three-pronged strategy by businesses to get their brand out there.

In this digital age, more and more companies are embracing paid amplification on social media channels. Utilized properly, it can be a powerful tool with which entrepreneurs can encourage unprecedented growth, but unfortunately, not everyone knows how to engage with their audience through paid social promotions. Here are three mistakes I commonly see others make when marketing with paid promotion.

Lack an Integrated Approach

Simply having a large promotional budget does not guarantee a successful connection with your target audience on social. The key to a successful social media campaign is engaging and channel specific content powered by the right amount of paid amplification. You need to create and leverage content that comes directly from the brand and brand advocates. This is extremely crucial to the process, as it will show readers and consumers that third parties are vouching for and talking about the brand. Therefore, an integrated approach of brand content, user generated content, and social ads is absolutely necessary, and it's a commonly overlooked aspect of social media promotion strategy.

No Attempt at Leveraging Paid Content and Engagement

Engaging content is your conduit to connect with your audience on social. Mostly brands don't consider the option of turning to paid influencers for interesting and relevant content. This is where paid word of mouth can boost your marketing strategy. Influencers' content and their following can spark organic conversations about your brand across social media platforms. There are millions of potential influencers and many companies are already starting to reap the benefits of working with targeted influencers on online and offline marketing campaigns. The key is to target and activate the right brand advocate/influencer who can bring your brand in front of the right consumers. Leading influencer marketplaces already connect hundreds of brands and agencies with the right influencers everyday. "Studies show that influencer content affects over 70% of purchasing decisions," says Rohit Vashist, CEO of Sverve. "Finding the right influencers, managing, and measuring their results is now possible with the technology Sverve brings to the market."

Forget to Manage, Measure and Update your Strategy

A successful marketing strategy requires more attention than simply creating a great integrated strategy and walking away expecting results. It's crucial to measure every part of your marketing strategy, including influencer activation, which is not an easy task. You need to manage work flow, measure both your paid and organic engagements, and frequently change up your marketing copy or imagery to keep your audiences coming back for more. Should you reach out to a company to help with paid promotions, including influencer promotions, getting involved with the right social media partner is crucial. It's more than just a financial transaction; it must be treated like the entrepreneurial relationship it is and be measurable. When measuring results, do a deep dive of how your integrated approach has performed. Examine how paid ads and influencer content have complimented each other and make appropriate adjustments for your next marketing campaign.

Marketers are still figuring out optimal social media marketing strategies. However, an integrated approach that combines owned and paid content with right amplification and performance based tweaks can yield great results.

References

- Digital-advertising, internet-marketing: webfx.com, Retrieved 25 June, 2019
- Digital-marketing: investopedia.com, Retrieved 14 March, 2019
- Types-digital-marketing: convertful.com, Retrieved 23 May, 2019
- What-is-electronic-media-advertising: pickeronline.com, Retrieved 18 January, 2019
- Television-advertising-india-types-merits-demerits: accountlearning.com, Retrieved 05 June, 2019
- Digital-marketing-sponsorships: martech.zone, Retrieved 25 April, 2019
- What-is-paid-media-and-how-is-it-used-by-online-businesses, ecommerce-answers: bigcommerce.com, Retrieved 13 May, 2019

5

Social Media Management

Media that can be created and shared by people in a social network is termed as social media. This chapter deals with various aspects of social media management such as business models in social media, social media marketing, social media advertising, paid social media advertising, social competitive analysis, social media sentiment analysis, etc.

Social Media

Social media refers to websites and applications that are designed to allow people to share content quickly, efficiently, and in real-time. Many people define social media as apps on their smartphone or tablet, but the truth is, this communication tool started with computers. This misconception stems from the fact that most social media users access their tools via apps.

The ability to share photos, opinions, events, etc. in real-time has transformed the way we live and, also, the way we do business. Retailers who use social media as an integral part of their marketing strategy usually see measurable results. But the key to successful social media is to not treat it as an extra appendage but to treat it with the same care, respect, and attention you do all of your marketing efforts.

Social Media Marketing is Fleeting

In the early days of social marketing, there was little competition for the dollar—not so today. For example, you can spend thousands of dollars on a Facebook ad campaign and, sometimes, get no return on your investment. By its very nature, social media is a short attention span media—it is much harder to get someone's attention with a Tweet then it was to get someone's attention with a newspaper ad. That's because ad headlines and copy are harder to write on Twitter or Instagram.

You must be Active on Social Media

One of the biggest mistakes retailers make is to open up accounts on every social media platform they think is relevant and then leave them alone with no activity. Having an account with any of the social media platforms does not mean your business is *into* social media any more than owning golf clubs makes you ready for the PGA. In fact, social media users are turned off by the retailer who opens accounts and does not engage with clients and the public and consequently become labeled a pretender. The reality is, it is better to not have a social media icon on your website if you are not going to actively engage with it—and actively means on a daily basis.

The other big mistake retailers make is to use social media to talk about what is important to them rather than talking about what is important to the customer. As a retailer, you may think it is great to shout that you have a sale going on; and in some regards, this would be true. But, if that's the only reason you are getting involved in social media it won't be beneficial. Your goal should be to provide content that is relevant to your customer and engage with them to the point that they want to share your post with others.

If you use social media you need to engage with your customers, involve them in a dialogue, and ask them for their opinions. Post a picture of two items you are considering carrying in your store and ask customers which one they like best. This creates a dialogue which leads to shared posts which leads to engaged followers. Plus, if you follow this example, it will also lead to enhanced margins because your back and forth conversation will prevent you from buying the item that won't sell as well.

Images are Key

Another thing to consider is that the most commonly-shared content on social media is an image. So, always include an image with your posts. This will dramatically increase your chances that one of your followers will share the post with their network. While building up a large network of followers is great, ultimately what you want is to have your followers—no matter how many you have—share what you're posting with their network, and those people will share your post with their followers, and so on.

This is the new form of "word of mouth" and it's what people mean when they say a post went "viral."

Social Media Management

Social media management is the process of creating, scheduling, analyzing, and engaging with content posted on social media platforms, like Facebook, Instagram, and Twitter. A social media manager may be employed by a brand, individual, or business to reach new customers online or to improve and maintain their reputation.

Social media managers are experts at handling social media activity, from responding to customer comments to developing strategy on how to achieve long term marketing goals by publishing original content. However, there are also social media management tools that give you control over your own strategy.

Even if your time is limited, social media management tools and services can make your social media presence a priority. And if you aren't making social media a priority at this point in the game, you're in trouble.

Social media plays an integral part in the business landscape. With 3.2 billion people using social media around the world, and 11 new users every second, it's safe to say the fad has turned into a global standard. Social media management tools and services can help you reach this huge audience and make running a social media campaign decidedly simpler.

If you're keen to kick start your business' social media strategy, there are expert services you can consult with. You can use our simple tool to get a few comparable quotes for digital marketing and social media management services.

Getting Started with Social Media Management

Engaging with your audience through social media is more important than ever. Customers interact with brands via Twitter, Facebook, Instagram, LinkedIn and more, and they expect fast responses and professional outputs. That's where social media management comes in.

Social Media Management Tools

If you're just dipping your toe in the social media marketing waters, do-it-yourself tools are a great way to get started. These platforms can help you manage your own campaigns with simple, comprehensive interfaces designed for the most novice of social media manager.

Plus, social media management tools are often very affordable, and many offer free versions to test out before you buy. However, if you want to really make a difference on social media, you›re going to need a bigger boat.

Social Media Management Services

While social media management tools can help your company increase the quantity of your content, improving the quality of your content is just as important when it comes to engaging your target audience.

Fortunately, social media management services are equipped with the knowledge and resources to manage your social media presence right. Through targeted posting, sponsored ads, and a wide range of social media tactics that are far beyond common knowledge, these services can bring your social media game to the next level.

The Key Elements of Social Media Management

Whether you hire a social media marketing service or take advantage of a wide range of tools, you'll be able to transform your strategy from drab to fab without spending too much or wasting too much time. You'll be able to:

- Manage multiple accounts across various platforms.
- Analyze social engagement.
- Schedule posts in advance.
- Receive comprehensive reports of analytics.
- Monitor comments and respond efficiently.
- Collaborate with team members on content.

As with any additional software or service your company takes advantage of, the ultimate goal of social media management is to save time and improve profits.

How can Social Media Benefit your Business

Social media management tools and services are designed to make marketing easier, which ultimately increases profits. After all, what's the point of paying for new software or services if they aren't going to improve your bottom line? Social media management tools and services come with a bevy of helpful benefits that will reinvigorate your marketing efforts and put your company in front of your target audience.

Fortunately, social media management services are equipped with the knowledge and resources to manage your social media presence right. Through targeted posting, sponsored ads, and a wide range of social media tactics that are far beyond common knowledge, these services can bring your social media game to the next level.

The Key Elements of Social Media Management

Whether you hire a social media marketing service or take advantage of a wide range of tools, you'll be able to transform your strategy from drab to fab without spending too much or wasting too much time. You'll be able to:

- Manage multiple accounts across various platforms.
- Analyze social engagement.
- Schedule posts in advance.
- Receive comprehensive reports of analytics.
- Monitor comments and respond efficiently.
- Collaborate with team members on content.

As with any additional software or service your company takes advantage of, the ultimate goal of social media management is to save time and improve profits. So how does social media management create specific benefits for your company?

How can Social Media Benefit your Business?

Social media management tools and services are designed to make marketing easier, which ultimately increases profits. After all, what's the point of paying for new software or services if they aren't going to improve your bottom line? Social media management tools and services come with a bevy of helpful benefits that will reinvigorate your marketing efforts and put your company in front of your target audience.

Social media management can help you:

- Save time – by scheduling posts in advance, rather than burdening yourself with remembering to post at peak hours during the day.
- Increase authority – by posting multiple times a day on a wide range of platforms.
- Understand your audience – by providing in-depth analytics that explain who is following you, where they're coming from, and what they want from your business.
- Improve customer support – by creating a simple pathway for customers to inquire about your company through social media and making it simple for you to respond.
- Take control of your brand's reputation – by allowing you to monitor comments and feedback more closely, and respond as quickly as possible.
- Foster innovation- by encouraging creative collaboration across new platforms, for each social media campaign.

Clearly, social media management has benefits. But, understanding how it works is only the first step in deciding whether or not you should purchase one of these tools or services for your own business. So, what's the next step?

How Much does Social Media Management Cost?

Social media management tools and services vary in costs, which is why it's so important to get a tailored quote before you make a decision. Above all, you'll want an accurate estimate of how much social media management tools and services will cost for the particular scale and needs of your business.

Cost of Social Media Management Tools

Most social media management tools charge by two important factors: the number of accounts you plan on managing and the number of posts you plan on scheduling in advance.

Social Media Accounts

The beauty of social media management tools is your ability to schedule posts for Facebook, Instagram, Twitter, and even LinkedIn from a single platform. However, depending on how many accounts you're looking to manage, the price could go up.

Whether you're popular on a wide range of platforms, or just have six different Twitter accounts that you want to manage, make sure you know exactly how much it costs to add extra accounts to your service, as it could cost you a pretty penny.

Social Media Posts

The primary purpose of social media management tools is to schedule posts in advance so you don't need to perfectly time out your day to hit those peak hours. However, if you're trying to take the "quantity over quality" approach, you might need to pay a little extra.

Even if you only have one account, some social media management tools will put a limit on the number of posts you can schedule in advance. The more posts you want to schedule, the higher the price, so make sure you take that into account when picking your tool.

Cost of Social Media Management Services

If you're looking to truly break open the potential of a social media campaign, social media management services are the best way to go.

The price is understandably a bit higher, but the results you'll see from such social media marketing specialists will be more than worth it.

Unlike social media management tools, these services offer everything from marketing strategy to paid advertising to improve your overall strategy on social media. Because of this, social media management services vary greatly in cost depending on a wide range of factors, including:

- The size of your company.
- How often you plan on posting.
- The type of services you require.
- Which platforms you want to share content on.
- The level of analytics you need.
- Whether or not you'll provide customer service through social media.

When it comes to social media management services, the varying costs make it imperative to get a customized quote before you make a decision.

Best Social Media Management Tools and Services

Now you know what social media management involves, its benefits, and the cost factors that will determine what sort of price quote you can expect, here are some examples of the companies that can help you.

Do it Yourself: Social Media Management Tools

If you'd prefer to be hands-on with your brand's social media, then there are some brilliant tools you can choose, to manage how you go about this. Social media for business shouldn't involve logging into a standard Facebook or Twitter account, just like you would with a personal page. Businesses need to be smarter.

Social media management tools can let you schedule updates, manage customer service comments efficiently and learn about trends in how your customers interact with your brand.

Some of the best social media management tools include:

- Buffer – a great, simple to use interface.
- Hootsuite – lets you schedule an unlimited amount of posts.
- Sprout Social – ideal for growing businesses.
- Hubspot – marketing tools included, and a free trial available.
- IFTTT – a super, free service to try.
- TweetDeck – for Twitter only, but with lots of handy features.

The question remains, is it smarter to attempt to tackle the social media feeds for your business yourself, or to trust this vital service to an expert? Done right, social media management can transform the way you interact with customers.

This isn't something you can easily fit in between all your other business tasks, so think carefully before attempting to do it yourself.

If you're confident in your ability to run a successful social media campaign, the above tools will be a great start. However, if you're interested in significant improving your company's presence on social media, the professional services listed below will not disappoint.

Business Models in Social Media

Business models in social networking present the description of the business. YouTube, Facebook and Twitter are three of the biggest social media platforms in the world right now. Making money is certainly not the aim of all social activities and some social networks have, indeed, started without any commercial ambitions. At a point of time, however, if a social network grows beyond its immediate social setting, the issue will be raised how money is to be made – if not for other purposes then for covering the costs of maintaining and developing the network.

As mentioned in the Twitter case, one of the co-founders of Twitter, Ewan Williams, has been cited for saying that "we're not worried about monetization, we're just worried about making a fantastic product". This resembles statements one could find before the so-called dotcom crash in 2000-2001, which caused business model analysts and developers to give greater emphasis to how money is actually made instead of just 'counting eyeballs'. There is, however, an ongoing discussion on how social networks are and will be making money. One only has to 'google' the words 'social networks' together with 'making money' and a range of websites will pop up.

An important difference between the pre-dotcom period and now is that the web in the first mentioned period, to a large extent, was dominated by one-way services, while web 2.0 services – as first Darcy DiNucci and later Tim O'Reilly have termed them - involving user participation, have presently grown in importance. This will have an influence on the role of attracting users without having a clear business model to start with. Network effects play a far greater role in web 2.0 services than in the first generation of web-based services.

The business model concept used here builds on the basic structure of the business model ontology developed by Dutch and Belgian researchers, presented, for instance, in one of its early versions in a paper by Edward Faber.

This conception differentiates between four design elements: Service design, organization design, technology design, and financial design. The sections on the three cases in the present paper use these four design elements as the structure for the description of the cases.

An important premise is that it is considered as virtually impossible to charge the individual users. This, of course, depends on the categories of services and of users. Some dating services, for example, are based on end-user payment. Furthermore, if dealing with business users and social networks involving business users, there may be greater possibilities for charging a fee for participating in the network. However, if dealing with residential users, there is a very low - if any at all - willingness to pay for such communication and interaction services on the Internet. Other modes of income have to be sought.

As we are dealing with platforms, there are, indeed, other sources of income. The economic characteristics of platforms are that they coordinate the demands of distinct groups of customers who are dependent on each other. All words are important here: Platforms coordinate the demands of distinct groups of customers who are dependent on each other. There are in other words indirect network effects between the different groups of users. Dating services are a core example.

YouTube is a video-sharing site where the residential users can hardly be characterized as distinct groups. But advertisers are distinctly another group and so are application developers. In the case of Facebook, the great mass of users must likewise, in an economic sense, be understood as one group. However, application providers are another group. The application developers which are verified by Facebook pay a fee to Facebook. Furthermore, advertisements are part of Facebook's business model. With respect to the Twitter case, application providers are also the second potential group of users.

If not fully developed yet, a clear development perspective for the social networks in question is to become two-sided or multi-sided markets/platforms. Other sources of money are, however, also possible. As at yet, the most important source of funding has hitherto been venture capitalists. They have put money into these operations based on the expectation that they eventually will be making money. This has functioned well - especially in a period of economic upturn. It may, however, become stricter in the coming years because of the present economic crisis.

An additional source of income will come from selling information on the users to advertisers. There are clearly privacy issues involved. However, information on users and their usage patterns can be made anonymous and still have great value to advertisers. There are thus different possibilities, and in the following three sections the actual and potential sources of income will be described together with a broader presentation of their business models in accordance to the business ontology presented.

YouTube

YouTube is an Internet based public video-sharing service, where the end-users upload and share video clips. On YouTube people can experience varying degrees of engagement: One can chose only to view the available content, or also to share videos with others and even to develop social relationships.

YouTube was created in mid-February 2005 by three former PayPal employees: Steve Chen, Chad Hurley and Jawed Karim, and in October 2006 YouTube was acquired by Google Inc for US$ 1.65 billion. Google has implemented a sophisticated advertising scheme and revenue sharing mechanisms to run the YouTube business. These are discussed in the following:

Technical Design

YouTube video playback technology is based on Adobe Flash Player and uses the Sorenson Spark H.263 video codec with pixel dimensions of 320 by 240. This technology allows YouTube to display videos with quality comparable to more established video playback technologies (i.e., Windows Media Player, QuickTime and RealPlayer). YouTube officially accepts uploaded videos in .WMV, .AVI, .MOV and .MPG formats, which are converted into FLV (Adobe Flash Video) Each YouTube video is accompanied by an HTML markup for embedding it in another page, unless the uploader chooses to disable this feature. This simple cut-and-paste feature is especially popular with users of social networking sites, and is also a key to the success of YouTube.

The video applications prior to YouTube were mainly based on peer-to-peer file sharing technology. YouTube chose the client-server model, which has been characterized as a step back in the development. The client-server architecture necessities huge amounts of investments in server parks and broadband links in a centralistic architecture, which has been considered being sub-optimal for video/audio sharing compared to peer-to-peer architectures.

In the beginning, the huge investment costs behind the service raised the question of how YouTube could get a return on the investments. In particular, this became important as the service became highly popular with huge amounts of upload of video content and because the business model was not entirely clear. However, the revenue model based on advertising and partner programs seem to be valid components of YouTube's business design.

Service Design

YouTube began as a video-sharing platform, but it also offers users a personal profile page – which YouTube calls a 'channel page'. This enables people to create friends and to develop social relationships. A channel page is the YouTube equivalent of what other social networking sites call 'profile' pages and includes personal information as well as a list of videos made by the participant, their subscribers, favorite videos, and subscriptions to other YouTube participants.

YouTube represents a service which is different from other video services and the traditional VoD systems. Many other video services and VoD systems prior to YouTube were driven by professional content. The quality and popularity of this content can often be controlled and predicted, while in YouTube the amount and quality of content are unpredictable and mechanisms like 'rating' are needed to enable users to get familiar with new content. When comparing traditional VoD services and YouTube, two main issues are mentioned in Zink et al. YouTube video contents are uploaded by anyone with access to the network. The content and quality of these video clips vary vastly. As a consequence, predicting how many new videos will be uploaded and their popularity within the YouTube community is very hard. 2) The manner in which content spreads from these two systems to the public is also different. In the VoD system, either the viewers expect regular updates on the content (in the case of news or TV series) or the content provider can announce new content (e.g., the upcoming of the latest block buster). In the YouTube system, it is often the case that a video clip has become extremely popular after viewers became aware of the clip and told their friends about it, discussed it in blogs, and put embedded links to the clip on their own web pages.

An important barrier for the development of the service has been the copyright issues, where people have simply used the platform for uploading copyrighted content without permission of the right holders. This has resulted in YouTube putting an upper limit of 10 minutes on video content, i.e., video content greater than 10 minutes is not allowed on regular the YouTube platform and can only be accessed as a premium service.

The participation and engagement of the users range from users viewing programs occasionally to users who are very active in uploading, commenting, rating and developing social relationships in the YouTube sphere. In a user study of YouTube users in the users are divided into the following 5 categories:

- Former participants, who no longer post videos but may maintain an account, watch videos on the site, and occasionally post a comment.
- Casual users, who typically do not have an account, tend to view videos when they wish to search for something specific, when they surf the site, or when someone prompts them with a link to a particular video.
- Active participants, who have an account and usually upload videos or at least participate by leaving comments on other people's video or channel pages.
- YouTubers or 'Tubers', who have a more intense engagement with YouTube in terms of the amount and type of their participation. They are often on the site daily and certainly weekly, sometimes for an hour or more per session. Many, although not all YouTubers, promote

their work both within and outside YouTube. They upload videos and closely attend to and participate in YouTube debates and discussions.

- YouTube celebrities, who share qualities similar to those of YouTubers. However, they are also quite well known both within and often outside of the site. YouTube celebrities influence the discourse, goals, and activities on YouTube through their videos, comments, bulletins, and other forms of interaction.

All categories of users generate advertising revenues, while as discussed below, category 4 and 5 can also get shares in the generated revenue by going into partnership programs with YouTube.

Organizational Design

YouTube is built on user generated content with the end-users acting as producers and consumers of the content. YouTube does not have any creative and content producing resources and their success lies in the provision of an easy to use, global platform, where the ordinary users and professionals upload and share videos with each other.

To create incentives for producers of both user generated content and professional content, YouTube has developed a partnership program, where the content generators get a share of the generated revenue. In the beginning, the content generators should contact YouTube to become part of the program, but in the past years YouTube has chosen a more proactive strategy, where they contact the popular content generators in order to bring them into the partnership program.

This partnership program may provide the solution to the copyright problem as it generates revenue to content providers, and professional content rights holders like Hollywood may see the You Tube platform as an opportunity for distribution of their content. It is not unrealistic that 'pay for content' can also be deployed for professional content as a supplementary revenue model for YouTube alongside with advertising.

Financial Design

The revenue model is so far based on advertisements. A number of different ways of advertisements are used in YouTube:

- In-video graphical and text advertisements: Around 15 seconds into a video, an 80% transparent overlay appears in the bottom 20% of the video. If ignored, it disappears after 10 seconds; if clicked, it plays the video ad over the top of the existing clip, then resumes your original clip when complete.
- Post-roll advertising: if you don't click on an overlay ad when it shows up in a clip you're watching, the video ad it would have played rolls automatically at the end of your video.
- Pre-roll advertising: Pre-roll ads are short video clips that you must watch before the video.
- Regular banners.
- Sponsored advertising: Sponsored video spots that works like sponsored advertising on Google: An advertiser buys a position for specific key words and when somebody types these key words the advertiser's video pops up above others with yellow background.

Fred Wilson the principal of 'Union Square Ventures' has on http://www.avc.com developed a simple model to calculate the YouTube's revenue model.

The model is very simplistic and the values used are not necessarily correct. However, it shows that because of the huge amounts of the viewers, even when advertisers are charged with a price as low as 15 US$ per 1,000 views, and even if 65% of this goes to content providers engaged in the partnership program, there will be more than enough left to cover You Tube's operating costs.

Facebook

Facebook was launched by a student, Mark Zuckerberg, at Harvard in February 2004. At the beginning, Facebook was just a student directory, the goal of which was to provide an important information and communication services to a pre-existing offline community. In the early days of Facebook, only users who could verify they had an .edu e-mail address for the college they attended could register. This restriction was made to ensure trust between the offline community and the online service created. Since then, Facebook has acquired over 300 million users and is the fourth largest site in the world after Google, Microsoft and Yahoo sites.

Worldwide unique visitors (June 2009)	
Google sites	844 million
Microsoft sites	691 million
Yahoo sites	581 million
Facebook sites	340 million

Target Group

Facebook provides a social network for all regular PC Internet users and recently also mobile users. Facebook's statistics page offers interesting information on user profiles and engagement. According to the statistics, more than 40 million users update their status every day, and they spend more than 6 billion minutes on Facebook every day. The average user has 130 friends on the site. The fastest growing segment is made up of people above 35 years of age. More than 70% of Facebook's users are outside the United States.

Since Facebook has been made available as a mobile service, more than 65 million active users access Facebook through their mobile devices. This kind of growth has important implications for infrastructure and for advertisement companies.

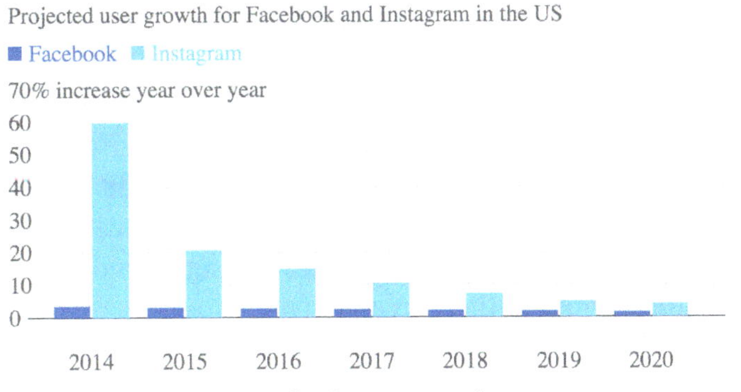

Facebook-user growth.

The graph shows that Facebook continues to grow in an extremely rapid pace. In just 14 months, Facebook has grown from 100 million to 300 million users.

Technology Design

Facebook Platform is a standards-based web service with methods for accessing and contributing to Facebook data5. A key feature which contributes to Facebook's success is its application platform, which enables the development of third-party social-networking applications. Facebook has opened up its core functions to all outside developers on May 24 2007 and already in November 2007, seven thousand applications had been developed on the Facebook Platform, with another hundred created every day. By July 2008, the number of applications had grown to 33,000, and the number of registered developers had exceeded 400,000. This growth has continued and in November 2009 the number of applications released by third party developers was as high as 350,000. Third party developers include: Microsoft, Amazon, Slide, RockYou, Box.net, Red Bull, Washington Post, Project Agape, Prosper, Snapvine, iLike, PicksPal, Digg, Plum and others. More than 250 applications have more than one million monthly active users.

In order to make the Facebook Platform better for both developers and users, Facebook has introduced new guidelines that have changed how applications are ranked in the application directory. Before, the focus was on total number of users, but going forward, user engagement becomes central. This change has helped drive the growth and distribution of applications which focus on user engagement and utility.

Service Design

Facebook services focus on building online communities that allows people to connect and communicate with friends. For users, Facebook's core service is completely free and ad supported. Users can upload pictures, create their profile and be friends with other users completely for free.

Facebook provides the user with a choice of who can view their profile. This prevents unauthorized users from accessing their information. Facebook provides a variety of ways for users to interact such as e-mail and instant messaging services. In addition to this, Facebook provides additional features such as the ability to create groups of users who share common interests, and facilitation of open or closed discussion forums. It is also possible to upload videos and other content. This can be sent as messages or shared by the use of the notes application.

One of Facebook's most popular features has been the ability to upload photos. Users can upload an unlimited number of photos from their cell phones or through the Java-based web interface, the only restriction being a 200-photos-per-album limit. Facebook also provides the feature to share the photos with a simple web link or send them via AIM or by e-mail. Users can also order prints online through a simple integrated interface. Users can, furthermore, set specific privacy settings for each of their albums, making them visible only to certain friends. Another important feature is the Facebook 'events' application, which can be used to organize events. This feature has been extremely successful when it comes to organizing parties. Along with organizing and joining events, users can also invite and recommend others to an event.

Facebook is, moreover, providing a few mobile options for its users. One of them is mobile web which is an alternative version of Facebook especially designed for mobile phones. Another option allows users to upload photos and notes from their mobile phones to Facebook. Users can send and receive text messages from Facebook friends. Recently, Facebook has implemented Facebook Connect which is Facebook's own approach to the single sign-on.

Organisational Design

The following actors are involved in the Facebook value chain: Facebook, application developers, access providers, handsets vendor, operators and users. Facebook is operated and privately owned by Facebook Inc. Access providers provide Internet and mobile access to Facebook. Users include private users as well as advertising companies.

An important part of the Facebook platform is services provided by application developers, particularly by games developers. The value that Facebook offers them is to tailor their applications for a social networking environment and to make it easy for Facebook users to access various applications, e.g., to find games and then play with friends.

According to Wireless Week, every handset vendor and operator is trying to get deals with Facebook and other social networks. Handset vendors are important players in the value chain.

According to operators, social networking applications are increasingly driving the growth of the mobile Internet audience. Therefore, handset manufacturers and operators are racing to be the first to bring phones with a user interface especially designed for the use of social network services like Facebook.

Recently, Facebook and Nokia are in talks about how to embed the social network into Nokia devices, mentioning the possibility of integrating Facebook contacts and activity with the device's phonebook. Even though Facebook already has a mobile site, this partnership would get it installed onto devices at the factory level, giving the community platform a strong foothold in the mobile market.

Finance Design

Revenue

At the beginning, Facebook's business model was based upon monetizing of the social network that has been built. The total number of users was more important than interaction between a user and a brand. As a result Facebook didn't make enough money from advertising services. Even though more and more advertisers spend their money on web advertising, only few of them had decided to invest in Facebook.

This situation has changed in year 2009. Facebook's management is expecting that revenue will grow from US$ 280-300 million to US$ 550 million in 2009. This implies a growth of 70% in one year. Expected sources of revenue are:

- $125 million from brand ads.
- $150 million from Facebook's ad deal with Microsoft.
- $75 million from direct sales of virtual goods.

- $200 million from self-service ads (mostly from social gaming companies on the platform, e.g., Zynga, but also 'performance advertisers' like online education companies).

Taking into consideration that Facebook has 300 million users in the world, revenue per user is still small. In comparison, Google makes 190 times the revenue of Facebook per page view.

From the data presented above, one can see that most advertising revenue comes from ad deal with Microsoft. Microsoft became the exclusive provider of standard banner advertising on Facebook using Microsoft's digital advertising solutions and the Microsoft ad Center platform in 2007.

During the second half of 2009, Facebook's revenue has become less dependent on the deal with Microsoft. Facebook started to make money on its new experimental advertising efforts and through sales of third-party brands and real-world goods as branded virtual gifts12. So far, companies offering virtual gifts include: Zynga, American Greetings Interactive, GreetBeatz, Somecards and Real Gifts, Sephora, Mars, Incorporated as well as 1-800-Flowers.com., Dell, eBay, Bud Light, Pizza Hut, Target, Dunkin' Donuts, Starbucks. Facebook is also launching a number of branding gifting campaigns, for example, for the Watchmen movie, Terminator Salvation movie, Britney Spears Circus tour, Budweiser, Johnnie Walker.

The largest Facebook app developer Zynga, which is a social gaming company contributes with as much as US$ 50 million per year in ad revenue to Facebook. Zynga sells virtual goods (reward points in Mafia Wars, chips in Poker etc.) to its players for US$ 500,000 a day. Members of Facebook purchase virtual gifts mostly for self-expression, social status and communication reasons. Approximately five million virtual goods are exchanged on Facebook daily, which means that this rare form of advertising is the form of ads that people like to receive. In comparison to traditional banners, this result is compelling.

According to the Piper Jaffray Report, 'Social Networking Coming of Age', the market for paid virtual goods is estimated at US$ 1.6 billion in 2009 and will be growing to US$ 2.8 billion by 2012.

A new feature implemented in Facebook can increase revenue by allowing advertisers to create, manage and monitor advertisements themselves. Advertiser can target their audience by choosing the preferred option regarding age, sex, location, time of the day as well as by language, place of work, education, status etc.

In addition, Facebook has extended its business opportunities by offering Facebook Ads in 15 currencies. Considering that 70 % of the users are from outside of US, this is important for many investors. It is expected that most revenue (app. 74%) will come from local, location-based ads. Local advertisers have found out that they can bring new customers into their business by targeting people who live nearby.

It is also expected that Facebook will generate significant revenue through payments or credits before the end of 2009. Unfortunately, Facebook has not disclosed exact numbers regarding their prediction of the revenue. In order to attract larger advertisers, Facebook has partnered with Nielsen15 to gain its credibility among advertisers. The Nielsen Company will provide information about how web content and online advertising on Facebook will affect consumer behavior. The management expects that this collaboration will help reaching the global consumer market through advertisements on Facebook.

According to a new report from Nielsen, year-over-year estimated online advertising spent on the most popular social network and blogging sites increased 119 percent, from about US$ 49 million in August 2008 to US$ 108 million in August 2009. In 2009, Facebook became the no.1 social networking side advertised on by 10 of the top 13 industries ranked by display ad impressions in US.

The share of Internet advertising had always been marginally less than advertising spending on local and national TV. This has changed in favour of Internet for the first time in 2009. According to the data presented in the report, all industries increase online ad spend on social networking sites in August 2009.

Cost

As Facebook continues to add new members and their associated content, it also needs to expand its abilities to serve by investing in infrastructure and staff. Facebook users upload more than 2 billion photos to the site each month and more than 14 million videos17. That will of course drive demand for more data centre space and more servers. More data centre space means more cost for the company. Facebook may spend well over US$ 1 million a month on electricity to power its servers and data centre space. The company has earmarked US$ 100 million to buy 50,000 servers this year and next.

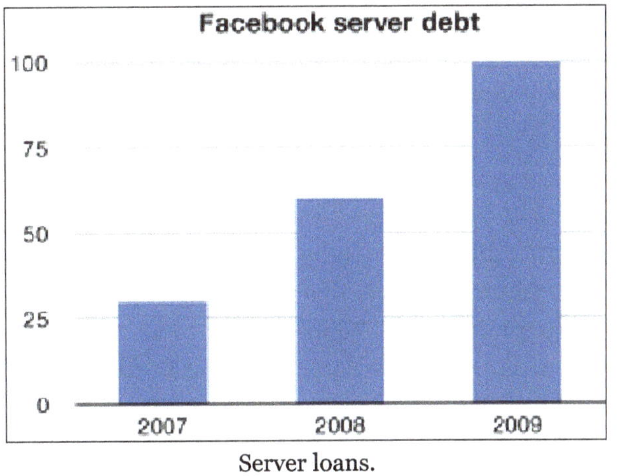

Server loans.

Facebook tries to solve the problem of high infrastructure cost by taking more control over its own data centres and infrastructure architecture. The company opened up its first data centre in Santa Clara in January 2009, and an international headquarter in Dublin, Ireland. These investments will allow for lowering total operating costs per server. At the same time, Mark Zuckerberg plans to hire more engineers and increase staff by 50%. Facebook currently has 1,000 employees. People are often the most substantial cost for a company and even though Facebook tries to reduce its cost, the company still plans to employ more staff.

With growing numbers of employees, Facebook spends at least another few million per month on payroll. The question is how much money Facebook will need to invest in the hardware to keep up with growth particularly in requirements for storage. According to various sources, Facebook has been buying one NetApp 3070 storage system per week just to keep up with all the user generated content. At up to US$ 2 million each, that means that they may have spent as much as US$ 30 million only in 2008.

Investors

The major resources of Facebook are the servers that keep the site running despite the heavy amounts of traffic. The growing audience could not be contained without external funding.

Facebook received its first investment of US$ 500,000 in June 2004. Paypal co-founder Peter Thiel, invested US$ 500,000 to buy servers to help support the rapid growth. Investment data is presented in the table below:

Date	type	Capital amount	Post-money valuation	Investors
09/2004	Seed	0.5M	Unknown	Peter Thie.
05/2006	Series A	12.7M	Unknown	Accel Partners.
04/2006	Series B	27.5M	Unknown	Greylock, Meritech Capital Series Partners, Accel Partners.
10/2007	Series C	310 M	15000M	Microsoft, Oliver Samwer, Alexander Samwer, Ka-Shing Li, Marc Samwer.
03/31/2008	Series C	40 M	Unknown	Clarium Capital Management, Greylock Partners, Meritech Capital Partners, Accel Partners, Microsoft.
05/2008	Dept	100 M	Unknown	TriplePoint Capital.
05/26/2009	Series C	200 M	10200M	Digital Sky Technologies will get preferred shares for it's 200 million.

Twitter

Twitter is a social network based on a micro blogging platform allowing users to post short messages and read messages from others. Twitter was founded in March 2006 and was introduced as a public service in October same year. Users are heavily represented only in a dozen countries. Twitter is most popular in North America, where 45% of the users are located. In 2008, Twitter introduced a Japanese version. Tokyo, New York, and San Francisco are the major cities with high adoption rates of users. In the US, the number of unique users have increased from 475,000 in February 2008 to more than 7 million a year later. In spite of this staggering growth, Twitter is still much less widespread than the most popular US Social network sites Facebook and MySpace.

Technical Design

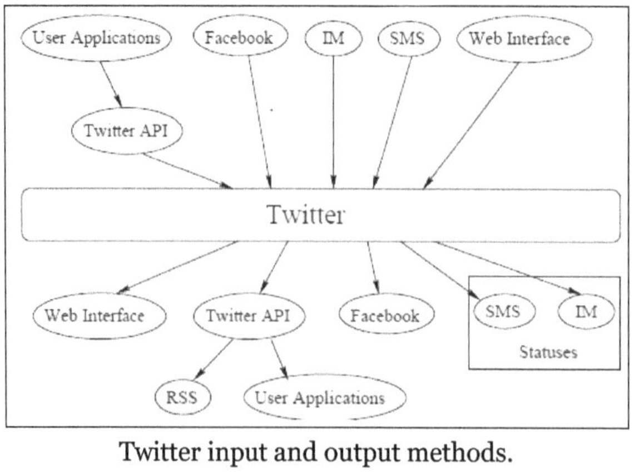

Twitter input and output methods.

Twitter provides a common platform for sending and receiving messages by the use of a wide range of delivery channels (figure). Twitter can be accessed via an Application Programming Interface (API) developed by a third party.

Service Design

The core services offered by Twitter are not very different from those offered on Facebook: Users can create their own homepage describing their profile. They can read and post messages (tweets), and they can send messages directly to another user. Posted messages are sent to all 'followers', i.e. those who have chosen to follow a certain user. The concept of followers is different from the concept of friends used on other social networking sites such as Facebook, Linkedin, and Plaxo. 'Friends' indicates a symmetric relationship, while you do not need to follow your followers on Twitter and vice versa. Furthermore, you can choose to follow any user without his prior acceptance. This implies that some users have many more ollowers than they follow. For instance Larry King has 1.3 million followers and follows only 81. Another important feature is that it is possible to do keyword search in the entire population of tweets. This enables users to see if anyone has posted something on a particular subject.

As other social networks, Twitter can be accessed on the Internet, but Twitter is deliberately designed as a mobile service. The formatting requirements for users' homepages are made in such a way that they are suitable for access via a mobile phone, and tweets are limited to 140 characters, so that they can be distributed via SMS. A hint on the intended value of the Twitter service follows from the preamble on the Twitter homepage. Here it is described how businesses can use twitter to build a community of customers and how they can keep them informed about what's going on in their business. This preamble is followed by a number of business cases on how private businesses have been successful in connecting to their customer by the use of twitter.

The most well-known delivered value has been the ability to report important news at a faster pace than any other media. This was for instance the case, when an aircraft landed in the Hudson River, and when an aircraft crashed in Schiphol Airport in February 2009. Twitter has also proven to be useful for reporting news from, for instance, Iran.

Organizational Design

The following actors are involved in the twitter value chain: Twitter, application developers, access providers, and users.

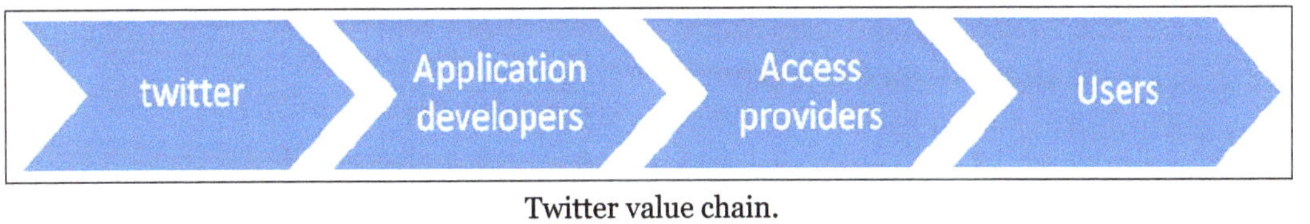

Twitter value chain.

Twitter is an independent company. It provides the software for the basic services and operates the common platform. The system is open and developers have free access to both platform and data, and several thousand applications have been developed by third parties for instance browser plugins, photo- and video-sharing applications that enhance mobile and computer based use.

Users include private consumers as well as businesses using Twitter as a channel for marketing. Users can be grouped into three different categories:

- Broadcasters: Those followed by a much larger number of users than the number they follow.
- Acquaintances: Those with reciprocity in their relationships, typically online social Networks.
- Users following a much larger number of people than following them.

The first group includes various online radio stations which use Twitter to broadcast the song they are playing right now, as well as news media and other businesses. The second is by far the largest group and includes private users. The last group is smaller than the others and includes spammers, who want contact to as many users as possible.

Financial Design

The financial design of the Twitter service is subject to vivid discussion on several blogs. So far the revenue Twitter is generating for itself is very limited. A little revenue is generated from users sending and receiving tweets on SMS, but this covers only a small fraction of the costs. Twitter neither charges subscription fees nor provides space for advertisements. Substantial revenues are generated by application providers, but in general these revenues are not shared with Twitter. Exec Tweets Twitter – a site linking to tweets from business executives – shares their revenue with Twitter, but this is an exception.

Revenues from advertisements or a fee imposed on businesses using Twitter as a marketing channel are obvious possibilities. There is a risk that especially advertising will reduce the perceived value of the service and that users will migrate to other platforms. The use of SMS as a delivery channel puts strict limitations on how to advertise without annoying users. On the other hand, it is very likely that companies would be willing to pay a fee for using Twitter to stay in contact with their customers. The focus on this application on the Twitter homepage could indicate that this option is seriously considered by Twitter. Other suggestions, which have been put forward, are to offer search engine facilities to companies or to sell the company and its customer base to, e.g., Google or Yahoo.

However, the company seems to be confident that it will be possible to leverage its huge population of users at some point of tome. Stone – a co-founder of Twitter has said that they will build the audience first and the revenue streams later. Ewan Williams – another co-founder – has the same opinion:" We are not worried about growing users, we're not worried about monetization, we're just worried about making a fantastic product".

Management Issues in Social Media

Juggling multiple social media channels on a daily basis is no easy feat; a good social media management tool is worth it's weight in digital gold. Customers, fans, and the general public are all following your social media accounts 24/7, in real time and with high expectations. They expect to see a steady stream of creative posts, informative content, sincere and meaningful interactions and engagement, and immediate responses to a majority of their questions and comments.

A unified platform for managing all of these disparate social media channels is not just a coveted luxury anymore; it's a necessity. Multiple companies have stepped in to fill this void, and each one offers a different user interface with different features and programming.

Manual publishing of social media content: Without a social media management platform, you essentially become responsible for manually cultivating and posting content to each of your social media channels on a daily and sometimes hourly basis. Efficiently leveraging your content across multiple social platforms becomes labor-intensive and cumbersome. eClincher, however, allows you to automatically and efficiently schedule content for posting to all of your social media channels. This publishing and scheduling tool includes auto-link verification, a tool to automatically shorten URLs, and the ability to preview a post before it gets published in its native environment. In addition, eClincher offers the Auto Post tool, designed to help you cycle or reuse your content without human intervention. Auto Post uses queues when each queue contains specific content that get published on a daily basis with a pre-defined schedule. Uploading your posts can be done with Bulk Upload where you can quickly upload hundreds of posts to your queues.

Engaging meaningfully with your audience: Followers who engage with your social media accounts all expect prompt, thoughtful, accurate responses—a daunting prospect for you to manage on a 24/7 basis. eClincher offers two important engagement tools to combat this challenge: live feeds of all social media activity from across all of your channels, as well as a universal inbox that aggregates messages, new followers, and notifications from all of your social accounts. The Unified Social Inbox is expertly designed to allow you to categorize and label every message, so you can, for example, keep track of all interactions with influencers, or all inquiries of a specific nature from potential customers. The Unified Social Inbox even comes with a search bar to easily find and retrieve archived messages at any time.

Finding the content that matters to you: Social media is a big, overwhelming space, but if you know where to look, it also comes with tremendous potential to gain real-time insights into news and trends relevant to you. eClincher has developed curated content feeds that allow you to filter out all of the noise and focus on just the trends, hashtags, industry influencers, and keywords that matter to you. Using the Custom Search Feeds feature, you are able to input specific search terms and then—on an ongoing, real-time basis—gain a pulse on what's happening in your corner of the world, who's talking about it, and how it relates back to you.

Having all platforms in one place: For a social media management platform to be useful, it needs to integrate with as many channels and complementary systems as possible. It also needs to be easy to use. eClincher offers integration with eight social media channels (Twitter, Facebook, Google+, LinkedIn, Pinterest, Instagram, Blogger, and YouTube), and also is fully integrated with popular third-party services including RSS/Atom feeds, Feedly, Pocket, and Canva. Finally, eClincher is designed to work on tablets and smartphones.

Trying to decipher convoluted analytics: If you're on social media for a purpose other than just pure fun, you care about analytics. Indeed, the powerful insights gained through analytics are what justify the investment of time and resources into your social media channels. And no matter how you use social media to market and promote something, you are using these analytics to help you plan and execute an audience engagement strategy. Additionally, many supervisors and managers expect to see this data on a monthly or even weekly basis. eClincher was built to capture real-time analytics data from sites like Twitter, Facebook, Google, LinkedIn, Blogger, YouTube, and Instagram (coming soon) – and display everything on one intuitive and visually engaging dashboard that cuts out needless clutter and confusion. Users also get unlimited access to analytics reports for all of their social media channels, which dramatically streamlines the reporting process.

Customizing the features that work for you: We all have different needs and wants in a social media management platform; some of us manage just a handful of social media accounts for a small business or a personal brand, while others maintain dozens of accounts across multiple brands and are constantly publishing, engaging, monitoring trends, and running analytics. eClincher has monthly plans that start at $15/month for users with up to five social media profiles. Pricing also is tailored to how many team members require access to the eClincher platform.

Managing social media channels does not have to be time-consuming, cumbersome, labor-intensive daily process that it is for so many of us. A social media management platform can take out a lot of the mundanity and guesswork that often accompanies running an organization's online presence. A solid social media platform should enable you to publish seamlessly, engage meaningfully with your audience, keep you informed through curated content feeds, bring clarity to convoluted analytics, and offer optimized, customized solutions for every user. With this newfound knowledge, you should now be able to leverage the power of social media to your advantage.

Social Media Marketing

Social Media Marketing (SMM) is a type of internet marketing which uses the benefits of social networking sites as a tool of promoting websites, thus increasing traffic towards them and learning from users' direct reactions.

SMM is based on the principle of organic search, which basically means that when the website or its connected social network page is more active, the website's position on search engines rises, i.e. it will be in seen the first few results.

Considering the fact that 90% of users searching the internet do not look any further than the first page of the search engine, and that 70% clicks on the first three results only, it is obvious that the position on the first page of the search engine is the only goal to strive for when optimizing a website.

What is SMM used for?

The main goal of SMM is to improve communication with users, increase brand visibility and reach more (potential) customers.

SMM is being done by creating quality content that the users of social networks share with their friends (via transmitting information electronically, i.e. Electronic Word of Mouth, or eWoM).

The point of SMM is to obtain direct feedback from users (or potential customers), so that the company gets a personal stamp at the same time, i.e. it appears more human-like.

By means of interactive options on social networks, the customers get the chance to be heard, either by asking questions or by making complaints.

This type of SMM is called Social Customer Relation Management (Social CRM), which can further lead to enhancing credibility and return on investment (ROI), of course, if the users are satisfied with content, relationship with the company and the service provided.

How to use SMM?

Social Media Marketing functions on the principle of Social Media Optimization (SMO), i.e. the improvement of company image on social networks.

Similarly to Search Engine Optimization (SEO), SMO attracts new, unique visitors to the targeted website.

Why would search engines care for social networks? Simply because many people use their social media to search for things, share links and thereby participate in building a strong network of links.

SMM, that is SMO, can be done in two ways:

- Active SMM promotion,
- Passive SMM promotion.

Active SMM Promotion

Active promotion means adding links (applications) which lead from the content on the website towards social networks (similarly to RSS and social media share buttons). Social networks which can be used as a means of SMM are the following:

- Facebook,
- Twitter,
- Google+,
- LinkedIn,
- Instagram,
- YouTube,
- Pinterest.

Each social network has its own Terms of use, which is different for natural persons and legal entities, i.e. companies.

What only companies get is the option of launching a paid ad campaign so as to reach wider audiences, thus improving traffic towards a website or a targeted web page.

Passive SMM Promotion

Passive promotion means promoting activities on social networks by updating statuses, publishing images, tweets or articles on blogs.

Users' reactions can be further analyzed in order to solve problems and remove dissatisfaction, and improve their brand experience.

What is useful especially is that that information is obtained in real time, which speeds up the entire process and opens the door to a new dimension of cooperation.

Social Media Advertising

Social media advertising is a category of digital advertising that places ads on social networking sites. It is one of two major social media marketing tactics: paid and organic.

Unlike paid advertising, organic marketing requires no upfront cash expense. But it does require the expense that comes with labor.

The difference between the two tactics lies in how the marketer reaches the target audience. A common organic effort in social marketing is simply regular and highly optimized posts in the social media account.

With paid social advertising, the marketer is trying to reach new audiences that he or she can't reach with organic efforts.

An effective social media strategy has a balance between the two tactics. Which one costs more in cash or labor? Which one has the best return on investment?

Some marketers find that they can get the results they want with a strategy that focuses 100 percent of their effort on organic tactics. Others find they have to place a heavy emphasis on advertising.

Marketing strategists constantly fine tune their efforts until they find the best balance between the two tactics.

Social Media Companies

The four largest social media companies at the time of this writing are in order of audience size according to Quantcast are:

- Facebook,
- Twitter,
- Linkedin,
- Pinterest.

What makes these sites attractive to advertisers starts with their vast reach.

The ability of advertisers to communicate with such a vast number is impressive. But in reality the attractiveness lies in segmenting that huge audience. The larger the audience, the greater the ability to target at a micro level.

A social network with 1 million users of whom 10,000 who have an interest in gardening is not attractive to a company such as Home Depot. But a network with 100 million users and 1 million gardening enthusiasts is more attractive.

Add the ability to segment those gardeners even further — landscapers versus flower gardeners — creates many opportunities for campaigns based on location, a specific sale or the time of year.

Geographic Targeting Appeal

Major social media sites have another appeal to advertisers — the ability to target users geographically.

Geographic targeting is available not only at the country level but also at the state, city and zip code level.

Social media companies are able to target down to the zip code level because they encourage users to provide personal information in order to maximize the usefulness of their accounts.

Again, mass reach provides great value. Having 10,000 users at zip code 55555 is more attractive to a Lowe's store located in that zip code than a network with only 50 users in the same zip.

Some users provide more information than others. So they don't have a complete profile on every one of them. But knowing the zip code of a user is only the start.

The networks also gain an understanding of age and sex. They track and grasp users' interests based on the social network groups they join or the comments they post.

That means advertisers can target geographically, demographically and psychographically.

Targeting Increases ROI

Any form of targeting potentially increases the return on investment for the advertiser because it is cost efficient.

An advertiser can spend $10,000 in a mass marketing campaign to reach 10,000 people, of which 9,900 aren't interested in that product or service. In reality, that advertiser has spent $10,000 to reach only 100 people who do have an interest.

The cost to reach that entire group is $1 per person, but the cost to reach the target is $100 per person.

With targeting, that same advertiser might spend $2,000 to reach that same audience of 100 people.

The cost to reach the entire target is $20 person — much higher than the first example — but the total cost is much lower. The cost to reach the target is usually higher per person with targeting because of the costs that go will developing a targeted solution.

Best uses of Social Advertising

OK, social media advertising has the ability to target in a cost efficient way. It has wide reach and rapidly growing acceptance.

All advertising provides either branding, response or a combination of both. Ads on these platforms serve three primary purposes. They:

- Promote the business' brand.
- Promote the business' social media presence.
- Send social media users to the business' Web site.

The ultimate goal of course is generating new clients and new revenue.

So it is up to the business to decide if a social media advertising campaign is beneficial. Then the business must decide how the campaign should be used to get the best return on investment for the expenditure.

Paid Social Media Advertising

Paid social media advertising is very different from traditional outbound advertising. Big data and machine learning allows you to find, target, and reach your audience with ease. Each platform is designed to facilitate the goals of your business, such as brand awareness, lead generation, website traffic, and more.

You can even access the native analytics for insights into how to enhance the performance of your social media advertising campaign. Whether you're looking for reach, engagement, or sales – the case for advertising on social media marketing has never been stronger.

Here are seven benefits to using paid social media advertising for your small business:

- Amplify your reach,

- Fit any budget,
- Enhance your targeting,
- Boost brand awareness,
- Maximize your content marketing,
- Gain access to mobile users,
- Gather market insights.

Amplify your Reach

Advertising on social media gives your brand instant visibility. Posts from friends and family now receive priority, so organic reach for brands on social media is declining steadily – especially on Facebook. The sheer volume of posts makes connecting with your audience a statistical improbability.

However, paid ads are guaranteed a place in the user's feed. Despite the noise of the larger social platform, this gives you a direct window to drive leads, website traffic, and sales.

To achieve the greatest reach, find where your audience spends their time online. The graphic below depicts the preferred platforms for each different age group.

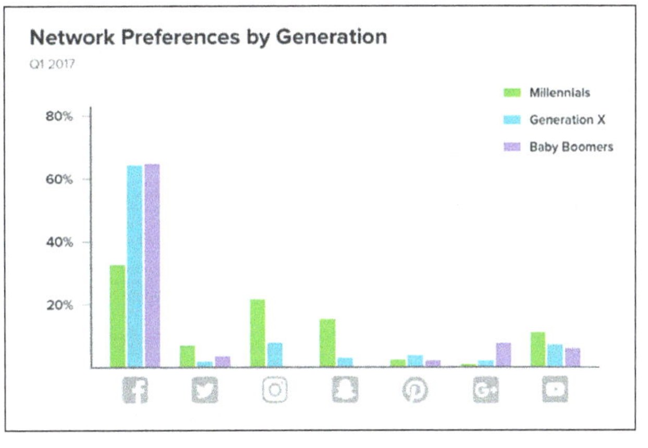

To maximize your impressions, align your social media advertising strategy with the behavior patterns of your audience.

Fit any Budget

Paid social media advertising is a cost-effective way to promote your business. Each platform uses the pay-per-click (PPC) payment model. This means that you pay only if the user takes the action you want.

Unlike conventional advertising, this lets you engage with niche markets at a discount. After a few ad cycles, you can refine your targeting to drive greater results and ROI.

We see that the average price-per-click for Facebook ads across all industries is $1.72.

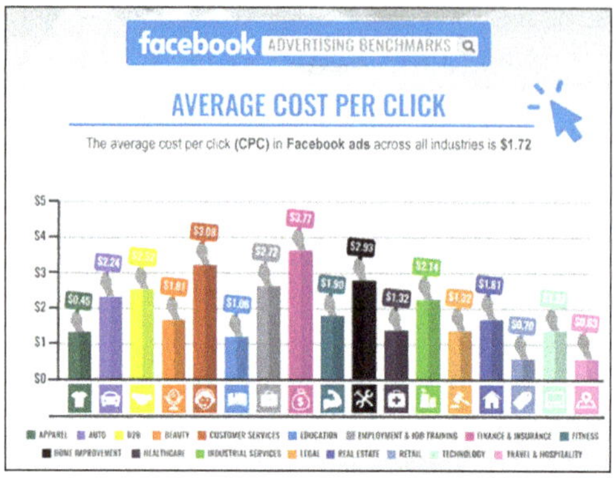

By comparison, the average cost per promoted Tweet is $1.35 and the average cost per 1,000 impressions on Instagram is $6.70. Though the cost is greater, Instagram boasts more engagement than other platforms, according to Forrester. If your product or service is visually-oriented, paying more for Instagram may drive better results at a lower end-cost.

When creating your ad budget, start small and invest where you see results.

Enhance your Targeting

Paid advertising on social media gives you complete control over who sees your ad.

Each platform offers a plethora of targeting parameters. Beyond basic user demographics, you can choose from psychographic factors such as interests, hobbies, personality types, and more.

Upload a list of contacts to target, or create a lookalike audience that resembles your existing contacts. This is a powerful way to both expand and engage your ideal audience at once.

Facebook also lets you retarget social users who've already visited your website. Simply install the Facebook retargeting pixel on your site and previous visitors will see ads for your company in their News Feed.

For example, Squarespace uses Facebook retargeting to promote a free 14-day trial to recent website visitors.

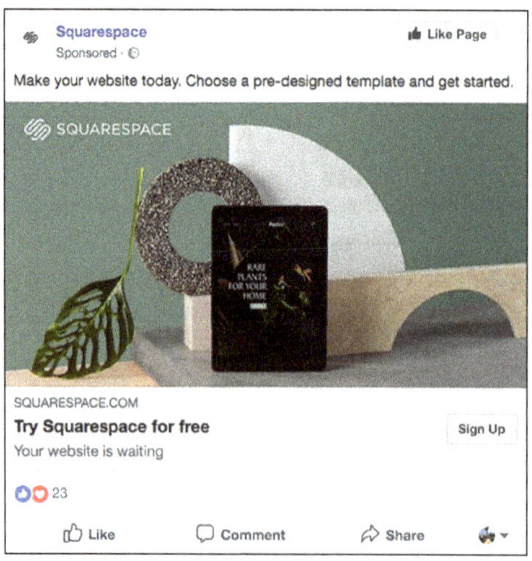

Leverage the various targeting options of social media to hook the attention of leads throughout your marketing funnel.

Boost Brand Awareness

Social media advertising is a cost-effective way to create exposure for your brand.

If your business appears in the news feed regularly, people will start to recognize you. Recognition will enhance your credibility, plus drive engagement and purchasing behavior.

Consider that 80% of its users follow at least one brand on Instagram. Of this majority group, at least 30% of users have purchased a product they discovered on Instagram.

When generating awareness, serve ads that are both informative and memorable. In the following example, UberEats uses an Instagram video to introduce their service to users at mealtime.

This captivating blend of motion, color, and text allows the delivery service to secure impressions and retain user attention throughout.

Maximize your Content Marketing

Social media is an ideal way to distribute your best content.

According to Sprout Social, 73.4% of users follow a brand because they're interested in its product or service. Nurture the curiosity of your followers with educational content that will transform them into qualified leads.

Aside from coaxing leads down the funnel, ads for content will help you to drive web traffic, boost engagement on social media, and improve the ROI of your content marketing.

Here we see Buffer use a Pinned Tweet to advertise their guide to scheduling Instagram posts.

A blend of diagonal lines, color symmetry, and relevant imagery grabs the attention and communicates value immediately. Investing in custom graphics will enhance the allure of your content assets and maximize the impact of your paid social media advertising.

Access Mobile Users Anytime

The penetration of social media advertising is unparalleled. According to Pew Research, 80% of time spent on social media is spent on a mobile device.

When users want to find, know, or purchase – a social media advertising campaign will help you to reach your audience in that moment. The most effective ads emulate the organic content of their native platform.

For example, TaskRabbit uses a sponsored Facebook post to appeal to mobile users' want for efficiency and productivity.

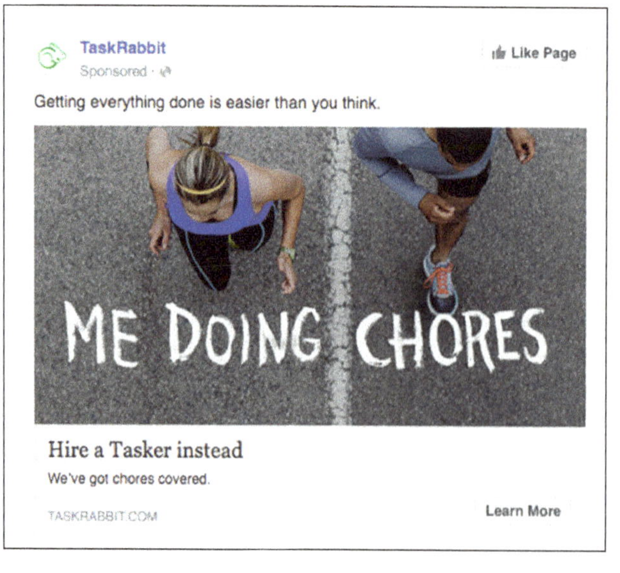

Language gives this ad a personal touch that imitates the tone of the Facebook feed. The brand uses minimal text with a strong image to instantly communicate its value proposition to quick-scrolling users.

Gather Market Insights

How did your audience interact with your ads? Which ad type was most popular? Did video convert better – and with whom? Use the native analytics within the social media platforms to assess and refine the performance of your advertising campaign. Look to KPIs such as clicks, comments, and profile visits to determine if your ads are creating an impact.

Facebook Insights is the gold standard of platform analytics. Seen below, you get detailed information on follower demographics, metrics like reach and engagement, plus the times that users visit your page.

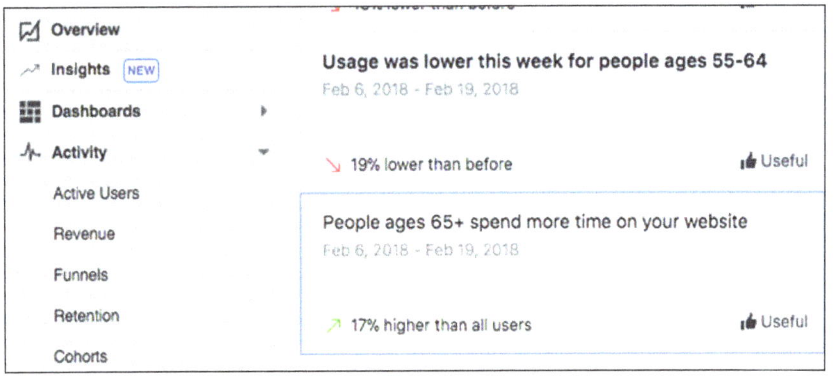

These data will allow you to identify your best targets and narrow your targeting parameters to most effectively drive conversions and impressions.

Equipped with information, you can benchmark your performance against competitors and establish what works.

Social Media Monitoring

Social Media Monitoring is often confused with other terms like Social Media Listening or Social Media Intelligence, but actually each of these monikers has its own place in your social analytics toolbox.

Social Media Intelligence is an overarching term covering a few key areas of social analytics, including Social Media Monitoring and Social Media Listening, with a focus on Competitor Analysis. It represents the sum of the parts (i.e., data) these other tools unlock.

Social Media Listening uncovers consumer insights you can apply to brand strategy. It's an ongoing task that focuses on getting to know your audience and their emotions, so you have a baseline understanding of the consumers you want your brand to reach. The goal is to learn what consumers care most about, and bring that into your customer experience at every level.

Social Media Monitoring is also an ongoing endeavor, but with a slightly different focus. If you think of Social Media Listening as creating a baseline for what your audience feels, Social Media Monitoring is about maintenance of that baseline.

Because technology has made the world "smaller" and more competitive, Next Gen AI Analytics is now the standard for achieving next level speed, accuracy, and control of analytics data.

But don't get overly caught up in the terminology. Think of it this way: If Social Media Monitoring is the instrument panel of your car, telling you how fast you're going, and whether you need gas or an oil change, Next Gen AI Analytics is the engine – powering everything and ensuring you can rely on what your instrumentation shows.

You need this level of precision because you're looking for anomalies – anything that stands out from the norm. These anomalies span the emotional spectrum from positive to negative – and both extremes require awareness and attention. This is why Social Media Monitoring is done in real-time.

Let's look at the negative side of the equation first, since social negativity is so damaging when it goes viral. There are three crucial things you're looking for in your monitoring:

Negative conversations – When consumers chat about your brand in a negative way on social media, they're likely not the only customers who feel that way. Here are some eye-opening statistics to keep in mind:

- Only 1 in 26 unhappy customers will complain to you; of the non-complainers, 91% just leave. This makes it all the more important to take care of those who do complain – to provide visibility for the ones who are silently watching. If they see you taking care of the others, they may give you another chance. But you can't take care of customer complaints unless you know about them.
- Overall, Americans tell more people about bad experiences (15 people on average) than about good ones (11 people on average). The problem is, misery loves company. Those 15 people might be happy to share a social post about a bad experience if they've endured similar. Any uptick in negative sentiment is definitely cause for concern. Your Social Media Monitoring tools *must* be backed by exceptional Natural Language Processing (NLP) and sentiment analysis capabilities.

On the other hand, when customer services problems are resolved well, 70% of formerly dissatisfied customers will give brands another chance. This is why the speed and accuracy AI Analytics brings to the table is so crucial.

The beauty of Social Media Monitoring tools – the best ones, at least – is you can set up alerts so you know when there's a spike in sentiment indicating a topic or post you shouldn't ignore. That way you can address issues quickly and stop angry posts from going viral.

These alerts use keywords you choose, as well as a metric called Passion Intensity that lets you know the strength of emotions in social posts. When Passion Intensity spikes, it's time to investigate why.

This careful attention is what allows brands like Buffalo Wild Wings to track sentiment around a potentially risky camaign – pumpkin spice flavored wing sauce.

Monitoring the conversation and sentiment showed them they were on to something even when some of the initial posts were skeptical.

Negative images – Because social media is becoming an increasingly visual medium, your tools also must monitor negative imagery. 100 million+ photos and videos are uploaded daily to Instagram alone.

Now consider this statistic: “Posts that include images produce 650 percent higher engagement than text-only posts.”

Given that, imagine the damage your brand could suffer if someone misappropriates your logo. Or how much visibility complaints with images could garner.

Your Social Monitoring software must include Image Analytics or you’re letting a huge chunk of content slip beneath your radar. Sadly, not all Social Media Analytics tools offer this feature.

Reputational threats – Of course the nightmare scenario for any brand is reputational damage from a viral post. This is why it’s so important to be alerted to and take care of anything brewing in the moment. Because anything left unresolved can pick up social steam and become viral in the blink of an eye. And that’s to say nothing of blatant attempts to do brands harm by any number of attackers.

Are there cases when you shouldn’t take action? Absolutely. Sometimes responding only fans the flames and does more harm than good – drawing more attention to something that would’ve just gone away on its own.

The most important thing is awareness – and knowing the data received is accurate. Some tools tell you there’s been a “breach,” as Lloyd’s Banking Group puts it, and send you into panic mode over nothing.

When your data is reliable, knowing about negative or potentially damaging posts means you can make smart decisions, and act – quickly – when it’s appropriate. Erring on the side of caution, by handling problems when they’re small, is always best.

This was the approach taken by FleishmanHillard when a real-life crisis incited a social crisis. By monitoring the conversation around a shooting in a national restaurant chain, they were able to understand how consumers were talking about the restaurant, if they were blaming the chain for the problem, and more.

What about Positive Sentiment?

Social Media Monitoring isn't all about gloom and doom. You also want to be alerted to positive swells in sentiment – because these are the users you can put to work as brand advocates and influencers. But don't stop at mentions of your own brand.

Monitoring the posts of your competition, their audience, and your industry overall, is the best way to spot opportunities your brand can take advantage of – like new trends, consumer problems in need of solving, and more.

Here's a look at a recent spike on the search "airlines":

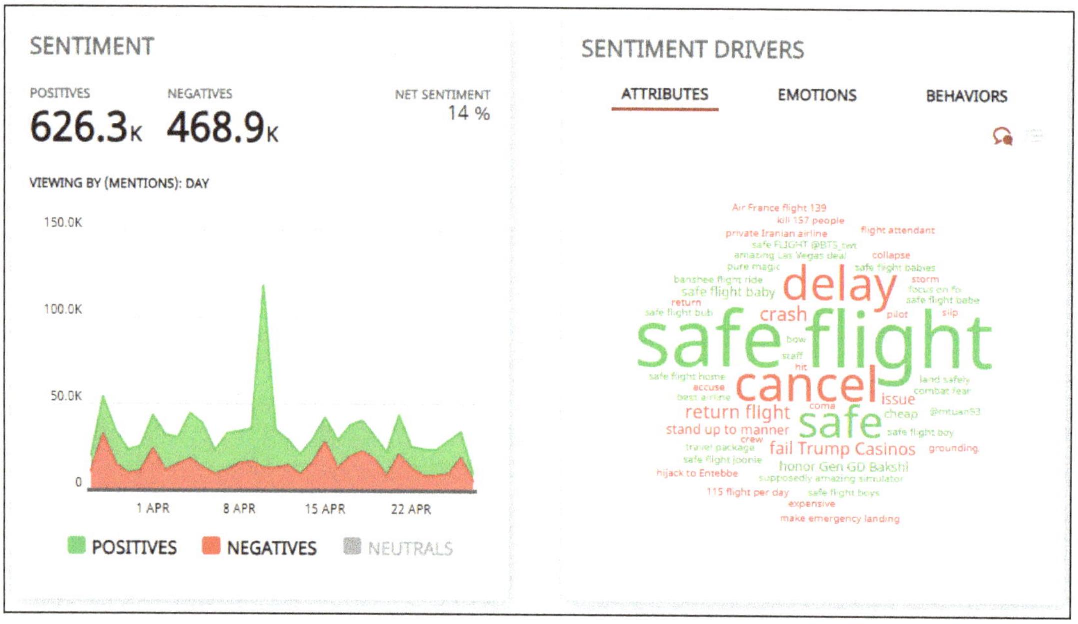

If you're an airline brand – or even a brand in the travel industry overall – understanding what's behind this sudden spike in positivity is important.

As we saw with Buffalo Wild Wings, you can use Social Monitoring to stay aware of sentiment around active campaigns, or to turn around operations overall by creating positive emotions out of negative through interaction.

Brand health is a big reason Social Media Monitoring should be part of your daily operations – but it's hardly the only one. Social Analytics uncovered through Social Monitoring are also not limited to the marketing department.

When you uncover data about customer service issues, it's not just about putting out that fire. It lets you identify if there's a specific area where you're not making par in your category, or where you're not living up to the expectations consumers have of your brand or products.

It's also how you know you're doing better than expected, or than competitors, and why. Imagine the money you can save by following the product launch of a competitor, and discovering consumers hate it? If you had a similar idea, you can avoid that loss – or offer a better version and claim that audience for yourself.

Identifying new influencers and monitoring the activity of current ones is another area where Social Monitoring comes in handy. Those positive sentiment spikes may lead you to a social celebrity worth putting to work for your brand. It also helps you see how influencers you already use are succeeding – by alerting you to content that is particularly engaging, for example.

Social Monitoring benefits all areas of brand operations from customer service, to marketing, to sales, to research and development. So when you spend on Social Monitoring Tools, you're making an investment that brings far-reaching returns.

Social Media Monitoring Tool

A question often asked – especially by smaller brands – is whether you really need to pay for Social Media Monitoring Tools. After all, there are a lot of free tools out there. That's true – and when you're just getting started, they're better than nothing.

But you have to remember, you get what you pay for. At a certain level, making do with free or subpar tools is like trying to hit a homerun for the Red Sox using a child's toy bat. It simply won't get the job done. But we understand that it's overwhelming to sift through the numerous solutions out there. Here's what matters:

Accuracy and speed: Social data is useless if it's inaccurate. The ability to speak multiple languages – including slang and emoji – is critical to this point. So is ability to analyze the sentiment behind posts and images. And it all has to happen in real-time. Today, that means AI Analytics driving your social data engine – because you don't have time to waste on inaccurate results, or data that takes too long to come through.

Integration: Social Media Monitoring, as we stated at the beginning of this post, is just one piece of the puzzle. It's the ongoing effort to track your established baseline. It only works well when combined with other modalities, like Social Media Listening. Additionally, you may want the ease of engaging back through social scheduling software, or combining CRM and other data. You want a Social Monitoring Tool that can interface with the tools you already use.

No 3rd Party Add-ons: They might seem cool, but they won't be under the control of your vendor. It's better to go with a vendor dedicated to innovating on their own. Otherwise you may fall in love with a feature that suddenly goes away.

Commitment to Innovation: This might not seem like a big deal – aren't all tools ultimately comparable at a certain level? Not quite. Tool providers that don't update their offerings regularly may fall behind when big changes happen suddenly – like Instagram's recent API changes. When your tools fall behind, they take you with them. Meanwhile, those who invested in best-in-class tools fly further past you.

Industry/Peer-recognized: The one thing the internet offers is transparency. If you're unsure of a tool's merit, the reviews will surely reveal all you need to know. Just as consumers rely on Consumer Reports when purchasing things like cars and appliances, there are places to look when you want reliable information about Social Media Analytics Tools. Trust Radius, Forrester and G2 Crowd are just a few where you can compare top solutions.

Social Competitive Analysis

Social Competitive Analysis (or Competitor Analysis) evaluates a competitor's social content, profile and overall strategies to identify strengths and weaknesses. Using this assessment, a brand can better position themselves in the market and create more compelling content.

What does a Social Competitor Analysis Look Like?

There are a variety of social listening tools that make competitive analysis much easier. When your competitors have a new ad campaign running, you can see exactly how consumers are responding and where their sentiment falls.

Understanding what your competitors' audiences love – and why – means you can offer the same thing, even if you never thought to before. Understanding competitor audience dissatisfaction gives you the chance to fill a need and gain new loyal customers.

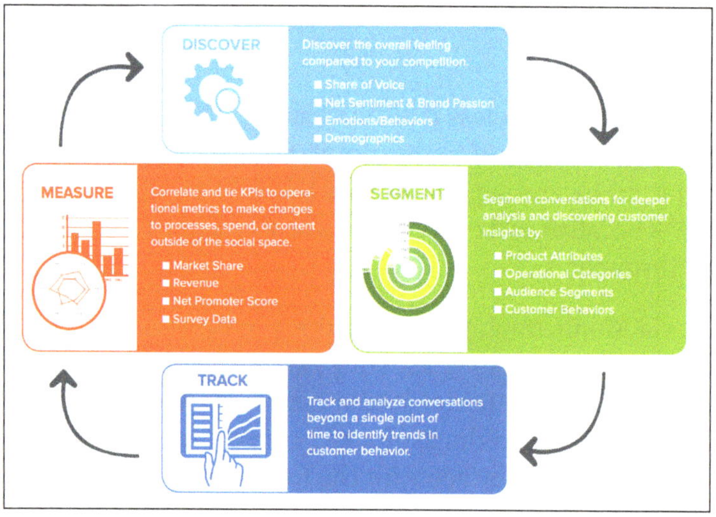

First Steps to Social Competitive Analysis

- Consider a Range of Competitors: Consider a wide range of competitors including established competitors, new entrants, and potential challengers within your category that may enter the market using Social Media Listening.
- Compare Apples to Apples: Maintain competitive topic definitions similar to brand topics to accurately benchmark share of voice, Net Sentiment, and Brand Passion KPIs.
- Segment Conversations for Deeper Insights: Use theme analysis to identify differences in volume and sentiment across sub-segments of the conversations – by competitor, operational segment, product feature, etc.

- Perform Ongoing Analysis: Extend ad-hoc competitive benchmarking as an ongoing analysis to identify trends and deviations to benchmarking metrics.
- Act upon Competitive Insights: Correlate KPIs to operational metrics (revenue, NPS, Survey data, etc.) and decide to improve processes, change spend, change resources, or develop new ideas to grow market share.

Best Practices for Social Competitive Analysis

- Understand which metrics matter – demographics, psychographics, and sentiment are more important than superficial metrics like mentions, likes, retweets, etc.
- Decide who merits your attention is analyzing sentiment, so you know which topics have the most passionate audience – those are the ones worth your time.
- Compare social content across platforms – look beyond the platforms you use to see where consumers are interacting with your competitors.

Social Media Sentiment Analysis

Social Sentiment analysis is the use of natural language processing (NLP) to analyze social conversations online and determine deeper context as they apply to a topic, brand or theme. Our net sentiment score and brand passion index show how users feel about your brand and compares across your competitors.

Identify Emotions and Depth of Feeling

Emotions – big bold, volatile, passionate emotions – are the driving force behind everything social users share. If you don't have a way to analyze all that shared sentiment, you can't possibly know what matters most to the people you want to love your brand. To make the most of Social Media Sentiment Analysis, you've got to monitor conversations to learn two key things:

- Whether consumers' emotions are positive or negative (Net Sentiment).
- How strong those emotions are (Passion Intensity).

When viewed through the lens of conversations about your brand, these combined metrics – measured on a scale from -100 to +100 – establish Brand Passion, a critical value in determining what actions you need to take next. To make that decision, you've got to look beyond your brand and get to know your audience intimately.

Ways you can use Sentiment

- Evaluating Your Brand's Health: To better understand consumer's feelings towards your brand, it's important to understand their social sentiment. This insight can lead to driving your understanding of feelings about your company, product, or service. The ROI can be significant by using an automatic sentiment analysis solution to obtain an overview of brand health.
- Dealing with a Crisis: Social sentiment can deliver signals into shifts in your brand health. A spike in negative posts about your brand can lead to a crisis. Your PR department can use social sentiment tools to find the root of the problem and establish a plan to correct this negativity.

Understanding the Competition: Social sentiment is great in providing a better understanding of how your product or brand is perceived compared to the competition.Once you understand your competitors sentiments, you can use to develop new and innovative ways to change the conversation about your brand.

References

- What-is-social-media-2890301: thebalancesmb.com, Retrieved 23 July, 2019
- Social-media-management-guide, digital-marketing: tech.co, Retrieved 04 March, 2019
- Business-Models-in-Social-Networking- 242178725: researchgate.net, Retrieved 13 February, 2019
- 6-biggest-social-media-management-challenges-how-to-solve-them: osmondmarketing.com, Retrieved 19 March, 2019
- What-is-social-media-advertising, online-advertising: promisemedia.com, Retrieved 14 January, 2019
- What-is-social-media-monitoring-sma-guide-part-2: netbase.com, Retrieved 18 June, 2019
- Social-media-sentiment-analysis: netbase.com, Retrieved 15 August, 2019

6

News and News Management

Freshly received notable information, related to important events, is called news. News broadcasting, online newsroom, news media, video news release, electronic news-gathering, news management, electronic newspaper, etc. are some of its components. This chapter closely examines these components of news and news management to provide an in-depth understanding of the subject.

News

News is an unpublished account of human activity, which seeks to interest, inform, or educate the readers. The first requirement of news is that a writing should not have been published anywhere before. It should come to the readers to the first time. It is like a hot cake coming straight from the over. Anything, which has come in print before, does not constitute news. It may be anything but not news. The second ingredient is human activity. News must relate in one way or the other to the human activity. Human beings must be involved in an event embodied in news. The Third important factor is that it should be of some interest to the readers. The interest may be physical or emotional. The fourth important pre-requisite is that it should be designed to impart some sort of information to the readers.

The information may be in respect of the reader's interest in specific fields. The best ingredient is that it should be of some education value for readers. The readers ought to be of the progress of the country and making in the specific fields. The countrymen have the right to know as to how strangers their country is. It is for the readers of the country. A news is tomorrows history done up in to-days meal package. News is the flow of tides of human aspirations, the ignominy of mankind and the glory of human race. It is the best record of the incredible meanness and the magnificent coverage of man. The news is current information made available to public about what is going on. It enables the people to make up their minds as what to think and how to act.

News is a truly, concise and accurate report of the event. A news is the report of an event and what an event itself. News means the record of the event that has taken place in a particular era. The significant element of news is that it is an event in which some kind of action takes place. It is a report in which the action is described narrated, highlighted or recorded. News is written in a comprehensive manner. There should be one audience or a class of readership. To whom the description is to be presented in print or on the air or on T.V. or movie screen. News should provoke into recipients or at least some of them to thought or action.

Examples:

A guide to advanced techniques in journalism brought out by the Editorial Study Centre of the Thompson Foundations has enumerated 20 categories of what makes news. These are "Novelty,

Personal impact, Local news, Money, Crime, Sex, Conflict, Religion, Disaster and Tragedy. Humour, Human interest, the Under-dog, Mystery, Health, Science, Entertainment, Famous people, Weather, Food, and Minorities".

A few examples of what makes news are given below:

- "Man bites dog". (Novelty).
- "Pay body recommends raise in pay of Federal Government employees". (Personal Impact).
- "A motorcyclist run over by a Niazi Bus Service near Anarkali, Lahore." (Local News).
- "Prices of T.V., Refrigerator and Cigarettes raised in Federal Budget". (Money).
- "100 persons died in the air crash". (Tragedy).

It is due to the fact that a journalist reports an incident in the same way as he sees it. Although it is possible that a particular journalist gives a dramatic touch to an incident while the others do not. But the original and genuine facts of the happenings are not to be changed at any rate.

Characteristics of News

The important characteristics of news are:

- Accuracy,
- Balance,
- Objectivity,
- Concise and Clear,
- Current and freshness.

You can read in detail the article about Different News Sources. But here I would like to tell you, we usually get most of your news about what is going on in the world today from the newspaper or radio or television or magazine or talking to people.

Elements of News

Following are different news elements:

- Immediacy or Timeliness,
- Proximity,
- Consequences,
- Prominence,
- Drama,
- Oddity,

- Conflict,
- Sex,
- Progress.

Importance of News

News is important for a number of reasons within a society. Mainly to inform the public about events that are around them and may affect them. Often news is for entertainment purposes too; to provide a distraction of information about other places people are unable to get to or have little influence over. News can make people feel connected too.

News is important as a social gathering space too, hence newspapers either online or physical place an emphasis on news. Where there are a lot of people gathered there is opportunity to advertise. This advertising sometimes can cause a conflict of interest in the way news is reported.

Importance of Local News

News from a local area is often important to advise people in a locality about activities that may have an impact on a community. This can allow a community to engage in decision making processes in a community. For example if a local community reports on a dangerous road or accident hotspot reporting these can be later used as evidence to lobby for funding to fix a problem.

Importance of National News

Often countries have a broad extent of distance and in some cases differing time zones. Having a national news focus can allow people to gain a sense of national perspective. This is particularly significant for countries that have a diverse range of population centres such as cities or towns. For example large cities many thousands of kilometres apart may still rely on each other for trade or resources of economic significance. So knowing the situations in other cities and towns becomes important.

Importance of International News

News from one country to another is important in todays global economy. Knowing what is happening in other countries gives people a perspective of each others ways of life and cultural differences. Certain kinds of news from countries that rely on each other for energy or other resources can often have a profound influence in overall global economics.

Electronic Newspaper

An electronic newspaper is a self-contained, reusable, and refreshable version of a traditional newspaper that acquires and holds information electronically. (The electronic newspaper should not be confused with newspapers that offer an online version at a Web site.) The near-future technology - researchers expect to have the product available as soon as 2003 - will use e-paper (electronic paper) as the major component. Information to be displayed will be downloaded through a wireless Internet connection. A number of versions of the future technology are in development, although there are two frontrunners: Xerox›s Palo Alto Research Center (PARC) is working on a newspaper that would consist of a single sheet of their e-paper (called Gyricon), while Lucent, in partnership with a company called E Ink, is working on a multi-page device (also called E Ink).

The Gyricon version consists of a single sheet of transparent plastic, containing millions of tiny bichromal (two color) beads in oil-filled pockets. Text and images are displayed through rotation of the beads that occurs in response to electrical impulses: a full rotation displays as black or white, and a partial rotation displays as gray shades. Nick Sheridon, a senior research fellow at PARC, has been working towards a viable electronic newspaper for over twenty years. Sheridon sees Xerox's device as consisting of a sheet of Gyricon wound around a spring mechanism in a lightweight cylinder. The user would pull the page out of a slit in the cylinder; in the process, the page would pass over a printer-like device which had downloaded data from the Internet through a wireless connection. To access another page, the reader would return the sheet to the cylinder, select the page, and draw the sheet from the scroll. The device could be carried like an umbrella, and would fit in a large purse or a briefcase. Sheridon projects that a Gyricon-based electronic newspaper could be available within three years. Currently, Gyricon uses 50-micron beads for a resolution of 200 dpi (dots per inch); the use of 30-micron beads will increase resolution to 300 dpi, slightly better than that of traditional newspapers.

Lucent's E Ink device uses electronic ink and combines thin, plastic, flexible transistors with polymer LEDs (light-emitting diodes) to create what are called smart pixels. The process involved - which is not dissimilar to traditional printing processes - uses silicon rubber stamps to actually print tiny computer circuits onto the surface. E Ink uses electronic ink for display: millions of tiny capsules filled with light and dark dyes that change color - charged dye particles move either up or down within the capsules - when exposed to an electric charge. According to Paul Drzaic, the director of display technologies, prototypes of the device have been running on watch batteries. Although the technology has been used for retail signs, Lucent says that an E Ink-based electronic newspaper is still at least 10 years away, because electronic ink has not been sufficiently developed to make complex displays practical.

IBM is also working on an electronic ink-based device. IBM's electronic newspaper is in a book-like format, and is constructed of 16 pages of flexible, fiberglass-reinforced paper, each about 8.5" by 11." The lightweight pages are bound by a rigid metallic bar, and covered with a clear, protective cover sheet. Charged dye particles move either up or down within the capsules - causing light or dark areas to appear in the display - when exposed to an electric charge. The whole device could be rolled or folded similarly to a traditional newspaper. Like the E Ink-based electronic newspaper, IBM's version is several years away.

The challenge involved in creating a viable electronic newspaper is to develop a device that has the desirable characteristics of traditional paper in addition to its own inherent benefits (such as being automatically refreshable). Like traditional paper, the electronic newspaper must be lightweight, flexible, high-resolution, glare-free, and affordable, if it is to gain consumer approval. Sheridon proposes that the Gyricon version could cost about the same as a year's subscription to a regular newspaper.

News Agency

News agency, also called press agency, press association, wire service, or news service is the organization wire service, or news service, organization that gathers, writes, and distributes news from around a nation or the world to newspapers, periodicals, radio and television broadcasters, government agencies, and other users. It does not generally publish news itself but supplies news to its subscribers, who, by sharing costs, obtain services they could not otherwise afford. All the mass media depend upon the agencies for the bulk of the news, even including those few that have extensive news-gathering resources of their own.

The news agency has a variety of forms. In some large cities, newspapers and radio and television stations have joined forces to obtain routine coverage of news about the police, courts, government offices, and the like. National agencies have extended the area of such coverage by gathering and distributing stock-market quotations, sports results, and election reports. A few agencies have extended their service to include worldwide news. The service has grown to include news interpretation, special columns, news photographs, audiotape recordings for radio broadcast, and often videotape or motion-picture film for television news reports. Many agencies are cooperatives, and the trend has been in that direction since World War II. Under this form of organization, individual members provide news from their own circulation areas to an agency pool for general use. In major news centres the national and worldwide agencies have their own reporters to cover important events, and they maintain offices to facilitate distribution of their service.

In addition to general news agencies, several specialized services have developed. In the United States alone these number well over 100, including such major ones as Science Service, Religious News Service, Jewish Telegraphic Agency, and News Election Service. Specialized services in other countries include the Swiss Katholische Internationale Presseagentur, which reports news of special interest to Roman Catholics, and the Star News Agency of Pakistan, which supplies news of Muslim interest in English and Urdu.

The major press associations in the United States have expanded their service to include entertainment features, and some feature syndicates provide straight news coverage as a part of their service. The Newspaper Enterprise Association distributes both news and features in the United States.

Despite the plethora of news services, most news printed and broadcast throughout the world each day comes from only a few major agencies, the three largest of which are the Associated Press in the United States, Reuters in Great Britain, and Agence France-Presse in France. Only these and a few others have the financial resources to station experienced reporters in all areas of the world where news develops regularly (in order to ensure access to well-organized transmission facilities) or to send them wherever news develops unexpectedly. These agencies are also equipped to distribute the service almost instantaneously.

The world agencies have established a variety of relationships with other agencies and with individual news media. Most of them purchase the news services of national or local agencies to supplement news gathered by their own staff representatives at key points. Reuters, like the Agence France-Presse, supplies a worldwide news file to be distributed by some national agencies along with their domestic news reports. The American services more often contract to deliver their service directly to individual users abroad.

News agencies in communist countries had close ties to their national governments. Each major communist country had its own national news service, and each news service was officially controlled, usually by the minister of information. TASS, the Soviet news agency, was the principal source of world news for the Soviet Union and its allies; it also made Soviet Communist Party policy known. Communist states outside the Soviet sphere, e.g., China and Yugoslavia, had their own state news services, which were controlled in similar fashion. China's Hsinhua, or New China News Agency, was the largest remaining news agency in a communist country by the late 20th century.

Most other countries have one or more national news agencies. Some depend on a common service, such as the Arab News Agency, which provides news for several states in the Middle East. Others are national newspaper cooperatives, such as the Ritzaus Bureau of Denmark, founded in 1866. A few, like the Agenzia Nazionale Stampa Associata of Italy, have expanded coverage abroad in a limited degree to supplement their domestic service but still depend on Reuters and Agence France-Presse for much of their foreign news. Germany since 1949 has built Deutsche-Presse Agentur into one of the more important news agencies in Europe, including extensive exchange with other national services. In Canada the Canadian Press is a cooperative news agency with headquarters in Toronto. The oldest and largest news agency operating exclusively in Britain is the Press Association, founded by provincial newspapers on a cooperative basis in 1868. It began active work on February 5, 1870, when the postal service took over the private telegraph companies that had previously supplied the provincial papers with news. It supplies news to all the London daily and Sunday newspapers, provincial papers, and trade journals and other periodicals.

The ability to transmit news rapidly greatly increased during the 20th century. Radioteleprinters that make possible fast automatic transmission of news messages linked all major areas. Picture transmission by radio and high-fidelity wires became well developed. From the major agencies, teletypesetter service, pioneered by the Associated Press in 1951, was available to newspapers wishing to have computerized typesetting done directly from news-service transmissions. By the 21st century, most news agencies had moved the bulk of their operations and transmission to computers.

News Broadcasting

News broadcasting is the medium of broadcasting of various news events and other information via television, radio, or internet in the field of broadcast journalism. The content is usually either produced locally in a radio studio or television studio newsroom, or by a broadcast network. It may also include additional material such as sports coverage weather forecasts, traffic reports, commentary, and other material that the broadcaster feels is relevant to their audience.

Television News

Television news refers to disseminating current events via the medium of television. A "news bulletin" or a "newscast" are television programs lasting from seconds to hours that provide updates on international, national, regional, and local news events.

There are numerous providers of broadcast news content such as BBC News, NBC News, CNN, Fox News Channel, RT, and Al Jazeera, as well as numerous programs that regularly provide this content such as *NBC Nightly News*. In addition to general news outlets, there are specialized news outlets, for example about sports ESPNews, Fox Sports News, and Eurosport News, as well as finances, including CNBC, Bloomberg Television, and Fox Business Network.

Television news is very visually-based, showing video footage of many of the events that are reported; still photography is also used in reporting news stories, although not as much in recent years as in the early days of broadcast television. Television channels may provide news bulletins as part of a regularly scheduled news program. Less often, television shows may be interrupted or replaced by breaking news reports ("news flashes") to provide news updates on events of great importance.

Radio News

Radio news is similar to television news, but is transmitted through the medium of the radio instead. It is based on the audio aspect rather than the visual aspect. Sound bites are captured through various reporters (generally through audio capture devices such as tape recorders) and played back through the radio. News updates occur more often on radio than on television – usually about once or twice an hour.

Structure, Content and Style

Television

Newscasts, also known as bulletins or news programmes, differ in content, tone, and presentation style depending on the format of the channel/station on which they appear, and their timeslot. In most parts of the world, national television networks will have bulletins featuring national and international news. The top-rated shows will often air in the evening during "prime time", but there are also morning newscasts of two to three hours in length. Rolling news channels broadcast news content 24 hours a day. The advent of the internet has allowed the regular 24-hour-a-day presentation of many video and audio news reports, which are updated when additional information becomes available; many television broadcasters provide content originally provided on-air as well as exclusive or supplementary news content on their websites. Local news may be presented by standalone local television stations, stations affiliated with national networks or by local studios which "opt-out" of national network programming at specified points. Different news programming may be aimed at different audiences, depending on age, socio-economic group, or those from particular sections of society. "Magazine-style" television shows (or newsmagazines) may mix news coverage with topical lifestyle issues, debates, or entertainment content. Public affairs programs provide analysis of and interviews about political, social, and economic issues.

News programs feature one or two (sometimes, three) anchors (or presenters, the terminology varies depending on the world) segueing into news stories filed by a reporter (or correspondent) by describing the story to be shown; however, some stories within the broadcast are read by the presenter themselves; in the former case, the anchor "tosses" to the reporter to introduce the featured story; likewise, the reporter "tosses" back to the anchor once the taped report has concluded and the reporter provides additional information. Often in situations necessitating long-form reporting on a story (usually during breaking news situations), the reporter is interviewed by the anchor, known as a ‹two-way›, or a guest involved in or offering analysis on the story is interviewed by a reporter or anchor. There may also be breaking news stories which will present live rolling coverage.

Television news organizations employ several anchors and reporters to provide reports (as many as ten anchors, and up to 20 reporters for local news operations or up to 30 for national news organizations). They may also employ specialty reporters that focus on reporting certain types of news content (such as traffic or entertainment), meteorologists or weather anchors (the latter term often refers to weather presenters that do not have degrees in meteorology earned at an educational institution) who provide weather forecasts – more common in local news and on network morning programs – and sports presenters that report on ongoing, concluded, or upcoming sporting events.

Packages will usually be filmed at a relevant location and edited in an editing suite in a newsroom or a remote contribution edit suite in a location some distance from the newsroom. They may also be edited in mobile editing vans, or satellite vans or trucks (such as electronic news gathering vehicles), and transmitted back to the newsroom. Live coverage will be broadcast from a relevant location and sent back to the newsroom via fixed cable links, microwave radio, production truck, satellite truck, or via online streaming. Roles associated with television news include a technical director, floor director audio technician, and a television crew of operators running character graphics (CG), teleprompters, and professional video cameras. Most news shows are broadcast live.

Radio news broadcasts can range from as little as one minute to as much as the station's entire schedule, such as the case of all-news radio, or talk radio. Stations dedicated to news or talk content will often feature newscasts, or bulletins, usually at the top of the hour, usually between three and eight minutes in length. They can be a mix of local, regional, national, and international news, as well as sport, entertainment, weather, and traffic reports, or they may be incorporated into separate bulletins. There may also be shorter bulletins at the bottom of the hour, or three at 15-minute intervals, or two at 20-minute intervals. All-news radio stations exist in some countries (most commonly in North America), primarily located in major metropolitan areas such as Chicago, Los Angeles, New York City, and Toronto, which often broadcast local, national, and international news and feature stories on a set time schedule (sometimes known as a "wheel" format, which schedules the presentation of certain segments focused on a specific type of news content at a specific point each hour).

News Broadcasting by Country

Terrestrial Television

Unlike in the United States, most Canadian television stations have license requirements (enforced by the Canadian Radio-Television and Telecommunications Commission) to offer locally produced newscasts (or any local programming, for that matter) in some form. Educational television stations are exempt from these requirements as are multicultural television stations, however some stations licensed as multicultural outlets do produce local newscasts in varied languages (such as the Omni Television station group). Canadian television stations normally broadcast newscasts between two and four times a day: usually at noon; 5:00, 5:30, and 6:00 p.m. in the evening, and 11:00 p.m. (there are some variations to this: stations affiliated with CTV usually air their late evening newscasts at 11:30 p.m., due to the scheduling of the network›s national evening news program *CTV National News* at 11:00 p.m. in all time zones; most CBC Television-owned stations formerly carried a 10-minute newscast at 10:55 p.m., following *The National*, these were expanded to a half-hour and moved to 11:00 p.m. during the fall of 2012).

Some stations carry morning newscasts (usually starting at 5:30 or 6:00 a.m., and ending at 9:00 a.m.). Unlike in the United States, primetime newscasts in the 10:00 p.m. timeslot are relatively uncommon (three Global owned-and-operated stations in Manitoba and Saskatchewan – CKND-DT, CFSK-DT, and CFRE-DT – and Victoria, British Columbia independent station CHEK-DT are the only television stations in the country carrying a primetime newscast); conversely, pre-5:00 a.m. local newscasts are also uncommon in Canada, Hamilton, Ontario independent station CHCH-DT, whose weekdaily programming consists largely of local news, is currently the only station in the country that starts its weekday morning newscasts before 5:30 a.m. (the station's morning news block begins at 4:00 a.m. on weekdays).

Like with U.S. television, many stations use varied titles for their newscasts; this is particularly true with owned-and-operated stations of Global and City (Global's stations use titles based on daypart such as *News Hour* for the noon and early evening newscasts and *News Final* for 11:00 p.m. newscasts, while all six City-owned broadcast stations produce morning news/talk programs under the umbrella title *Breakfast Television* and its flagship station CITY-DT/Toronto's evening newscasts are titled *CityNews*). Overall umbrella titles for news programming use the titling schemes "*(Network or system name) News*" for network-owned stations or "*(Callsign) News*" for affiliates not directly owned by a network or television system (although the latter title scheme was used on some network-owned stations prior to the early 2000s).

CBC Television, Global, and CTV each produce national evening newscasts (*The National*, *Global National* and *CTV National News*, respectively), which unlike the American network newscasts do not compete with one another in a common timeslot; while *Global National* airs at the same early evening time slot as the American evening network newscasts, *The National*'s 10:00 p.m. Eastern Time slot competes against primetime entertainment programming on the private broadcast networks, while *CTV National News* airs against locally produced 11:00 p.m. newscasts on other stations. *The National*, which has aired on CBC Television since 1954, is the longest-running national network newscast in Canada. All three networks also produce weekly newsmagazines: CBC's *The Fifth Estate*, Global's *16x9* and CTV's *W5* (aired since 1966 and currently the longest-running network newsmagazine in Canada).

CTV's *Canada AM*, which has aired since 1975, is the sole national morning news program on broadcast television in Canada, although it has since been relegated to semi-national status as most CTV owned-and-operated stations west of the Ontario-Manitoba border dropped the program during the summer and fall of 2011 in favor of locally produced morning newscasts. The Sunday morning talk show is relatively uncommon on Canadian television; for many years, the closest program having similarities to the format was CTV›s news and interview series *Question Period*; Global would eventually debut the political affairs show *The West Block* in November 2011, which closely follows the format.

Cable Television

Canada is host to several 24-hour cable news channels, consisting of domestically-operated cable channels and news channels operated outside Canada or North America. Domestic national news channels include CTV News Channel and Sun News Network, which offer general news programming; Business News Network, which carries business news; and The Weather Network, which offers national and local forecasts. The Canadian Broadcasting Corporation operates two national news networks: the English-language CBC News Network and the French-language Réseau de l›information (RDI). Other Canadian specialty news channels broadcasting in French include general news networks Argent and Le Canal Nouvelles, and MétéoMédia, a French-language sister to The Weather Network.

The Canadian Radio-television and Telecommunications Commission authorizes carriage of some cable channels from foreign countries on domestic cable and satellite operators provided that they are linked to a Canadian network. Amongst news channels, all four major U.S. cable news networks: CNN, HLN, MSNBC, and Fox News Channel are available on most providers, along with channels from outside North America such as Al Jazeera English from Qatar, BBC World News from the United Kingdom, Deutsche Welle from Germany, and RT from Russia.

Regionally-based news channels are fairly uncommon in Canada in comparison to the United States. Two 24-hour regional news channels currently exist in the country: the Toronto-centered CP24 and the Vancouver-focused Global News: BC 1 (although CHCH-DT, a general entertainment station with a rolling daytime news block on weekdays (currently from 4:00 a.m.-4:30 p.m.) that has existed since August 2009 and hour-long local newscasts nightly at 6:00 and 11:00 p.m., serves as a *de facto* regional news channel for Southern Ontario's Golden Horseshoe region); CityNews Channel formerly operated as a competitor to CP24, although that channel shut down after a year-and-a-half of operation in May 2013.

Broadcast Television

Local Newscasts

Local TV stations in the United States normally broadcast local news three to four times a day on average: commonly airing at 4:30, 5:00, 5:30, or 6:00 a.m.; noon; 5:00 and 6:00 p.m. in the early evening; and 10:00 or 11:00 p.m. Some stations carry morning newscasts at 4:00, 7:00, 8:00, or 9:00 a.m., midday newscasts at 11:00 or 11:30 a.m., late afternoon newscasts at 4:00 or 4:30 p.m., or early evening newscasts at 5:30 or 6:30 p.m. Many Fox affiliates, affiliates of minor networks (such as The CW and MyNetworkTV), and independent stations air newscasts in the final hour of primetime (i.e., 10:00 p.m. in the Eastern and Pacific time zones or 9:00 p.m. in the Mountain and Central time zones in the U.S.). Stations that produce local newscasts typically broadcast as little as one to as much over twelve hours of local news on weekdays and as little as one hour to as much as seven hours on weekends; news programming on weekends are typically limited to morning and evening newscasts as the variable scheduling of network sports programming (if a station is affiliated with a network with a sports division) usually prevents most stations from carrying midday newscasts (however a few stations located in the Eastern and Pacific time zones do produce weekend midday newscasts).

From the 1940s to the 1960s, broadcast television stations typically provided local news programs only one to two times each evening for 15 minutes (the normal length for many locally produced programs at the time); usually these programs aired as supplements to network-supplied evening news programs or leadouts for primetime programming. Reports featured on local and national television newscasts during this time were generally provided via film or still photography; eventually, videotape began to be used to provide live coverage of news events. The 1950s also saw the first use of airborne newsgathering; most notably, in 1958, Los Angeles television station KTLA began operating the "Telecopter", a helicopter equipped for newsgathering use that was the most advanced airborne television broadcast device of its time.

The modern-day coverage of major breaking news events came to fruition following the assassination of John F. Kennedy on November 22, 1963; the news of Kennedy›s death was first announced by Eddie Barker, the news director at KRLD-TV (now KDFW) in Dallas, who passed along word from an official at Parkland Hospital; Barker's scoop appeared live simultaneously on CBS and ABC as a result of a local press pool arrangement. Many local and national news organizations such as Dallas station WFAA-TV and CBS News provided continuous coverage of the events and aftermath for five days. The November 24, 1963 assassination of Kennedy›s accused killer Lee Harvey Oswald by Jack Ruby was fed to NBC by a remote unit on loan to its Dallas affiliate WBAP-TV (now KXAS-TV) from competitor KTVT, and was the first murder to have been witnessed live on U.S. network television. The coverage provided by the local stations eventually led to further investments and technological developments to provide real-time news; newsgathering vehicles equipped with satellites began to be used on the local and national levels beginning in the 1970s. During the 1960s and 1970s, many stations began to provide additional news programming, beginning with midday news programs; in the late 1970s, the first local morning news programs debuted.

Additional changes in local news content came during the 1980s and 1990s; in January 1989, WSVN in Miami became the first to adopt a news-intensive programming format; rather than fill its schedule with syndicated content as other Fox stations did at the time it joined that network, Ed Ansin (owner of WSVN parent Sunbeam Television) chose instead to heavily invest in the station's news department, and replace national newscasts and late-prime time network programs vacated as a result of losing its NBC affiliation (the byproduct of an affiliation switch caused by CBS and WSVN's former network partner NBC buying other stations in the market) with additional newscasts. This model was eventually replicated by many other stations affiliated with the post-1986 television networks as well as some news-producing independent stations (beginning with Fox›s 1994 deals with New World Communications and SF Broadcasting that saw several major network stations change their affiliations), and also resulted in even NBC, CBS, and ABC affiliates adopting similar scheduling formats (tweaked to account for the larger amount of network programming that those networks carry). In 1990, WEWS-TV in Cleveland conceived a concept known as the "24-Hour News Source" (which has its origins in a news format used by short-lived Boston independent station WXPO-TV when it signed on in 1969), in which supplementary 30-second long news updates were produced at or near the top of each hour outside regular long-form newscasts during local commercial break inserts shown within network and syndicated programming. The format spread to other U.S. television stations (most notably, WISH-TV in Indianapolis, one of the few remaining users of the concept), most of which eventually disposed of the hourly update format by the early 2000s.

Since the early 1990s, independent stations and stations affiliated with a non-Big Three network have entered into "news share agreements," in which news production is outsourced to a major network station (usually an affiliate of ABC, NBC, or CBS), often to avoid shouldering the cost of starting a news department from scratch or because of a lack of studio space. These commonly involve Fox, CW, and MyNetworkTV affiliates (and previously affiliate stations of the now-defunct predecessors of the latter two networks, The WB and UPN) and in some cases, independent stations; however such agreements exist in certain markets between two co-owned/co-managed Big Three affiliates. News share agreements are most common with stations co-owned with a larger network affiliate or whose operations are jointly managed through a shared service or local marketing agreement. In cases where a station with an existing news department enters into a news share agreement, it will result either the two departments merging or the outright conversion of newscast production from in-house to outsourced production. Minor network affiliates involved in news share agreements will often carry far fewer hours of local newscasts than would be conceivable with an in-house news department to avoid competition with the outsourcing partner's own newscasts, as a result, minor network affiliates involved in these NSAs often will carry a morning newscast from 7:00 to 9:00 a.m. (in competition with the national network newscasts instead of airing competing with the Big Three affiliates' newscasts) or a primetime newscast at 10:00 p.m. Eastern and Pacific or 9:00 p.m. Central and Mountain Time, with limited to no newscasts in other traditional news time periods (midday, late afternoon, or early evening).

Because of the increased presence of duopolies and outsourcing agreements since the early 2000s, the number of minor network affiliates and independent stations that produce their own newscasts has markedly decreased compared to when duopolies were barred under Federal Communications Commission rules prior to 2000 (as of 2013, there are at least 15 minor network affiliates or independent stations that produce their own local newscasts, most are located within the 20 largest U.S. media markets). Duopolies and outsourcing agreements have also affected Fox stations in a similar manner; although Fox is considered to be a major network on the same level as NBC, ABC, and CBS and has urged its affiliates since the early 1990s to broadcast local news, about half of its stations broadcast local news programming through news share agreements with many of the remainder operating their own news departments. Several stations affiliated with Spanish-language networks (such as Univision and Telemundo) also broadcast their own newscasts, these stations often produce a substantially lower weekly newscast output compared to its English-language counterparts (usually limited to half-hour broadcasts in the evening, and often airing only on weeknights).

Unlike international broadcast stations which tend to brand under uniform newscast titles based solely on network affiliation, U.S. television stations tend to use varying umbrella titles for their newscasts; some title their newscasts utilizing the station's on-air branding (such as combining the network affiliation and channel number with the word "News"), others use franchised brand names (like Eyewitness News, Action News and NewsChannel) for their news programming. Conversely, the naming conventions for a station's newscast are sometimes used as a universal on-air branding for the station itself, and may be used for general promotional purposes, even used in promoting syndicated and network programming (such as KFOR-TV in Oklahoma City, Oklahoma, which uses the uniform news and general branding NewsChannel 4). Many stations title their newscasts with catchy names like Daybreak, Good Morning (city or region name), First at Four, Live at Five, Eleven @ 11:00, or Nightcast. These names are intended to set one station apart from the rest, especially for viewers who are chosen for audience measurement surveys. If the respondent was unable to provide a channel number or call letters, the newscast title is often enough for the appropriate station to receive Nielsen ratings credit.

Network News Programming

The Big Three broadcast television networks produce morning and evening national newscasts (America This Morning, Good Morning America, and ABC World News are broadcast by ABC, CBS broadcasts the CBS Morning News, CBS This Morning, and the CBS Evening News, and NBC produces Early Today, Today, and NBC Nightly News) as well as weekly newsmagazine series (NBC›s Dateline; ABC's 20/20 and Nightline; and CBS's CBS News Sunday Morning, 48 Hours, and 60 Minutes). Network morning newscasts usually air at 7:00 a.m. (English-language network morning shows air live in the Eastern Time Zone and tape delayed for the remaining time zones, while the Spanish-language morning shows air live in the Eastern, Central, and Mountain time zones and are tape delayed in the Pacific Time Zone); network evening newscasts usually are broadcast live at 6:30 p.m. on the East Coast and broadcast live in both the Eastern and Central Time Zones, with a secondary live broadcast (otherwise known as a 'Western Edition") at 6:30 p.m. Pacific Time. Today was the first morning news program to be broadcast on American television and in the world, when it debuted on January 14, 1952; the earliest national evening news program was The Walter Compton News, a short-lived 15-minute newscast that aired on the DuMont Television Network from 1947 to 1948.

All four major English networks and the two largest Spanish networks also carry political talk programs on Sunday mornings (NBC›s Meet the Press, ABC's This Week, CBS' Face the Nation, Fox's sole news program Fox News Sunday, Univision's Al Punto, and Telemundo's Enfoque); of these programs, Meet the Press holds the distinction of being the longest-running American television program as it has aired since November 6, 1947. The U.S. is one of the few countries in which broadcast networks provide overnight or early morning national news programs, in addition to those airing in the morning and early evening. CBS and ABC are currently the only networks that produce overnight news programs on weeknights in the form of Up to the Minute and World News Now, respectively; NBC previously produced overnight newscasts at different times, both of which have since been cancelled: NBC News Overnight from 1982 to 1983, and NBC Nightside from 1991 to 1998 (NBC currently does not offer a late night newscast, although the network currently airs rebroadcasts of the fourth hour of Today, and sister network CNBC's Mad Money on weeknights).

Spanish-language news programs are provided by Univision, which produces early and late evening editions of its flagship evening news program Noticiero Univision seven nights a week (and was the only nightly newscast on the major Spanish networks until Telemundo resumed its weekend newscasts in October 2014), along with weekday afternoon newsmagazine Primer Impacto and weekday morning program Despierta America); Telemundo, which has a daily flagship evening newscast Noticiero Telemundo, along with weekday morning program Un Nuevo Día and weekday afternoon newsmagazine Al Rojo Vivo; MundoFox, which produces the weekday-only flagship newscast Noticias MundoFox, along with a weekday afternoon newsmagazine MundoFox ¡Y Ya!; Estrella TV, which produces the weekday-only flagship news program Noticiero Estrella TV and the primetime newscast Cierre de Edición; and Azteca América, which produces morning, early and late evening newscasts on weekdays under the umbrella title Hechos. In the cases of Univision and Telemundo, both of their evening news programs compete with national evening news programs on their English-language competitors.

Fox, The CW, and MyNetworkTV do not produce national morning and evening news programs (although Fox made a brief attempt at a morning program from 1996 to 1997 with Fox After Breakfast; many CW and MyNetworkTV affiliates and independent stations air the syndicated news program The Daily Buzz, while some Tribune Broadcasting-owned CW and MyNetworkTV stations air a similar program called EyeOpener).

Cable Television

24-hour news channels are devoted to current events around the clock. They are often referred to as *cable news* channels. The originator of this format from which the name derives is CNN (which following its 1980 launch, spun off other national and international networks using the brand such as CNN International, CNN en Español, and CNN-IBN), originally standing for Cable News Network in reference to the then-new phenomenon of cable television. As satellite and other forms of television have evolved, the term "cable news" has become something of an anachronism, but is still in common use; many other television channels have since been established, such as BBC World News, BBC News Channel, Sky News, Al Jazeera, Newsmax TV, ABC News 24, France 24, STAR News, Fox News Channel, and MSNBC. Some news channels specialize even further, such as ESPNews (sports news; sister channel to ESPN); The Weather Channel (weather, although its status as a specialty news channel has become ambiguous due to its recent incorporation of non-news entertainment programming) and WeatherNation (weather); CNBC, Bloomberg Television, and Fox Business Network (financial news).

Conversely, several cable news channels exist that carry news reports specifically geared toward a particular metropolitan area, region, or state such as New York City's NY1 (which focuses on the entire New York metropolitan area) and News 12 Networks (which serves portions of the area outside Manhattan), Orlando's News 13 (which is also carried in areas surrounding Greater Orlando), Tampa, Florida's Bay News 9, and Washington, D.C.'s NewsChannel 8. These channels are usually owned by a local cable operator and are distributed solely through cable television and IPTV system operators. Some broadcast television stations also operate cable channels (some of which are repeated through digital multicasting) that air the station's local newscasts in the form of live simulcasts from the television station, with rebroadcasts of the newscasts airing in time periods between the live broadcasts.

A term which has entered common parlance to differentiate cable news from traditional news broadcasts is network news, in reference to the traditional television networks on which such broadcasts air. A classic example is the cable news channel MSNBC, which overlaps with (and, in the case of very significant breaking news events, pre-empts) its network counterpart NBC News; in some cases, viewers may have trouble differentiating between the cable channel and either a counterpart network news organization or a local news operation, such as is the case with Fox News Channel and the Fox network's owned-and-operated stations and affiliates (most of which use the *Fox (channel #) News* brand for their newscasts), due to the network›s controversially perceived conservative-leaning political content that differs from the Fox broadcast stations› independent and generally nonpartisan reporting. Most U.S. cable news networks do not air news programming 24 hours a day, often filling late afternoon, primetime, and late night hours with news-based talk programs, documentaries, and other specialty programming.

Radio

More often, AM radio stations will air a 6½-minute newscast at the top of the hour, which can be either a local report, a national report from a radio network such as CBS Radio, CNN Radio, NPR, Fox News Radio, or ABC News Radio, or a mix of both local and national content, including weather and traffic reports. Some stations also air a two-minute report at the bottom of the hour.

FM stations, unless they feature a talk radio format, usually only air an abbreviated weather forecast. Some also air minute-long news capsules featuring a quick review of events, and usually only in drive time periods or in critical emergencies, since FM stations usually focus more on playing music. Traffic reports also air on FM stations, depending on the market.

In some countries, radio news content may be syndicated by a website or company to many stations in a particular region or even the entire country. A notable example is Israel, where there are groups of radio stations that broadcast the same hourly news capsule by an Israeli news website and television station. There are currently two groups of local Israeli stations: one broadcasts news from YNET, the other broadcasts them from Channel 10. Israeli Army Radio general public stations broadcast the same news capsule every hour, and IBA's Kol Israel stations broadcast theirs.

Online Newsroom

With physical newsrooms shrinking and the need for engaging content growing, the time to transform your news site into a successful online newsroom is now. According to a recent survey, 85 percent of journalists agreed that online newsrooms were an increasingly important tool for sourcing content and building news stories; however, 65 percent of online newsrooms are not meeting media expectations.

Simple, quick and engaging newsrooms with easy-to-find information, appealing content and downloadable visuals attract and engage media – and, can accomplish other business goals as well, such as engaging employees, generating leads and establishing thought leadership.

Here are 5 easy tips for creating a successful online newsroom:

Storytelling is Key

Effective storytelling is the foundation of PR and journalism. A good narrative is based on the "a-ha moment" that emotionally resonates with a reader. When interviewing someone for a story, look for the facts or anecdotal details that will connect the story with your audience.

Where do most content creators go wrong? By focusing on the brand or product, rather than drawing the audience in by connecting on a personal, emotional level. No matter how boring or dry your information is, it is your job to make it interesting. Find a personal or emotional element and let that drive your story, then layer in your product or brand throughout the rest of the story.

Focus on Visuals

We've all seen them – a company's online newsroom (media page, news page, press release page or whatever you want to call it) full of lists of company press releases. In today's world, people refuse to settle for boring. To attract readers, whether they're clients, future customers, employees, journalists, etc., your content must be engaging. Eliminate the clutter and replace them with videos, photos and captivating headlines.

When it comes to headlines, readers love lists and how-to's. Put yourself in your readers' shoes. What would make you want to open an article? Give your readers short, catchy, bite-size previews of the content you want them to read.

Run your Communications Department Like a Newsroom

The key to managing a successful online newsroom is drafting your "A Team." Identify the key players in your organization who can help streamline the process of creating content, posting it to your website and amplifying it across your various communication channels (i.e. email, social media, etc.). When it comes to running your online newsroom, adopt the newsroom mentality, which includes brainstorming, developing an editorial calendar, breaking down the silos by involving other departments (i.e. marketing, human resources, PR, internal communications, IT) and pushing out good stories with engaging visuals. An online newsroom isn't just a temporary campaign – it's the way to communicate both internally and externally.

Re-think how you Pitch Content

If a journalist won't write your stories, then do it yourself! Figure out the right way to tell the story and then pitch it. Instead of blasting a hundred reporters and news desks, do your research and carefully think about your target audience and the outlets they're interested in. Instead of sending long-winded pitches or press releases, write and post a compelling story paired with engaging visuals and pitch the link. Send this with a personal introductory note to the journalist about why you think they'd be interested. This makes the journalist's job easier, and increases your chances of having them share your story.

Importance of Metrics

Before implementing a new online newsroom strategy, establish your business purpose. For example, is your goal to increase sales? Generate leads? Become a thought leader? Whatever your business purpose may be, it's imperative to identify metrics to measure the success of your online newsroom. For example, if your company is putting out a monthly email newsletter linked to your online newsroom, establish a quantifiable goal for open rates to measure the value of doing this.

Online newsrooms aren't for everyone, so if it doesn't make business sense, don't do it! However, if done correctly, this tactic can add tremendous value and help you achieve your business goals. An online newsroom isn't just a communications strategy – it's a business strategy.

News Media

The news media are those elements of the mass media that focus on delivering news to the general public or a target public.

These include print media (newspapers, newsmagazines), broadcast news (radio and television), and more recently the Internet (online newspapers, news blogs, etc.).

Broadcasting is the distribution of audio and video signals (programs) to a number of recipients ("listeners" or "viewers") that belong to a large group.

This group may be the public in general, or a relatively large audience within the public. Thus, an Internet channel may distribute text or music worldwide, while a public address system in (for example) a workplace may broadcast very limited ad hoc soundbites to a small population within its range.

In a broadcast system (television), journalists or reporters are also involved with editing the video material that has been shot alongside their research, and in working on the visual narrative of the story. Broadcast journalists often make an appearance in the news story at the beginning or end of the video clip.

In television or broadcast journalism, news analysts (also called news-casters or news anchors) examine, interpret, and broadcast news received from various sources of information.

Anchors present this as news, either videotaped or live, through transmissions from on-the-scene reporters (news correspondents).

News films ("clips") can vary in length; there are some which may be as long as ten minutes, others that need to fit in all the relevant information and material in two or three minutes.

News channels these days have also begun to host special documentary films that stretch for much longer durations and are able to explore a news subject or issue in greater detail.

A newspaper is a lightweight and disposable publication (more specifically, a periodical), usually printed on low-cost paper called newsprint.

It may be general or special interest, and may be published daily, weekly, biweekly, monthly, bimonthly, or quarterly. General-interest newspapers are usually journals of current news on a variety of topics.

Those can include political events, crime, business, sports, and opinions (either editorials, columns, or political cartoons).

Many also include weather news and forecasts. Newspapers increasingly use photographs to illustrate stories; they also often include comic strips and other entertainment, such as crosswords.

A newsmagzine, sometimes called news magazine, is a usually weekly magazine featuring articles on current events. News magazines generally go more in-depth into stories than newspapers, trying to give the reader an understanding of the context surrounding important events, rather than just the facts.

Online journalism is reporting and other journalism produced or distributed via the Internet. The Internet has allowed the formal and informal publication of news stories through mainstream media outlets as well as blogs and other self-published news stories.

Journalists working on the Internet have been referred to as J-Bloggers, a term coined by Australian Media Academic Dr Nicola Goc to describe journalists who blog and bloggers who produce journalism. "J-Bloggers: Internet bloggers acting in the role of journalists disseminating newsworthy information, who subscribe to the journalistic ideals of an obligation to the truth and the public's right to know."

By covering news, politics, weather, sports, entertainment, and vital events, the daily media shape the dominant cultural, social and political picture of society. Beyond the media networks, independent news sources have evolved to report on events which escape attention or underlie the major stories.

In recent years, the blogosphere has taken reporting a step further, mining down to the experiences and perceptions of individual citizens.

Video News Release

A video news release is a segment of video that is designed to resemble a real news report; however, instead of being created by a news agency, it is made by a public relations specialist, an advertising agency, or a corporation. A VNR is given to television newsrooms and are used as a tool to shape the opinion of the public, to promote the products or services that a business offers, to publicize an individual, or to support some other type of interest, with the intent of gaining attention.

Elements of a Video News Release

A good VNR will contain each of the following elements:

- A professional news reporter, someone who has on-air experience with the news, or an actor.
- Interviews with experts who usually have legitimate expertise in a topic, though that expertise may be biased.
- Eye-catching visual elements, such as a company's logo.
- Demonstrations of the products or services that are being discussed.
- A short run time; typically no longer than 2 minutes.

Things to Avoid

If you want a video news release to be effective and meet your objective, you are going to want to stray away from certain things. The following things should be avoided when creating a video news release:

- Highly promotional. Though the goal of a VNR is to promote a company, a product, a service, or a person, it shouldn't appear too promotional. If it does, it will be viewed as an advertisement rather than "news".
- Excessive producing. Some producing is fine, but too much can detract from the value of a VNR. If it's too produced, news agencies won't be able to put their own spin on it, which is what they intend to do.
- Inappropriate visuals. Video news releases should contain visuals, but they should contain the right visuals. In other words, images should match the content that is being shared.

Benefits of a Video News Release

A VNR can provide several benefits, and if done correctly, can serve as a powerful part of a public relations campaign. Some of the most notable benefits that VNRs offer include:

- Audio and visual elements of the story, which makes it more engaging than a written press release.
- They show journalists and viewers the story you are aiming to share rather than having them imagine the story after they read it.
- They can boost the credibility of a company, organization, or individual, as they highlight expertise.
- They are much more attention-grabbing than standard press releases, which means that they can be a highly effective marketing tool.

- They're more effective than standard press releases because viewers can easily obtain the information they contain in a very short span of time.

Criticisms of Video News Releases

Though they can be an effective marketing tool, not everyone agrees with them. In fact, critics have referred to video news releases as deceptive propaganda that tries to influence viewers under the disguise of real news. This is particularly true when it is not made clear that a VNR isn't real news. In fact, that's why many people refer to video news releases as "fake news".

Disadvantages of Video News Releases

In addition to being largely criticized, there are other disadvantages associated with video news releases. Some of these disadvantages include:

- Costly production. A steep investment is required to create a video news release.
- High competition. There are so many organizations, business owners, and private individuals that create video news releases, which makes the competition very high.
- They involve a complex, highly technical process.
- It can be difficult to create an effective VNR that will have an impact on viewers.

How VNRs are Distributed

It used to be that video news reviews were distributed to news agencies via video cassette. However, today, they are fed through satellite, which makes them easier to assess. Once a news agency receives a video news release, they give it a once over and read any accompanying documentation that may be necessary. After reviewing, news agencies decide how they can incorporate the VNR, which is based entirely on their discretion. For example, they might choose to showcase the entire video, or they may decide to incorporate it with a news story.

Organizations that use Video News Releases

A VNR can be a tool that any type of business, individual, or organization can use. Some examples of industries that use these public relations tools include:

- Government agencies, such as the US Department of Health and Human Services.
- Large corporations that sell a collection of products.
- Small businesses that offer unique and specific services.
- Vehicle manufacturers.
- Cosmetic companies.
- The food industry.

Virtually any type of business can use a video news release as a way to market what it is that they offer, to boost brand awareness, to establish authority, and to connect with and engage with their target audience; however, companies, organizations, or individuals that intend on marketing themselves to the general public can use VNRs.

Electronic News-gathering

Ever since the advent of television, news has been a vital part of programming. Like radio news, it allowed audiences to get news as it was breaking rather than having to wait for the newspaper. But TV also had the advantage over both radio and newspaper of being able to beam film footage of a newsworthy event into the audience›s living rooms.

Electronic news gathering changed the way we receive information from around the world.

However, the problem with early TV news was that film footage wasn't available until hours after an event occurred. Thus watching news break on the television simply consisted of a talking head behind a desk in a studio reporting what was happening -- not much better than simply listening to the coverage on the radio. Live footage on television was a rare event indeed, reserved for huge, planned events, like the coronation of Elizabeth II in 1953. Live feeds took planning, big equipment and circuits provided by the telephone company to transmit the feed.

It wasn't until electronic news gathering (ENG) developed in the 1970s and '80s that TV news crews could quickly set up live video signals to send back to the studio and into people's homes, drastically changing the face of television news. ENG refers to the electronic technologies that allow news crews to report from remote locations outside a studio. Before ENG came about, TV news footage shot outside of the studio was recorded on film, which had to be brought back to the studio for time-consuming processing and editing before it was ready to air. Editing for instance, involved manual cutting and spicing of the film by a trained employee. Often, an anchor reporting a late-breaking story on the 6 o'clock news would have to end a story by promising the audience "film at 11."

The BBC attempted to streamline this process as early as 1962 with the Mobile Film Processing Unit using three different vehicles -- a processing truck, an editing truck and a truck for converting film projection to television. The trucks would race to cover a story and then send the footage through microwave links to the studio. But it turned out that this so-called "three-ring circus" of trucks didn›t work so well and was more trouble than it was worth, only lasting a few years.

The real advancement that ushered in the age of ENG was videotape. We spoke with Jonathan Higgins, an expert in the field of ENG and author of two books on the subject, who helped explain how ENG changed news reporting.

How Electronic News Gathering Changed the News

Although it had been around since the 1950's, videotape technology improved throughout the 1970s and '80s. It originally used large 2-inch-wide tape and required bulky equipment. Then came the Sony U-matic in 1971, which used 3/4-inch tape, and then finally the Sony Beta in the 1980s that used 1/2-inch wide tape and became the industry standard. This also resulted in smaller video cameras.

Videotape did not have to undergo the cumbersome processing of film. Although at first, editing videotape was just as difficult as editing film, this too was solved by advances in tape decks throughout the 1970s and 80s, which allowed simpler electronic editing. And, as opposed to film, videotape was cheap and reusable. Videotape also resulted in more thorough news reporting because it meant crews needed less time to process and edit, giving reporters more time to cover a story.

By the time videotape technology advanced, the capability for microwave transmission was well established (and used in the 1960s by the BBC's ill-fated Mobile Film Processing Unit). But the convenience of videotape finally allowed crews to more easily use microwave links to quickly send their footage back to the studio. It even made live feeds more possible, as in the police shootout with the Symbionese Liberation Army in 1974. Also in 1974, KMOX, a station in St. Louis, Mo., was the first to abandon film and switch entirely to ENG. Stations all over the country made the switch over the next decade.

ENG technology also faced dramatic advancements during the digital age of 1990s and 2000s. Videotape was gradually abandoned in favor of digital video recording, which made editing even easier and even allowed journalists without special technology training to edit the footage on a laptop. TV crews also began using digital signals for their microwave transmission instead of analog. Perhaps most significantly, however, is how crews began using satellite links to transmit their feeds instead of land-based links. Because a view of the sky establishes a line of sight for the microwaves, this allowed video feeds to be instantly sent half-way around the world.

News Management

The News Management System is a TOOLIP™ module for publishers, that allows the end-to-end management and monitoring of articles (from creation to publication). Specifically the NMS provides the following functionalities:

- Easy customization and refresh of web pages with configurable rules and content areas.
- Various ways of capturing User Generated Content (e.g. user comments, user ratings, polls and surveys).

- Complex workflows for drafting, approval and publication of news.
- Content Metering for content-based subscription models.
- Support for multiple news formats (audio, video, galleries).
- Easy to use advertisement engine that integrates with the ad server of your preference.
- Integrated social tagging and sharing mechanisms.

References

- What-is-news-meaning-definition-and-sources-of-news: studylecturenotes.com, Retrieved 19 April, 2019
- Importance-of-news: clearlyexplained.com, Retrieved 09 February, 2019
- Electronic-newspaper: searchmobilecomputing.techtarget.com, Retrieved 16 March, 2019
- 5-tips-creating-successful-online-newsroom: buzzbinpadillaco.com, Retrieved 18 June, 2019
- News-media: sciencedaily.com, Retrieved 16 July, 2019
- Electronic-news-gathering: people.howstuffworks.com, Retrieved 23 May, 2019

Permissions

All chapters in this book are published with permission under the Creative Commons Attribution Share Alike License or equivalent. Every chapter published in this book has been scrutinized by our experts. Their significance has been extensively debated. The topics covered herein carry significant information for a comprehensive understanding. They may even be implemented as practical applications or may be referred to as a beginning point for further studies.

We would like to thank the editorial team for lending their expertise to make the book truly unique. They have played a crucial role in the development of this book. Without their invaluable contributions this book wouldn't have been possible. They have made vital efforts to compile up to date information on the varied aspects of this subject to make this book a valuable addition to the collection of many professionals and students.

This book was conceptualized with the vision of imparting up-to-date and integrated information in this field. To ensure the same, a matchless editorial board was set up. Every individual on the board went through rigorous rounds of assessment to prove their worth. After which they invested a large part of their time researching and compiling the most relevant data for our readers.

The editorial board has been involved in producing this book since its inception. They have spent rigorous hours researching and exploring the diverse topics which have resulted in the successful publishing of this book. They have passed on their knowledge of decades through this book. To expedite this challenging task, the publisher supported the team at every step. A small team of assistant editors was also appointed to further simplify the editing procedure and attain best results for the readers.

Apart from the editorial board, the designing team has also invested a significant amount of their time in understanding the subject and creating the most relevant covers. They scrutinized every image to scout for the most suitable representation of the subject and create an appropriate cover for the book.

The publishing team has been an ardent support to the editorial, designing and production team. Their endless efforts to recruit the best for this project, has resulted in the accomplishment of this book. They are a veteran in the field of academics and their pool of knowledge is as vast as their experience in printing. Their expertise and guidance has proved useful at every step. Their uncompromising quality standards have made this book an exceptional effort. Their encouragement from time to time has been an inspiration for everyone.

The publisher and the editorial board hope that this book will prove to be a valuable piece of knowledge for students, practitioners and scholars across the globe.

Index

CPSIA information can be obtained
at www.ICGtesting.com
Printed in the USA
LVHW062021100122
708212LV00002B/368

9 781647 283520